Praise for *Overcoming Spiritual Myopia*

"St. Paul worries about us seeing the world through a dark and distorting lens. Margaret Placentra Johnston offers you a clear lens, a corrected lens, that invites you to see what is without distortion and illusion. Hers is a perspective much needed and rarely offered. Read this book if you want to see; put it aside if you prefer to be blind."

—Rabbi Rami Shapiro, *Holy Rascals: Advice for Spiritual Revolutionaries*

"Spirituality is often described as a sense of oneness and that everything is connected and interdependent. Sadly many people cannot handle that level of openness and inclusivity. Instead they get lost inside their own limited beliefs. *Overcoming Spiritual Myopia* is an intelligent and inspiring analysis of this lack of vision. Margaret Placentra Johnston carefully and clearly explains this myopia and also the ways to deconstruct, heal and transcend it. This is a very useful conceptual and practical book for any serious contemporary spiritual seeker."

—Dr. William Bloom, leading British spiritual educator, founder and director of the Spiritual Companions Trust (http://www.spiritualcompanions.org) and author of many books, including *The Endorphin Effect* and *The Power of Modern Spirituality* (http://williambloom.com)

"If you don't know what 'spiritual myopia' is, you could be suffering from it... But, don't worry! Understanding and remedy are at hand in Margaret Placentra Johnston's comforting new book. A wise and warm-hearted Doctor of Optometry, Margaret is a wizard concerning not only conventional sight, but also inner vision, in-sight. She is a person who wants everyone to see clearly and so contribute to a better, safer, happier world. So, without hesitation, let me commend *Overcoming Spiritual Myopia* to you."

—(Dr.) Larry Culliford, former psychiatrist, the author of *Seeking Wisdom—A Spiritual Manifesto,* and a regular blogger with *Psychology Today* (see www.ldc52.co.uk)

Overcoming Spiritual Myopia is a meaty inspiring highly readable sequel to *Faith Beyond Belief*. Margaret Placentra Johnston offers us a path to spiritual health and well-being that can affect not only the individual but have global impact. Her work is deeply scholarly yet accessible to any thinking person.

Overcoming Spiritual Myopia offers three gifts

- the concept of spiritual myopia,
- how spiritual myopia affects us and the global community, and
- a new consciousness as a "cure."

Margaret gently pulls us into a way of understanding spiritual thought as it has evolved beyond religion. Overcoming Spiritual Myopia is both an excellent literature survey and a support for the position that spiritual myopia can be cured. Margaret presents a positive hopeful message for anyone willing to consider personal/spiritual growth as a path to a better life and world.

—Reverend Margaret J Shepherd, MBA, MDiv.,
author of *The Visionbuilders' Manual: 9 Steps to Visionary Success for your Company, Career or Cause*

Margaret Placentra Johnston, both a practicing optometrist and spiritual teacher, uses the very apt metaphor of myopia, more commonly known as nearsightedness, to describe particular deficiencies of spiritual perception that keep our vision of a more inclusive and loving view of the universe out of focus.

In *Overcoming Spiritual Myopia,* Johnston visits both past and future as she casts a discerning eye on the vast sweep of human religious development. Using the lens of spiritual development theory from her first book, *Faith Beyond Belief,* Johnston looks back at history and how the focus on narrow and provincial understandings that are too near to us has distorted our vision and caused us to lose sight of the original intention of religion's wisdom teachings. According to this theory, individuals pass through four levels of spiritual development—lawless, faithful, rational, and unitive—on their way to maturity. Distortions of spiritual vision (personification, literalism, fundamentalism, triumphalism, binary logic, and need for certainty,) each of which Johnston elaborates upon, prevent us from reaching the more mature, inclusive, "unitive," level where one can "connect in a beneficent way to everyone and everything in the universe." Her spiritual development theory is eminently useful in understanding and dealing with these distortions of spiritual vision so prevalent in our contemporary world.

Johnston's work not only describes but prescribes. She has culled from the literal mountains of contemporary books on new age spirituality rare gems of insight and wisdom from such authors as Don Cupitt, Wayne Teasdale, and Harvey Cox. Readers benefit from both her extensive research into the subject as well as key insights from the author's personal journey. These insights are then applied methodically and effectively to the problem of spiritual myopia with a clarity and conciseness made possible by her painstaking research and competent thoughtfulness. There are no shortcuts to spiritual growth, but having a good guide is certainly expedient. I heartily recommend Johnston as one. Here she offers humanity better vision of a more promising world.

Overcoming Spiritual Myopia is a tour de force in spiritual development literature.

—(Dr.) Fred Howard, author of *Transforming Faith: Stories of Change from a Lifelong Spiritual Seeker*, minister, Valdosta Unitarian Church

In *Overcoming Spiritual Myopia,* Margaret Placentra Johnston presents an insightful view of the evolution of human spiritual development, not just individually, but also of humanity as a whole. She offers helpful perspectives on religion, the Bible, how and why humans perceive the Bible the way we have and how we can perceive it more clearly. Issuing a call to interspirituality, Johnston inspires a commitment to spiritual advancement which may help save humanity and the earth.

—Rev. Carol E. Richardson, author of *Truth and Illusion: The Politics of Spirituality*

"I feel so good reading this book. It gives me hope!"

—Sharron Dorr, editor

I generally am not one to go too deep into books of this nature. But, the first chapter will have you hooked. *Overcoming Spiritual Myopia* offers a way to help us understand ourselves and the world at large. Dr. Johnston has made this not only an easy read, but an experiential read that raises our awareness about religion, spirituality, and life in general. A must read!

—Sister Jenna
Director of Brahma Kumaris Meditation Museums
Host of America Meditating Radio Show

Overcoming Spiritual Myopia

A View Toward Peace Among the Religions

MARGARET PLACENTRA JOHNSTON

MPJauthor.com

Copyrighted Material

Overcoming Spiritual Myopia: A View Toward Peace Among the Religions

Copyright © 2019 by Margaret Placentra Johnston. All Rights Reserved.

No part of this publication may be reproduced, stored in a retrieval system or transmitted, in any form or by any means—electronic, mechanical, photocopying, recording or otherwise—without prior written permission from the publisher, except for the inclusion of brief quotations in a review.

For information about this title or to order other books and/or electronic media, contact the publisher:
Margaret Placentra Johnston
MPJauthor.com
mpj@mpjauthor.com

ISBN: 978-1-7321648-0-2 (print)
978-1-7321648-1-9 (eBook)

Printed in the United States of America

Cover and Interior design: 1106 Design

Publisher's Cataloging-In-Publication Data
(Prepared by The Donohue Group, Inc.)

Names: Johnston, Margaret Placentra.

Title: Overcoming spiritual myopia : a view toward peace among the religions / Margaret Placentra Johnston.

Description: [McLean, Virginia] : Margaret Placentra Johnston, [2018] | Includes bibliographical references and index.

Identifiers: ISBN 9781732164802 (print) | ISBN 9781732164819 (ebook)

Subjects: LCSH: Spirituality. | Religions--Relations. | Religions (Proposed, Universal, etc.) | Religion and science. | Social evolution.

Classification: LCC BL624 .J64 2018 (print) | LCC BL624 (ebook) | DDC 204.4--dc23

The phrase "standing on the shoulders of giants" is often attributed to Isaac Newton, but the idea was not original to him. In a treatise on logic called Metalogicon, the 12th century theologian John of Salisbury wrote "Bernard of Chartres (a French philosopher of that time) used to compare us to dwarfs perched on the shoulders of giants. He pointed out that we see more and farther than our predecessors, not because we have keener vision or greater height, but because we are lifted up and borne aloft by their gigantic stature."

In all humility I want to claim the status of one such dwarf. Each of the authors whose work I reference here—as well as that of many others I could not mention—is far more schooled in a certain field than I. It was only when I allowed information they each shared to coalesce in my mind that the concept of spiritual myopia occurred to me. From this arose the perspective that spiritual myopia is a widespread ill we in our culture must work to overcome if we are ever to enjoy a healthy society. Hence this book.

As a dwarf perched on the shoulders of the giants whose work collectively informed the spiritual myopia concept, it is to these giants that I gratefully dedicate this book.[1]

Also by Margaret Placentra Johnston

Faith Beyond Belief: Stories of Good People Who Left Their Church Behind (Quest Books, 2012)

GOLD WINNER of the 2013 Nautilus Book Awards in Religion/spirituality (Western)

Contents

List of Illustrations	xiii
Acknowledgments	xv
Introduction	1

1. **The Basics: Defining Myopia** — 13
   - What Is Refractive Myopia? — 13
   - What Is Spiritual Myopia? — 17

2. **Looking Back through Time: Perspective** — 25
   - The Evolution of Religion — 25
   - Christianity: The Belief Element — 29
   - Technological Evolution — 34
   - The Spread of Knowledge — 38
   - Modernity and Beyond — 39

3. **Spiritual Development Theory: A Key Element in Spiritual Vision Correction** — 45
   - The Faithful: Stage Two of Four — 48
   - The Rational: Stage Three of Four — 54
   - The Lawless: Stage One of Four — 59

Contents

4. **Signs and Symptoms of Spiritual Myopia:
   A Disease of Insularity** — 63
   - Personification — 63
   - Literalism — 69
   - Fundamentalism — 71
   - Triumphalism — 74
   - Spiritual Blindness — 75
   - Binary Logic and the Need for Certainty — 79

5. **New Lenses for Spiritual Clarity: Indulging in a
   Bird's-eye View** — 83
   - Cultural Intermixing — 84
   - The Perennial Philosophy — 93
   - The Westar Institute — 97
   - The New Physics — 103
   - Big History — 105
   - The Interfaith Movement — 108

6. **The Unitive Level in Spiritual Development:
   Even Clearer Vision** — 113
   - How Does One Get There? — 114
   - A Few Characteristics — 121
   - By Their Fruits Ye Shall Know Them — 127
   - A Few More Characteristics — 132

7. **Human Cultural Evolution: A Hopeful Outlook** — 139
   - Ontogeny Recapitulates Phylogeny — 139
   - A Bigger Story — 147
   - This is Not Relativism — 150
   - The Age of the Spirit — 153
   - The New Spirituality — 155

CONTENTS

8. More Universal Perspectives: Further Vision-Opening Opportunities — 159
    Interspirituality — 159
    Isn't the Bible the Inspired Word of God? — 161
    Reports of Direct Spiritual Experience — 164
    Near-Death Experiences — 165
    What about Prayer? — 168
    What about Miracles? — 171
    What about Revelation? — 172

9. Overcoming Spiritual Myopia: The Prescription — 175
    Treatment — 176
    Prevention — 185
    Conclusions So Far — 187

10. Prognosis: A Transformed Society — 193
    The Pains of Healing — 196
    What Individual Spiritual Maturity Might Look Like — 200
    What a Spiritually Mature Society Might Look Like — 223

Afterword — 233

Suggested discussion questions — 235

Notes — 239

Bibliography — 249

Index — 253

Things you can do to help promote (or refute) awareness about Spiritual Myopia — 267

About the Author — 269

List of Illustrations

1. Sketch of normal eye, myopic eye, and eye with glasses correction — 14
2. The development of religions over time — 28
3. Faithful-stage Traits — 50
4. Comparison of Faithful- and Rational-stage traits — 58
5. Lawless-stage traits (far left) compared to those at the Faithful and Rational stages — 61
6. Universal-stage traits (Mystic, far right) compared to those at the Lawless, Faithful, and Rational stages — 127
7. A pendulum and its fulcrum — 198

Acknowledgments

Before publication, *Overcoming Spiritual Myopia* was evaluated by several beta readers. Rather than attempt to list them all and risk forgetting one of them, I will thank them as a group. Each one offered some comment that led me to change something in this book. One comment caused me to spend about three months rewriting an entire chapter! For these opinions, I am very grateful.

Sharron Dorr served as my editor, and I can't thank her enough for her insight and revisions that surely have improved this book. Lisa Hagan from Lisa Hagan Literary offered the opinion that this book was too serious for most traditional publishers. She suggested that publishers think people are too upset by the political climate to focus on serious topics. I am grateful to her for saving me the trouble of writing a proposal and spending a year or more with bated breath hoping a traditional publisher would pick up this book.

I also want to thank Quest Books for having the confidence to publish my first book, *Faith Beyond Belief: Stories of Good People Who Left Their Church Behind*. That they have stopped putting out new books is a great sorrow. However, I also want to thank them for

Acknowledgments

the numerous books they published in the past, many of which have informed this work. Readers will see many Quest Books listed in the bibliography.

I especially want to Sister Jenna of the *America Meditating Radio Show*. In exchange for a mere thirty-minute interview on her show, she extended a most generous invitation to a retreat with some of her other show guests at the Brahma Kumaris Peace Village Retreat Center in Haines Falls, New York. It was among these beautiful beings of light and love that I was surrounded by enough positive vibrations to gain clarity in my intent for the book and to clear my heart of some random muck that had been holding me back from creating it. In addition, I want to thank whichever Peace Village volunteers maintain the labyrinth at the property. It was here on the last day of our seminar in 2015 that I was finally able to spell out the content for this book. Also, I want to thank the many people who made the retreat possible—Antonia, Kanu, Sister Kala, and others.

Introduction

Some say we are on the threshold of an overall, society-wide spiritual transformation. Beneath the notice of conventional society, a grass-roots, underground mindset adjustment continues to grow and swell. Conventional news sources will not touch it because it cannot be explained in the short, simplistic news bites to which our society has grown accustomed. It is not sensational, so pithy headlines cannot be written about it. Even to begin to appreciate this transformation requires the kind of sustained attention our conventional media have weaned us away from in recent decades. It requires a more sophisticated form of reasoning, and deeper thought than the dumbed-down, black-and-white (binary) logic in which our news sources—some more egregiously than others—attempt to portray reality.

Also, even those involved seem to lack clarity on what comprises the transformation. Some vaguely drone on and on about spiritual evolution and how this transformation will spawn an idyllic world in which everyone is equal, everyone has what they need, everyone is fulfilled, and everyone is nurtured and happy. Others write complex treatises that are far beyond the comprehension level of the ordinary

Introduction

person. But even the most involved participants, the self-proclaimed ring leaders of this transformation, fail to articulate clearly for the masses exactly what this evolution will consist of and how exactly we are going to get there. The factors leading to and involved in the transformation are not sufficiently explicit; this obliqueness keeps it from being recognized and from spreading as quickly as it might. When someone in the conventional world receives a hint of it, it sounds like nonsense because our airwaves are dominated by the opposite type of message: life is really all about competition, getting ahead of the other guy, convincing people that they are wrong and we are right, and hoarding resources for ourselves, lest we should experience lack of some comfort or security. The conventional world rebels against, refuses to acknowledge, and sees no value in any transformation that could threaten to alter the current order.

I write, not as a leader of this potential transformation, but as someone who sees our society crying out for a major update in our conventional beliefs and a reframing of our mainstream values. This book attempts to cull as simply as possible some of the factors that play into this transformation. It aims to call readers to responsibility in reconsidering some of the outmoded values that certain religious, political, and media leaders continue to inspire. Our insular religions have played an important part in human history. They still serve a vitally important purpose. But so many factors in today's world render the *insular* aspects of the traditional religious message untenable that, without an update in focus, peace among the religions remains an increasingly hopeless fantasy.

In my profession as a Doctor of Optometry, I have spent a lifetime correcting physical myopia (shortsightedness or nearsightedness) for my patients. *Overcoming Spiritual Myopia* uses the term *myopia*

Introduction

metaphorically to imply that many of our conventional beliefs and values were set down before a number of historical, scientific, sociological, and cosmological discoveries were made. Now that we have access to improved information, we are called to update our understandings accordingly. Failing to do so leaves us mired in an inexcusable myopic blur, while doing it will allow the transformation to move forward.

Ever more information is available now that challenges us to clarify our vision about important concepts. Some new information offers improved spiritual vision, broader understandings, and improved values, resulting in a far more universal and inclusive sense of responsibility toward our fellow human beings and all other elements of the universe. We are confronted with the choice either to allow these new perspectives to inform and improve our understandings or to dig in our heels and reject them without consideration. Human nature is often inclined to choose comfort and ease over an open-minded, dynamic, and energetic engagement with new insights.

One tool we can use to open our hearts and minds to newer understandings is to realize that the historical founders of our religions, the writers of our holy books, and even our current religious leaders have only been able to share wisdom based on the information available to them in their time. The beliefs they have offered have been fine for their period in human knowledge. When limited information about the galaxies was all we had, it was completely acceptable to hold earth-centric religious beliefs that only offered citizens from certain parts of one lonely planet a form of "salvation," assuring them a place in the heavens above or eternal punishment in the depths below. Now that more advanced cosmological realities

INTRODUCTION

have become known, we must learn to forgive ourselves for believing things that now seem so simplistic.

When some in the conventional world hear of spiritual notions that are not connected to organized religion, they are likely to dismiss them hastily as very superficial and totally invalid. But a new kind of spirituality is arising now that, far from being superficial and invalid, represents instead a *necessary result* of the various factors discussed in this book. It is not an indication of people trying to escape reality. It is not about people with poor reality testing or over-easy acceptance of woo-woo, wish-fulfilling fantasies. Rather, it consists of those willing to engage with reality more fully, more authentically, and more vigorously than one may do through the avenues typically available in the conventional world. One need only read a few books on the topic (see the bibliography for examples) to recognize that this transformation—this move toward a new spirituality—appeals to those willing to feel both the cold and the warmth of our deepest reality, to embrace the difficult as readily as they bask in comfort, and to live with more vigor. As opposed to the lonely hermit meditating alone all day on a mountaintop, the new spirituality appeals to those ready to focus on this life, doing their utmost to enhance truth and right actions in our current reality, without concern for their own personal salvation in the next life.

Now, anyone turning on any news station at any time or any day will certainly be convinced that the opposite is true. News stations are forced to focus on the negativity because it is only sensational news that sells. Focusing on single, isolated incidents, which are usually negative, also makes news bites easier to understand. As this transformation is a quiet one, a calm one, and a complex one, it is not likely to be reported on. The factors that drive our media are

Introduction

holding it back, and notice of this is being inhibited by the effect that the constant negativity in the news often has on our souls. In addition, I suspect that there are factors motivating some of our political and religious leaders to preserve more conventional understandings and values. Yet in these times a broader understanding is not only possible but also necessary. People with competing insular views cannot live peacefully in an ever more interconnected and globalized society. Unless we want to allow increasing strife, we must seek a bigger story, one that includes and validates wisdom from all religious and spiritual traditions. If we are ever to see the transformation to a new spirituality become manifest as a step toward interreligious peace, we must be willing to correct the spiritual myopia in which conventional understandings and mainstream values seek to keep us mired.

At the time I wrote my first book, *Faith Beyond Belief: Stories of Good People Who Left Their Church Behind,* I thought that book's message was revolutionary. I feared retribution from confirmed literalists who resented my pointing out the value in moving beyond religious literalism. Despite having read hundreds of books on the spiritual path and having run my manuscript by almost as many preliminary readers who would surely have corrected me, I worried that I may have misrepresented the concepts my book contained. Rather, as it turns out, quietly waiting in the wings was an army of people who considered the need to reason oneself beyond religious literalism and insularity to be a matter of course.

While these readers mostly admitted that my presentation told the story in a different way—"It has been reheated, and it tastes better than ever!" wrote one reviewer—some expressed a mild disappointment that it mainly reiterated things they already knew. These commenters were probably already relatively spiritually aware and were looking to be introduced to new spiritual *depths.*

I realize now that I should have been more explicit about my mission. My intended audience was not people already on the spiritual path. I had written *Faith Beyond Belief* in the hope of alerting members of our more conventional society to the very *existence* of such a path; I wanted to communicate that there *is* a choice beyond the literal belief level that does not limit a person to stark, literal atheism. My hope was also perhaps to invite conventionally minded readers to dirty their shoes a bit in the mud of the paradoxical, but more comprehensive, world beyond black-and-white spiritual and even cultural reasoning.

In *Overcoming Spiritual Myopia,* my mission once again is not so much to convey spiritual (or cultural, or scientific, or historical) depth for those already on the path to spiritual mastery. Rather, my purpose is to cull together the many factors that, when taken together, call the average person to consider ways in which an authentic personal spirituality differs from the over-easy wish fulfillment most of our society thinks it is. I also strive to show how, in its most authentic form, a deep spirituality is far more demanding than the "Follow the rules and you will be saved!" mentality common in conventional religion. Our world is becoming too sophisticated and too complex for conventional thought, and we should welcome an alternative viewpoint.

Personally, I continue to straddle conventional society and what we might call the spiritual community. Willing neither to lose my grip on conventionality (which my profession calls for) nor to abandon my deep interest in full-blown, post-conventional thought, I feel I can be of most service by introducing conventional readers to post-conventional thought and to what is being called the "new spirituality"—a greatly improved idiom over the old "New Age." I aim to describe

Introduction

entry points by which the average person might be introduced to the growing world of spiritual awareness.

John Mabry, in *Growing into God*, describes for us what Awakening is. He writes in very religious terminology; but my claim is that, as is the case with many who write on such topics, he means it mostly metaphorically. Furthermore, I claim that the same concepts apply to those people who are spiritual but NOT religious. Mabry says, "[God] shows us just a little bit, enough to turn us from our intended course, and promises that if we will come with him, he will show us much more. This is the essence of Awakening. It is a minor miracle—sometimes dramatic, sometimes subtle, but usually it is enough to make us go, 'Whoa! What was that?' and start us searching in a direction we might not have gone otherwise."[1] Awakening is a brief experience of Union, whereas enlightenment is a permanent state of union.[2] It is "a conversion—a transformation, if you will—of one's very perception of Reality. When we are born for the first time, it is into a world that revolves around us. When we have an Awakening experience, we are born again, but this time into a world in which the locus of importance is elsewhere—in fact, *everywhere*. Awakening is a momentary flash of insight when we are granted a glimpse of the Universe as God sees it."[3]

How can we translate these insights into terminology the conventional world might recognize? I am trying to bridge the gap between conventional understandings and the unitive view held by mystics—not only within the general spirituality community but also within the growing numbers of the everyday kind who may already be lurking unnoticed in the form of your accountant (yes, really) or your TV repairman, as well as those few, exceptional individuals whose writings have stood the test of time through the centuries. According to spiritual development theorists, the mystical, or unitive, worldview is

Introduction

both more mature than other positions AND very close to what large numbers of ordinary people are approaching in today's world. It is only by making certain connections that go largely unnoticed in the conventional world that we can recognize how much of our general culture, and most of traditional religion, is designed to lead us away from spiritual maturity—and ever deeper into a seemingly hopeless spiritual myopia.

A few commenters claimed I repeated myself in my first book. In defense of my style, I would like to point out that in treating complex topics it is sometimes necessary to write in a circular fashion, first introducing a concept and then returning to it in more depth after presenting other supporting concepts. If reality occurred in a straight line, I would be able to treat one topic at a time as a separate function. Everything being interconnected as it is, this is not possible.

When my children were young, I once marched into the principal's office demanding an explanation for why they were taught to tell time, first in kindergarten, then in the first grade, and then again in the second grade. The principal kindly informed me of the concept of a "spiraling curriculum," which had not been around in the days when I obtained my master's degree in education. The idea is to present a subject quickly in the year it is introduced. At that point, it's not worth spending a lot of time on it, because, while some students will be ready to learn it upon first exposure, many others will not be ready and will not grasp the concepts. The next year, the same subject is presented again, in only slightly more depth. The students who learned it when it was first presented will likely gain new perspective, while those who were not ready the first time may have become ready to pick up the basic lesson. Teaching the subject a third time has the same goal—to pick up the students who were not ready for it the first or second time.

Introduction

I wrote both *Faith Beyond Belief* and *Overcoming Spiritual Myopia* around the idea of a spiraling curriculum, introducing a concept and then moving on to something else before treating the topic in more depth. Because spiritual development is such an emotionally thorny issue, some who see no validity to it on first presentation may gain some appreciation as successive presentations are offered in a different manner.

Spiritual myopia—the central metaphor of this book—calls for some explanation of how I am using the word *spiritual*. The typical definition limits the *spiritual* to that which is experienced more individually and the *religious* to that which is involved with established human institutions. I want to offer a further concept: Spirituality as discussed in this book also refers to that which calls us beyond the limitations of institutional religion, but it means to avoid the cheap emotional appeal of escape from reality, as well. My concept of spirituality offers to help us develop a posture toward reality that is more personally demanding, more creative, and more alive than that which is provided by either institutional religion or the fluffy, escapist, will-o'-the-wisp methods typically connected with what was once called "New Age spirituality."

The kind of spiritual vision we discuss here invites a person to involve himself fully in the inevitable mysteries of our existence. It calls a person to go beyond the need to resolve those mysteries into the myopic and misleading certainties offered by most of our religious institutions *and* to resist the appeal of the over-easy, wish fulfillment tactics offered by the vision of the now outdated New Age.

Chapter 1, "The Basics" begins—predictably—with a cursory lesson about *myopia* as the term applies in the eyecare world. This is followed by an explanation of how I am using that concept as a metaphor for a

Introduction

shortsightedness in the way much of society approaches the timeless human need for religious and/or spiritual connection.

Chapter 2, "Looking Back through Time," sweeps the reader through a very condensed view of the evolution of religion and the changes that led up to mainstream society's current religious understandings, especially regarding Christianity.

Chapter 3, "Spiritual Development Theory," reintroduces and summarizes the theory that was the core concept of my first book, *Faith Beyond Belief*. This concept is crucial in understanding the myopia involved in the explicit proclamations of most of our traditional religions.

Chapter 4, "Signs and Symptoms of Spiritual Myopia," discusses ways in which some core religious tenets have been distorted into misleading notions that cause shortsighted spiritual vision.

While most readers will be aware of the factors discussed in Chapter 5—"New Lenses for Spiritual Clarity"—lumping them into a single chapter is meant to focus the readers' attention on how these influences in today's society, when taken together, call us beyond traditional limited spiritual understandings.

Chapter 6, "The Unitive Level in Spiritual Development Theory," continues the discussion begun in chapter 3. It completes the discussion of spiritual development theory as it applies to the individual, and then it discusses how traits and values typical at the highest spiritual level—when properly understood—promote a healthy society.

Chapter 7, "Human Cultural Evolution," discusses how civilizations tend to pass through the same stages in their general evolution as humans do individually. Premodernity, modernity, and postmodernity are compared to the individual development stages described

Introduction

in spiritual development theory. A hopeful view of the human future is presented.

Chapter 8, "More Universal Perspectives," furthers the discussion begun in chapter 5, adding factors in our postmodern society that call us to more universal spiritual understandings.

Chapter 9, "Overcoming Spiritual Myopia," pulls together how, when viewed as a whole, all the elements of the prior chapters invite us to remove the blinders consciously that provincial religious understandings impose and to overcome our spiritual myopia. Suggestions are offered to prevent spiritual myopia in the upcoming generations.

Chapter 10, "Prognosis," offers an optimistic view of what a society cured of its spiritual myopia would look like and discusses how that state of being could contribute to enhanced peace among the religions, an enhanced life experience for all people, and a more responsible posture toward the universe, as well.

Thank you in advance for trusting that *Overcoming Spiritual Myopia* has something of value to offer you.

1
The Basics: Defining Myopia

What follows is a brief foray into a technical concept that is basic to my optometric profession. I have rendered it in the simplest explanation possible. I want to be sure readers are easily able to make the connection between the very common visual disorder called *refractive myopia* and the spiritual counterpart I am calling *spiritual myopia*.

What Is Refractive Myopia?

If you wear glasses to help you see better from a distance, you know what it means to be nearsighted. You can see pretty well up close, but you can't see too well far away. The medical term for nearsightedness is *myopia* (my oh' pee a.) Myopia is a very common visual disorder. A recent study estimates that about 42 percent of the U.S. population is myopic, as is about 30 percent of the world population.[1]

In myopia, parallel rays of light entering the eye (such as those that emanate from an object one is trying to view from a distance) come to a point focus in front of the retina, rather than on it, resulting in a blurry image. Glasses or contact lenses that correct myopia cause the parallel rays of light to "bend" farther out, so that they come to a point focus *on* the retina, where clear vision results. Glasses and contact-lens prescriptions that eye doctors write to correct myopia extend the person's vision out into the distance so that they can see the world more clearly.

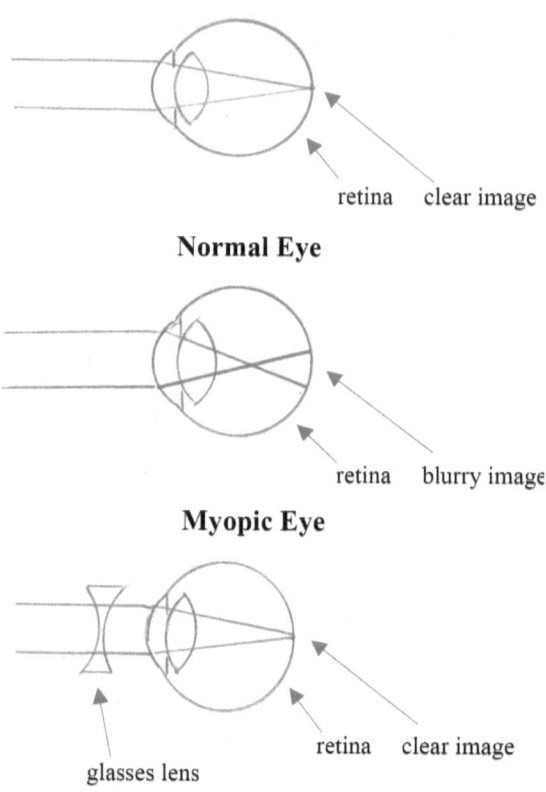

Figure 1. Sketch of normal eye, myopic eye, and eye with glasses correction

The Basics: Defining Myopia

Refractive errors, like myopia, are caused by some combination of genetic and environmental factors. If the eyeball is too long, or the surfaces of the eye are too curved (the refractive elements are too strong,) myopia results from strictly genetic factors. But the incidence of myopia is said to be rising, which is more likely due to environmental factors. A recent study estimated that, by the year 2050, 49.8 percent of the world's population will suffer from myopia.[2]

While we have no official explanation, there is a very good chance that myopia is increasing thanks to the ability of the human body to adapt to changing needs. Young people, and even not so young people, now spend much of their day looking at one electronic device or another (or several at once!). Whether it be a computer screen, a phone, or a tablet, these devices are all viewed at arm's length or closer. When looking at something so close, the eye muscles have to work to create that focus. Only when looking at something twenty feet away or farther are the focusing muscles at rest. If the eye is not given the chance to relax into distance focus, it will adjust its natural, resting point of focus to something closer than twenty feet, causing myopia.

When you look up the word *myopia* in the dictionary, the first definition describes this refractive error in the eye's focusing mechanism. However, a second, metaphorical definition is offered: "a lack of foresight or discernment: a narrow view of something."[3] It is this second definition that forms the central analogy of this book: Most of our current society suffers from a form of spiritual myopia (or short-sightedness) that comes from restricting our perspectives to that which is close to our immediate experience and rejecting wisdom that could result if our point of focus were expanded to include more of reality. *Overcoming Spiritual Myopia* offers you driving glasses for the soul!

Chapter 1

Besides myopia, several other common refractive errors exist in the physiology of the eye. *Farsightedness* (hyperopia) is a bit more complex than myopia. Here, the eye's resting point of focus is farther than the usable distance. Parallel rays of light entering the eye come to a point focus at a spot that is virtually behind the retina. A relatively young person who is only a little farsighted may be able to see well at both far and near, but she will need to use eye-focusing muscles to bring the focus forward, constantly exerting energy to see clearly at any distance. In an older person, those focusing muscles will have broken down, so that the person can no longer use energy to make them work. If the person has a severe degree of farsightedness, they probably cannot focus on anything at any distance, far or near. So, it is complicated.

Astigmatism is a condition in which an eye focuses differently in the vertical meridian than it does in the horizontal meridian. Vertical parallel rays of light reach the retina at a different point than horizontal ones do, resulting in a distorted image at any distance. And *presbyopia* is something that happens to nearly everyone beginning around the age of forty. Here, the eye-focusing muscles lose flexibility in such a way that the person can no longer switch focus from one distance to another. A presbyopic person with good distance vision will start having trouble seeing close things.

But we need not concern ourselves too much with all the above terms. For the purpose of this book, it is enough to know that in myopia a person's vision is limited to that which is very close, and the person is blinded to the wider world. Myopia is the most prevalent cause of limited vision.

In contrast to these refractive *errors,* the state of having perfect focus, in which the eye sees perfectly, is called *emmetropia*. Parallel rays of light naturally come to a point focus exactly on the retina, resulting in clear

The Basics: Defining Myopia

vision when viewing distant objects without using any focusing effort or eyewear. Emmetropia simply means that the vision is unhindered by any type of refractive error. In a cultural sense, emmetropia would be the state of being able to appreciate concepts universally, that is, understanding that there is more to reality than one's own experience.

What Is Spiritual Myopia?

Just as refractive myopia is the most common vision problem, spiritual myopia is the most prevalent spiritual error, at least in the Western world. Both ailments result in a lack of perspective that comes from our focus being limited to objects or concepts that are too near to us. Both ailments afflict a person with the inability to see the big picture.

At this point, we could begin to draw all sorts of analogies, comparing other spiritual weaknesses with other refractive errors. We all know of someone who spends tremendous energy trying to save the world from various kinds of ills, while failing to notice or attend to the needs in his own family or community. We could, if we wanted to, call that a type of spiritual farsightedness.

Most of us are aware of someone whose notion of spirituality is tied up in seeking out all sorts of paranormal or supernatural experiences. And, of course, there are many who think that just burning incense and maybe wearing a certain type of beads will make them a spiritual person. We might label these efforts spiritual astigmatism because, while they may help the person concerned feel better about him- or herself, they contribute little to the greater good. Attempts to connect to an "other" reality, while ignoring or even wishing to escape from our current, everyday reality may be harmless placebos, but they are distortions that may blind a person to spiritual opportunities based on a more comprehensive type of spiritual perception.

Chapter 1

In contrast, in spiritual emmetropia a person's spiritual perceptions are simply not clouded by any of these limitations. While I can hardly think of a less elegant or less poetic term than *emmetropia*, none of its synonyms seem to work well here. Spiritual *clarity, lucidity,* or *purity* sound too definite and imply too much know-it-all-ness. If I were to use any of those terms it could sound as if I am trying to direct people to a certain conclusion about something that, in fact, has no definite endpoint, no objective truths that all should share.

Later in this book, I will begin using the term *spiritual emmetropia*, or *spiritual emmetrope*, to describe a person who suffers from few or none of the all-too-human tendencies that manage to limit our spiritual vision. While I question whether too many pure spiritual emmetropes exist in real life now, the factors discussed in this book point us to an appreciation of what spiritual emmetropia might look like and allow us to perceive it, not only as a goal, but also as a clearly emerging possibility. Only when we can appreciate ways in which the conventional world suffers from a serious and destructive spiritual myopia can we begin to see ways in which a spiritually emmetropic society would offer an improvement over our current one.

While spiritual emmetropia defines no specific endpoints, some traits are commonly found. They will be considered in more detail throughout this book, but I will introduce a few of them here. Spiritual emmetropia tends to bring a person to the point of wanting to connect in a beneficent way to everyone and everything in the universe. In his book, *Creative Faith*, philosopher and former Anglican priest Don Cupitt uses these terms: "The saint desires to be able to live and to love the whole world of human life in a purely affirmative and generous way."[4] Readers should not be put off by his use of the word *saint*. Cupitt makes clear that he is talking about mature, responsible, and

The Basics: Defining Myopia

fulfilled life in *this* world, not some ethereal, otherworldly existence above the fray of everyday struggles.

A fuller expression of spiritual emmetropia would not limit itself to *human* life but would demonstrate an affirmative and generous love for all forms of life, including animals, nature, and our environment. In its fullest expression, spiritual emmetropia would even include aspects of our existence that are not discoverable through the use of our everyday five senses—the inner reality that only comes to fruition when the mind is calm and the heart is open to a larger reality. Hopefully, as this book proceeds I will be granted the privilege of finding words that will add to the existing understanding of this concept.

Meanwhile, we will return to our consideration of spiritual myopia. While other spiritual defects also deter our cultural progress, it is spiritual myopia that requires the most attention. In fact, much in our conventional Western society seems designed to *cultivate* spiritual myopia, limiting our focus too closely on ourselves and our own little part of reality. As I have said, this book is designed to show how this is so and prescribes a remedy.

Spiritual myopia exists in several different forms in our society. One aspect of it is the need to have definite answers. Starting with our school years, we are taught that there are right answers and wrong answers on our tests. We are taught about the scientific method by which a hypothesis may be definitively determined to be either correct or incorrect. If only we use a specific set of techniques, and follow specific principles of reasoning, we are sure to arrive at a definite piece of reliable information. This form of inquiry has brought immeasurable improvements to our living situation. Just look at the scientific developments in the last hundred and fifty years. But expecting that kind of reasoning to provide definitive answers about everything

Chapter 1

in our reality is one of the signs and symptoms of spiritual myopia discussed in chapter 4. It holds back appreciation of the spiritual complexities of our existence.

Triumphalism is another symptom of spiritual myopia. Once our scientific inquiry or our personal experiences have brought us to a certain conclusion, we tend to become arrogant or scorn anyone else whose inquiries or experience may have brought them to a different conclusion. We are inclined to feel superior to anyone who thinks differently. Or else, we feel sorry for them or, even worse, feel it our duty to convince them to abandon their truth and accept ours instead. In this book, we will see how indulging in triumphalism limits our perceptions and keeps us from appreciating the many multidimensional aspects of the full depth of the spiritual reality.

Another particularly dangerous aspect of the spiritual myopia prevalent in our society is the failure to appreciate that whatever affects one person (or even one animal, or one plant) affects all of us. We cannot cause, wish for, or even *allow* bad things to happen to anyone or anything else in the universe without harming ourselves in the process. We cannot wish to be better, smarter, or wealthier than others; we cannot aim to win in a game in which there must be a loser. This concept is easy to dismiss when taken literally, as the typical Buddhist mantra seems to suggest: "We all are one." But appreciation of how the concept of oneness is true at the figurative level is a key factor in correcting our spiritual myopia.

Counterintuitively, central to the spread of spiritual myopia are the efforts of some leaders in the world of organized religion. Certainly, our religions do a lot of good for certain types of people. But, as our world evolves, it is becoming evident that a particularly pernicious assumption underlies the traditional religious message.

The Basics: Defining Myopia

Until we recognize the spiritual myopia involved, our religions may be doing more harm in the big picture than good. While it is easy to see that violent zealots who are creating wars, blowing up buildings, and killing people in the name of religion are spiritually myopic, some conventionally sanctioned religious attitudes suffer from the same lack of vision. Any clergyman preaching an exclusive message about his or her own religion and claiming that all other religions are wrong is spreading spiritual myopia; he is blinding his congregation to the more inclusive spiritual vision available in spiritual emmetropia.

Just as refractive myopia has suffered a dramatic rise in recent decades, it seems that in some ways spiritual myopia is on the increase, as well. Surely, confusion about this phenomenon abounds. At one time, say, back in the 1950s in the United States, there were certain prescribed "correct" ways of dressing, behaving, thinking, and so on that few dared breach—at least outwardly. It was almost as if outward appearances trumped inward reality. If a lady went out wearing a nice dress, gloves, earrings, nylon stockings, high heels, and makeup, it could almost be assumed that her inner life was also totally in order. This outward appearance belied the probability that her opportunities for personal authenticity may have been limited by societal expectations that kept her confined to cooking and cleaning the house.

The 1970s questioned that static view, creating an upheaval of all our societal norms. Suddenly, women were freed to create authentic lives, people of color were encouraged to demand equality, and the disabled were given advantages such as special parking spaces. Whereas before that time "normal" people didn't want to be reminded of those who were different or less fortunate, now such people were invited to venture out into the world freely and live meaningful lives, equal to those of anyone else.

Chapter 1

Though some people are unwilling to admit it, these changes represented societal *progress*—a more solid form of justice, greater equality, and more inclusiveness. Most of all, these changes brought on a new type of freedom for women and minorities—one that had formerly only been accorded to white men. It allowed women and minorities a chance to enjoy an authentic and fulfilled creative life.

But for some people, these changes threatened the social order they felt was holding everything together. Out of a sense of fear, those unable to perceive the progress involved began to fight back, trying to hold the old order in place. Some reverted to a rather stagnant and fear-based form of religion. The fundamentalist movement that had begun in the mid-nineteenth century as a reaction against the liberal and progressive views of that time experienced a strong resurgence in the 1970s and '80s. Our social culture was opening to broader understandings, but the fundamentalists failed to appreciate the advantages those changes offered. While progressive forms of religion were progressing, fundamentalist forms of religion became louder and louder in their protests, trying to enforce *regression* to a less evolved stance, and caused mass confusion in the general society.

To generalize broadly, fundamentalist religion and conservative social movements suffer from overly unsophisticated reasoning processes. They portray a simplistic universe that can be subjected to black-and-white, predetermined rules. A belief is either true or false. To be "good," you just have to follow the rules. Going forward, we will see how such limited reasoning is but another sign of spiritual myopia. We will also see how portraying our reality in black-and-white terms blinds people to appreciation of broader, more sophisticated, and more nuanced forms of truth.

The Basics: Defining Myopia

Simplistic reasoning, and the spiritual myopia it invokes, also give people permission to gloat over others whose worldview differs from theirs. We see this every day in the various media outlets that display intolerance and insular small-minded thought patterns like a badge of honor and encourage their unsuspecting audience to do the same. Once we come to recognize tolerance and acceptance as hallmarks of spiritual clarity, we can appreciate intolerance and rigidity as symptoms of a spiritual myopia that detracts from wholesomeness of life for everyone.

While some factions insist on putting their finger in the proverbial dike, hoping to hold back change, various forces in our world today compel us toward increasing awareness. Change is inevitable; our challenge is to find a way to incorporate new perspectives so that we more closely approach a spiritually emmetropic vision and work toward an enhanced existence for all beings. Trying to hold back change is to seek shelter by burying one's head in the ground.

To begin our exploration, we will first review some factors that have contributed to the spiritual myopia with which most of our mainstream society is struggling today.

2

Looking Back through Time: Perspective

It is a fact. Things change over time. Some people resist change. Others welcome it. But over large swaths of time, certain changes are inevitable. To ignore or to think we can stem the tides of change is a spiritually myopic tactic. Below are discussed some changes the recognition of which is necessary in overcoming spiritual myopia.

The Evolution of Religion

The oldest known religion still being practiced today is Hinduism. It began in India about four thousand years ago. But it was by far not the first religion. We have evidence that, as far back as 300,000 BCE, Neanderthals had intentionally buried their dead in some type of grave and, in some cases, marked the grave. This practice indicated their awareness of death, respect for the deceased, and sense of hope for something beyond their everyday reality.

Chapter 2

Also, we have evidence that as early as 300,000 BCE ancestor worship, shamanism (in which a selected individual enters an altered state of consciousness to communicate with spirits or animals), and animism (which concerns the belief that all things have a soul or spirit) were practiced.[1]

Around 35,000 BCE, god and goddess worship began to develop. Shinto practices arose in Japan around 14,000 BCE, and in 9130 BCE the first man-made temple was built, apparently for use in shamanistic or animistic worship.[2]

Polytheism (the belief in many gods and goddesses) was common among many ancient societies such as the Sumerian, Egyptian, Greek, Chinese, and Celtic. While all these societies developed their sense of their gods separately, the gods they dreamed up and then worshipped tend to follow certain common themes. For the most part, each of these ancient societies had creator deities, water deities, mother goddesses, and love deities.[3] For example, the Chinese had a water deity they called *Mazu*, the Greeks called their water god *Poseidon*, the Romans' water deity was *Neptune*, and the Celts' water deity was *Lir*. Why, we might ask ourselves, would all these different cultures come up with the common idea of a water god? Water has always been a powerful force strongly influencing human well-being. Before humans had the scientific knowledge we enjoy today, water must have seemed most mysterious, and almost supernatural. The same could be said of the other god themes—creation, motherhood, and love—of which for the most part we still lack a full understanding even today. Could there be something universal to all humans calling them to seek connection with forces more powerful than they themselves?

Looking Back through Time: Perspective

Hinduism is a term that applies in general to various religious traditions of India. Its origins can be traced back to around 2000 BCE. The Hindu god system is very complex and may include as many as 330 million gods. The particular gods vary according to the different sects within Hinduism. At least some of the Hindu gods are arranged around much the same themes as the original polytheistic religions are. There is a god of rain, a god of fire, a god of the moral law, etc. However, at its core Hinduism is not strictly speaking a polytheistic religion. There is a crucial difference: Hindus acknowledge that all their gods are just different representations of the same entity—the one, supreme entity that has no form and is beyond time, space, and causation. In fact, Hindus see all of creation and everything in it as part of God. So, out of their diversity of gods, there is unity of all living things as part of the same god.

Judaism as a nationality arose in the Middle East with the patriarchs Abraham, Isaac, and Jacob around 1900 BCE. But Judaism as a religion began with the story of Moses receiving the Ten Commandments on Mount Sinai around 1400 BCE. Judaism is largely considered to be the first strictly monotheistic religion. It recognizes only one God, who is characterized as a specific supreme being, separate from humankind and the rest of creation. Judaism is focused not so much on dogma or beliefs but rather on action and relationships. It includes 613 commandments, which are listed in the Torah, plus other laws and customs that its adherents must observe.

Buddhism and Jainism in India, along with Zoroastrianism in the Middle East and Taoism and Confucianism in China, all began around 600 BCE. Of these, only Zoroastrianism is strictly monotheistic. In general, the others can be said to be nontheistic religions.

CHAPTER 2

This means that their adherents concern themselves with values and spiritual connection while not necessarily involving belief in a god or gods.

Christianity, of course, is a monotheistic religion. In its literal interpretations, the Christian God is a being separate from humans and separate from everything else in the universe. There are, however, a few within Christianity who interpret the word *God* in a less literal

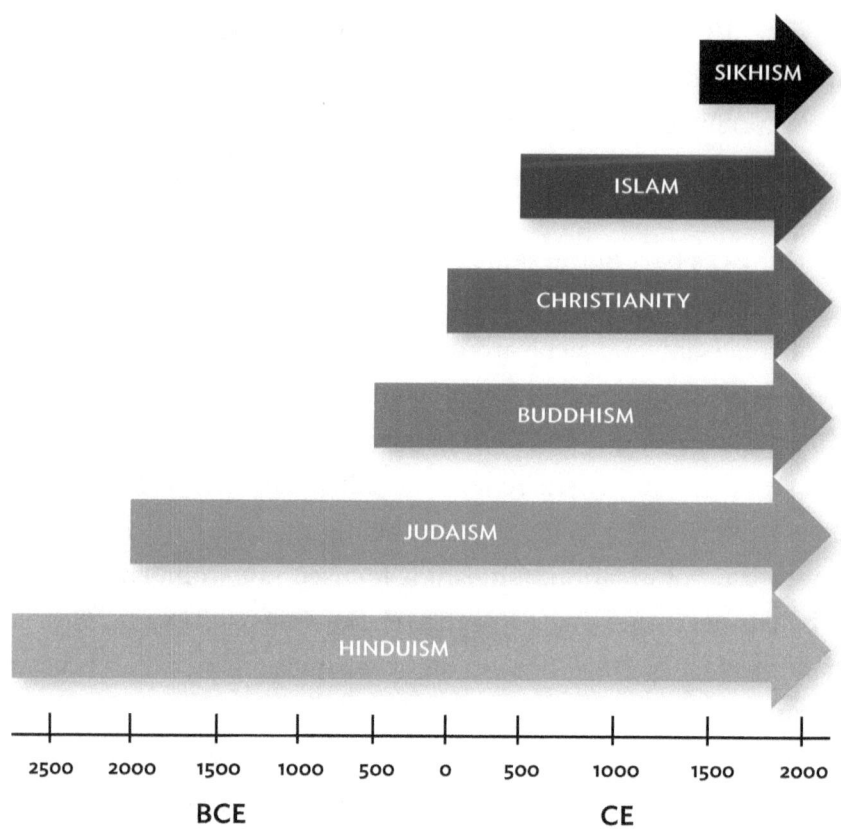

Figure 2. The development of religions over time

sense. They see God as something of which we are all part (Christians and non-Christians alike, believers and nonbelievers, animals, plants. and rocks. as well) and as something individuals can experience directly, as opposed to relying on Church teachings. Their God or god is something that includes all of creation, rather like that of the Hindus. What is tricky is that such Christians often use religious words in much the same way as those who hold literal beliefs do, so it is hard to recognize them.

More recent religions are essentially monotheistic. They include Islam, formed in the Middle East around 600 CE; Sikhism, formed around 1500 CE in India; and Baha'i, which arose in the Middle East around 1900 CE.

In short, every culture about which there is a recorded history has practiced some form of spirituality or religion. What drove all these people from all different cultures and eras to delve beyond their everyday, "here-and-now" reality and acknowledge a sense of something *beyond* it? What common factor in their humanity drove them to form notions of a god or gods? As we look at the overall history of religion, we may want to ask ourselves, could these developments represent an *evolution* in religious thought?

Even specific religions change over time. Since Christianity remains the chief religion in the West, we will look at it in terms of how it developed in the first place and then how it has changed since the time of Jesus.

Christianity: The Belief Element

We can divide the recorded history of the Western World into three segments: antiquity, premodernity, and modernity. In each of these time

Chapter 2

frames, people have held a different view of life. A basic grasp of these different eras is necessary to understand the impact of Christianity as it arose in the first place and as it has morphed over time.

Antiquity is considered to have spanned from the seventh century BCE to about the fourth to sixth century CE. This was the time of the Greek and Roman Empires. It has been described as a golden age of culture and learning. Huge advances were made in literature, science, architecture, and philosophy, and under these improvements the culture flourished.

One thing often not considered, however, is that this was a golden age *only for the aristocracy.* That controlling class comprised only about 1 to 2 percent of the population at the time. Nearly all the rest were peasants living at barely a subsistence level. Their main concerns centered on having enough food for the day, enough seeds to plant for the next year. In the world into which Jesus was born, such peasants were controlled and exploited by two oppressive systems: a Jewish domination system overlaid by the Roman imperial domination system.[4] Debts were imposed that often caused the peasants to lose the land they needed to sustain themselves.

Also, in this time, individual lives were considered to have no importance. The peasants—again, 98 to 99 percent of the population—were regarded rather in the way some of us today might see bugs: if we don't want a bug in our house, some of us still feel free to kill it. Similarly, in antiquity human lives were not valued in the way that most of us, at least, value them today. So, relative to what we currently enjoy, antiquity was a chaotic and lawless time for most human beings.

In the middle of all this turmoil, Jesus arrived, and his message was revolutionary. However, its appeal to the society of the time

LOOKING BACK THROUGH TIME: PERSPECTIVE

may have been quite different from the way it has been portrayed over the centuries since then. In his 2009 title, *The Future of Faith*, Harvard theologian Harvey Cox explains how he has had to alter his understanding of early Christianity since his seminary studies in the 1950s. Over the ensuing decades, several sources have revealed much new information showing that the traditional teachings about early Christianity have been misleading. Some of the most important new insights resulted from the unexpected discovery in 1946 of some ancient Christian documents that had been hidden in caves for millennia. The Gospel of Thomas is a key example. In her *New York Times* bestseller, *Beyond Belief: The Secret Gospel of Thomas*, Bible scholar Elaine Pagels tells us that certain passages in Thomas's gospel take us in a very different direction than, for example, the Gospel of John. Similar to the language of mysticism, the Gospel of Thomas suggests that "the image of God is hidden within everyone, although most people remain unaware of its presence."[5] More precise and more scientific archaeological efforts and the refinement of historical research methods also caused Cox to expand his understanding. He proposes three major alterations to the traditional view of early Christianity that should be made now in the light of this new evidence. These are described briefly below, but for greater detail see Cox's description in *The Future of Faith*.[6]

First, Cox points out that early Christianity was extremely diverse and multifaceted among the various little groups of followers in different locations. There was no standardized theology among them, no single pattern of governance, no uniform liturgy, and no commonly accepted scripture. Because in those days there was no form of mass communication, Christianity developed in little separate local groups, each of which had a somewhat different understanding of what Jesus's message had been about. These groups were united only in the powerful sense that they were all engaged in spreading Jesus's message. The "official" version of Christianity that emerged three hundred years later at the hands of Constantine, with all its hierarchies and official beliefs, was only one out of a range of other possibilities.

Second, Cox tells us the actual apostles never claimed authority for themselves. Rather, they "placed their confidence in the authority of the Spirit's presence among the people."[7] The concept of apostolic authority was "read back" into Christian history by those in later years who wanted to claim authority for themselves.

Third, Cox says that the Roman Empire in those days dominated and tyrannized those under its rule. The first Christians understood themselves as a movement centered around an alternative to this tyranny. According to Cox, "The first Christians understood themselves as an essentially anti-imperial movement."[8] This claim includes a disclosure that may be surprising to some: that the *upcoming* end-times scenario relished by fundamentalists over this last century is but a distortion of biblical texts. Rather than the end of the world, what was to end with the battle of Armageddon in the book of Revelation was the *imperial world* of Rome.[9]

Peasants in the time of Jesus, living at subsistence level, just hoping for the physical means to survive the day or the year, had little concern for existential answers and little interest in an afterlife. Jesus's message was popular not because it was suddenly offering people a chance for salvation in the next world. Rather, it was popular because the peasants were being told that God loved them as they were in the here and now, despite their lack of comfort and their suffering at the hands of the society they lived in. They were told that their lives *each* had value *in this world*. Jesus's message equalized people,

Looking Back through Time: Perspective

and this was exciting news that introduced a degree of order into the reigning chaos of those times. Hence, early Christianity was, in fact, not so much about supernatural beliefs or salvation in the next world. It was about values (justice and equality) and a way of life *in this world.*

The time of premodernity is considered to have run from about the fifth to the fifteenth centuries CE. This was the time of the Middle Ages. Regarding medieval Europe, it has been called the "Dark Ages" when compared to the supposed light of antiquity that came before it and the light of the Renaissance that came after it. Christianity in this time was heavily influenced by the Roman emperor Constantine. He was a controversial figure who lived from 272 to 337 CE and was a convert to Christianity.

Constantine had been disturbed by the variation among the different little groups that followed and celebrated Jesus's message. So, he set out to impose conformity onto the Christian message. Under his influence, members of the Council of Nicea established specific beliefs that all Christians were supposed to hold. They also threw out various books of the Bible that contained anything that might have been confusing or that referred to anything numinous or mystical. What they kept were the nuts and bolts, law-and-order parts of the religion. Some scholars now say that Constantine's keen interest in the content of Christianity was born more out of political ambition than sincere religious interest. In fact, it seems that the specific beliefs delineated as essential to the official religion under his influence were designed to control people—to impose rules, structure, and hierarchy over the individual.

Constantine's actions not only instituted conformity of belief but also refocused the emphasis of the Christian message around specific beliefs about God and the afterlife. In fact, it was only around this time that Christians "decided" that Jesus had been both divine and human. Whereas during the first few centuries CE, the Christian message had been focused on a way of life in this world and on the values of equality and justice, under Constantine's influence in the third or fourth century, Christianity came to be centered on specific supernatural beliefs.

Harvey Cox spells this out very clearly in *The Future of Faith*. He calls the time from Jesus's birth to the time of Constantine the "Age of Faith," because, in those days, Christianity was centered on values and a way of life in this world. Cox applies the term the "Age of Belief" to the years beginning with the time of Constantine—because that is when Christianity became belief centered—up to almost the present day. Lamenting Christianity's departure from Jesus's original message over the last fifteen hundred years, Cox offers the hopeful prediction that something new is coming up now, which he calls the "Age of the Spirit." Later chapters in this book will consider this idea more fully, as well as the distinction between belief and faith. In the next few pages, we will look at some other factors that caused changes in the general worldview.

Technological Evolution

With the advent of modern technology, we, in the eye-care field, now have many means of correcting refractive myopia beyond the old ways. Recent inventions have eased the hardship of the thick, myopia-correcting glasses I was forced to wear as a child. Laser vision correction for myopia flattens the cornea, thus extending the point at which light focuses within the eye out to the macula (where it needs to focus if clear vision is to result) and eliminating the need for glasses.

Looking Back through Time: Perspective

In cataract surgery, surgeons now implant a lens in the eye that has roughly the correct refractive power so that the patient barely needs glasses after the surgery. Specialty contact lenses allow many people with more complicated prescriptions to use them. All these advances have been developed in the years that I have been practicing optometry, such that my recommendations to a patient are very different now from what they were when I finished optometry school in 1982. These changes represent *progress,* and all eye doctors have had to adapt their way of practicing to accommodate them.

Technology is also causing sweeping changes in our culture, and religion is not immune to its effects. In fact, while technology seems to be causing an increase in visual myopia by keeping us tied to computer screens all day long, it may actually be helping to correct myopia of the spiritual type. This section, together with the next few chapters, begins to describe how this could be so. People not wanting to limit themselves to the "old ways" will do well to update their spiritual understandings accordingly.

Until the printing press was invented in the fifteenth century, books had to be painstakingly copied by hand, one by one. Obviously, books were very expensive then. The average laborer was unable to read and was unlikely ever even to see a book. So "knowledge" was limited to the scribes and scholars and members of the privileged classes. What books did exist centered around the teachings of the Church. Religious truth was limited to the province of religious leaders and was dispensed to the masses by them. As ordinary people had no way of studying the Bible (or any other religious text) themselves, they were dependent upon a leader to tell them what to believe. People in those days followed an authority that came from something outside themselves, namely, their religious leaders. In this way, the aristocracy exerted a level of power and control over the common person.

With the invention of the printing press in 1445, all that began to change. Gutenberg is the man credited with the invention of movable type—a crucial feature of the printing press. His first project was to print a set of two hundred illustrated Latin Bibles. Each copy cost about three times the annual salary of the average clerk of the day. The first books were printed in Latin and focused mostly on religious topics. But soon books were being produced much less expensively, and over time people demanded them on a wide variety of topics— travel manuals, medical manuals, poetry, almanacs, etc. By the year 1500, half a million books were in circulation. Literacy rates soared as books were quickly coming into the hands of the average person. Knowledge of all sorts was becoming widely available.

Eventually the writings of the ancient Greeks and Romans emerged from where they had been hidden for many centuries. People were able to study the early philosophers and were introduced to a different approach to life than what the religious aristocracy had taught them. Whereas writings before the printing press had been mostly on religious topics focused on saving one's soul in the interest of heavenly reward, now people were considering issues of philosophy, art, science, and government. Readers were coming to place more emphasis on life on this earth and on the importance of the individual and the intellect.

Dramatic cultural and societal changes came about in the sixteenth century, and the printing press is considered to have been a major factor that spearheaded these changes. The cultural shifts that consequently arose have been referred to as the Renaissance (1300 to 1700 CE) or the Reformation (1517 to 1648 CE). The term *Renaissance* refers mostly to the advancements that arose at that time in art and architecture and in the general culture. The term *Reformation* refers mainly to the religious change that fragmented Christianity into the various Protestant religions, as differentiated from Catholicism.

Martin Luther was a German Augustinian monk born in 1483 who held a doctorate in theology from the University of Wittenberg. He is often credited with having sparked the Protestant Reformation. He took issue with the Church's practice of selling indulgences. (An indulgence in those days referred to a piece of paper a person could purchase from the Church in exchange for God's forgiveness of his or her sins. The indulgence would supposedly reduce the time the person would have to spend in Purgatory atoning for such sins after death, thus permitting quicker entry into heaven.)

In a time when very few people would ever dare publicly to challenge the authority of the religious aristocracy, Luther had the nerve to post his famous ninety-five theses (or complaints against the Catholic teachings of the time) on the door of the Wittenberg church. Thanks to the printing press, copies of Luther's theses were disseminated first throughout Germany and eventually throughout Europe. Besides rejecting the validity of Church-issued indulgences, Luther's ninety-five theses further challenged Church authority by insisting that the Christian truth was found within the Bible, which by that time could be read by any literate individual. This overthrew the reigning assumption of the time that the pope had sole authority to "dispense" religious "truth" down through the Catholic hierarchy to the people.

Not surprisingly, Luther was excommunicated from the Church for this insubordination, but his actions had already spearheaded a new thought pattern: that it was okay for an individual to challenge the religious authorities. Our various Protestant religions have their roots within Luther's rebellion against papal authority.

At the same time, a general movement was also arising in the overall culture that we now call the Renaissance. This included a similar thought pattern in that it also asserted the importance of the individual in a way that challenged the authorities of the day. Where the medieval times had been characterized by religious piety, obedience, and submission to religious authorities, during the Renaissance the individual began to enjoy an elevated status. Emphasis was shifted away from salvation in eternity as the goal of human life and toward the importance of personal development and individual interests in *this life*. Great emphasis was put on human dignity and on the power of human reason to deliver truth. Science and the arts rose in importance, and there was a new excitement surrounding human development and exploration of human potential.

The Spread of Knowledge

Between the spread of knowledge that took place in the Western world during the Renaissance thanks to the printing press and the cultural shifts in attitude that accompanied it, the power that the aristocracy was able to exert over common people was greatly diminished, and quality of life for the common person was greatly enhanced.

Along with knowledge comes truth. The more we know, the more of reality we can "see" and the closer to the truth we can live. The average person during the Renaissance had far greater access to knowledge than did his predecessors, was less spiritually and culturally myopic, and therefore was able to live in greater truth. As a result, his life was improved. The changes in the Renaissance represented human *progress*—improvement in the lives of common people.

LOOKING BACK THROUGH TIME: PERSPECTIVE

The spread of knowledge and the accompanying changes in attitude that mushroomed during the Renaissance continued into what we now call the Enlightenment era, which spanned the years from around 1620 to 1789 CE. During that time scientists and philosophers alike laid out specific methods of inquiry through which it was assumed that natural laws and factual truths could be learned. Impressed with their own progress, humans began to place major importance on their own abilities to reason things out, so this time has also been called the Age of Reason. Individual rights and individual freedom came to be seen as important, as did free speech and free thought.

Huge advancements took place in medicine, mathematics, and physics. For the first time, humans realized that they could discover the nature and the laws of the universe through their own efforts. This was very different from the prior assumption that such information could be revealed only by divine sources. Eventually, people got the idea that information obtained through human reasoning was actually superior to information that had supposedly been divinely revealed. For the first time, scientific authority began to overtake religious authority in importance. Furthermore, it came to be assumed that, as ever more knowledge was obtained, the quality of human life could be continually improved. The idea that knowledge equals progress became unquestioned. Technological progress came to be seen as a major value, along with the notion that all progress is good—at any cost. Most of these notions regarding human reasoning, information, and progress survived into what we now call the modern era.

Modernity and Beyond

Modernity is considered to include the Enlightenment era and is thought to have continued up to the late, or perhaps just the middle,

Chapter 2

of the twentieth century. For the purposes of this book, three factors about modernity are important to understand.

First, as mentioned, modernity marked the first time when humans got the notion that they could discover natural, scientific, and philosophical truth through their own methods, instead of needing to rely upon divine revelation.

Second, impressed with their own discoveries, humans began to value technological progress very highly. What took priority was the assumption that all progress was good and that our scientific discoveries would one day bring us to ultimate truth. No consideration was given to the costs such progress might impose on our environment, and a strictly rational and materialist view of the universe arose.

Third, as people began to question revealed religious truths, we found that some of them conflicted with recent scientific discoveries. Logical and scientific weaknesses were detected in the religious myths that had previously been accepted unquestioningly. Because we now were placing greater trust in reason and the scientific method, scientific authority replaced religious authority. This era of modernity—which extends *almost* up to the present day—is often called "secular" modernity.

The secular mindset that emerged with the Enlightenment is crucial to understanding modernity. As secular modernity saw through the logical and scientific weaknesses in the religious myths, it also moved away from the *next-world* focus of traditional religion. Secular modernity concerned itself with here-and-now values in *this* life, making the best use of the life we have here on Earth. This emphasis was seen as part of the *progress* society was undergoing throughout the time of modernity.

Assuming that the myths traditional religion put forth needed to be either believed or rejected on a literal level, secular modernity largely rejected them and tried to distance itself from religion altogether. This attitude ignored the important fact that every civilization since the beginning of time has sought some form of spiritual connection or religious expression.

Modernity failed to appreciate a very important, basic universal human drive. We could express this drive in a number of ways, but the way the broadest number of people would accept might be to say that all humans need to find meaning in life. What might be less obvious is that true meaning comes not from meeting our selfish desires for money and worldly accomplishments but from finding ways to connect with something greater than ourselves.

Many people today may find authentic meaning in ways that have nothing to do with religion. Our connections with our family, our friends, our profession, our community, or even our hobbies may be compelling enough to deliver us beyond self-absorption. Some experience a transcendent feeling when they are out in nature—under a starry sky or before a vast ocean, for example. People will describe these feelings variously, but often the description will include a sense of awe and a feeling of being a very small part of something much, much bigger. We may not even realize that these sorts of *everyday* activities have the power to draw us outside of ourselves, or that they offer a healthy avenue of authentic spiritual connection.

But not everyone can access connection outside the limits of religion. For some, the only way to find meaning is through spiritual seeking or specific religious beliefs. Hence, to dismiss all forms of religion and spirituality as false or useless is to deny some people the chance to find fulfillment in life. In some camps, secular modernity has been accused of having stripped the meaning out of life. In its haste not to be duped by simplistic existential explanations, secular

Chapter 2

modernity seems to have thrown the spiritual baby out with the bathwater.

The modern era is considered to have begun to fade around the middle to the end of the last century. Few people seem to realize this, but, if you call something *modern* today, you are actually saying that it arose somewhere between the seventeenth and the twentieth century. Here in the twenty-first century, that which is "modern" is now outmoded. What is arising now is a new era that will make full use, and even improve upon, all of modernity's scientific advancements. It seems that some parts of our culture haven't quite caught on yet, but we are now entering *postmodernity*—an era that calls us to challenge many of modernity's most prized assumptions.

The rest of this book attempts to shed light on how postmodern, (i.e. *current*), realizations can take us beyond both the gifts and the spiritual handicaps we humans brought upon ourselves in the modern age. While it is not yet entirely clear just what form our civilization will take in the future, the use of the word *postmodernity* implies that we at least recognize that some aspects of modernity are being left behind. It goes without saying that my use of both terms—*modernity* and *postmodernity*—applies only to the Western world. Conditions elsewhere are too different to apply to this discussion.

A large part of what is causing the shift beyond modernity has to do with enhanced communications brought to us through the Internet. Chapter 5 will address this factor in a different context. For now, suffice it to say that what the printing press did for the Enlightenment, the Internet is doing for the twenty-first century. Knowledge has become a commodity; we can say that the Internet is causing further democratization of knowledge. Before the Internet, access to advanced knowledge on any topic was controlled by the intellectual and political elite.

Looking Back through Time: Perspective

Knowledge was power. Now, as the average person gains the potential to acquire knowledge on any topic she might choose to research, the elite are losing power. With a few clicks of a mouse, a middle-school student may easily surpass his history teacher's knowledge about a certain historical event. A parishioner who has spent a few evenings researching a certain theological point may find justification in challenging his clergyman's proclamations. With a great deal of research, a person like me can write authoritative books on a topic completely outside the field in which she has been formally trained.

Also losing power in postmodernity are what we might call metanarratives—grand, overall explanations that account for everything. In the past, these explanations may have been seen as holding everything together. What we could call the traditional Christian message is one such metanarrative that may be subject to losing power in the coming decades. In fact, new religious and spiritual realizations lie at the heart of what postmodernity "threatens" to bring us. Given that the more knowledge we can access, the clearer our vision becomes and that we cannot hold back inevitable change, our challenge as modernity fades into its postmodern cousin is to examine our current spiritual vision willingly. And, if it is found to be myopic, the open-minded and open-hearted among us will agree to don new lenses that will afford us enhanced spiritual clarity.

Two related concepts are crucial in the development of the type of spiritual understanding this book attempts to share. Both enjoy solid substantiation by various types of experts and are accepted as a matter of course in certain camps. Yet both are largely ignored by the media and rarely discussed in the conventional society. Certain factions seeking to hold back their recognition in the hope of controlling others may even actively suppress them.

Chapter 2

Many expert theorists have described the way individuals develop spiritually. I have amalgamated their works into what I have called spiritual development theory and describe it in detail in chapter 3 (and in even more detail in my earlier book, *Faith Beyond Belief: Stories of Good People Who Left Their Church Behind*).

Studying individual spiritual development can also bring hopeful recognition of a larger process—human cultural evolution (as discussed in chapter 7). Without the perspective afforded by considering these two concepts together, the average person is restricted to a limited spiritual focus. The following pages may be countercultural, but they offer a hopeful glimpse of a transformed world that may one day be possible, if these two concepts come to be appreciated by the larger society.

3
Spiritual Development Theory: a Key Element in Spiritual Vision Correction

My first book, *Faith Beyond Belief: Stories of Good People Who Left Their Church Behind* is about spiritual development theory. That book highlights the work of about twelve theorists who have described stages an individual person may go through in attaining spiritual maturity. The theorists come from different academic and spiritual backgrounds, different parts of the world, and even different centuries. They all use different terminology and describe a different number of stages. Some of them are even known to deny any connection with the stages the others describe. Yet, from a bird's eye view, the commonalities in the trajectory they have all laid out are unmistakable. While I believe I may be the first person to draw extensive connection among the works of these theorists, and the first to name the concept *spiritual development theory*, I feel it has huge importance in allowing peaceful coexistence among adherents of various religious traditions, as well as huge importance in correcting the spiritual myopia from which most of our mainstream society suffers so severely.

For many years, I have had a Google Alert set up to inform me whenever the term *spiritual maturity* appears on the Internet. Often a piece will come through in which someone describes spiritual maturity as a specific endpoint of deep engagement in a particular religion—for example, the person has grown closer to Jesus. But this kind of involvement is part of the spiritual myopia this book seeks to correct. A study of the spiritual development theorists—and there are many more than twelve; I just could not discuss them all in one book—exposes quite a different trajectory.

Spiritual development theory proposes that, on the road to spiritual maturity, we become less attached to one single set of religious truths and instead come to appreciate a more universal, less dogmatic spiritual perspective. This perspective would tend to replace the exclusive beliefs that apply only to our insular religious tradition with an all-inclusive sense of universal connection. Rather than viewing our religious stories as strictly factual, historical accounts, this new perspective would lead us toward a metaphorical appreciation of the message the stories in our tradition were meant to illustrate.

Though some of the theorists discussed in *Faith Beyond Belief* define as few as two stages, and one as many as twelve, I find that the process of spiritual development is most easily described in terms of four stages: the Lawless, the Faithful, the Rational, and the Unitive. It must be noted that these stages are not limited to any specific religion. They describe a process that is common to people of all faiths, including even nondogmatic traditions such as Buddhism. Two further disclaimers pertain:

1. Although we use the term *stage*, no one individual exists wholly at any one stage. Compare the stages to the words *introvert* and *extrovert*. No given person is either a hundred percent introverted or a hundred percent extroverted. We all slide along a continuum, more extroverted in some situations, more introverted in others, some years trending to more extroverted overall, some less so. Yet the terms *introversion* and *extroversion* do shed light on an important factor in our personality. The terms illustrate a concept of which we could otherwise have no understanding. The words *optimist* and *pessimist* provide an additional example. No one person is completely optimistic about all situations all the time, and no one is completely pessimistic. But the fact that we have these words does allow us to understand something important about ourselves. Awareness of the optimist-versus-pessimist concept can even inspire us in the direction of the trait we view as being more favorable. Similarly, an understanding of the stages can inspire us in a more favorable direction spiritually.

2. Just as we do not use the words *introvert* or *extrovert* or *optimist* or *pessimist* to judge a given person, so the spiritual development stages are offered not as a means of judgment but more as a tool that helps us understand an important concept. No one ever exists completely at any one spiritual stage. Our journey along the spiritual development trajectory proceeds neither in a straight line nor in an orderly manner. And while only a very few people ever reach the uppermost stage overall, I believe that each and every one of us carries at least a few traits of the upper stages, mostly without even realizing it. Similarly, each

of us could easily be pulled down, temporarily or permanently, into a prior stage in the presence of certain provocative life circumstances.

The Faithful: Stage Two of Four

Though it is not the first stage, I like to begin with what I call the Faithful stage, the second out of four, because it is the one most descriptive of the typical, explicit religious mindset in our culture. This is what most of us understand as popular religion. That is, religion as preached from the typical pulpit (which is a bit different from religion as it is discussed among theologians.) A person at the Faithful level obtains her religious truths from a source that comes from outside herself. Her minister, rabbi, imam, or priest tells her what she should do and believe, and those directives are backed up by the holy book to which her religion ascribes. This type of outlook harks back to the days when the only people who could read were the elite—often religious scholars. It was their job to dispense information to the masses who had no other access to religious truths. The ordinary person was essentially a child with no personal authority, especially in spiritual matters.

Another attribute of the Faithful stage is that the people in it tend to hold understandings that are completely *literal*. Within Christianity, adherents of this stage believe that Moses really did cause the waters of the Red Sea to part just long enough for all the Israelites to walk through, and really did wave his staff to cause the same gap to close over the entire Egyptian army, drowning every one of them. And Mary, the mother of Jesus, was a virgin in a biological sense of the word. Faithful adherents also see God as a specific being, completely external to the person and separate from our world. The Faithful-level person accepts all these concepts in a literal sense, both because he accepts the authority of the religious leaders who offer them and because he finds himself disinclined to question the science behind them.

Another Faithful-level trait is to be very attached to one's own group and to see that group as being more important, more real and more right than all the others. We can say that the Faithful-level person is *ethnocentric*; what happens to those outside his own group concerns him far less than what happens to those inside his group. Also, what happens to those outside his group concerns him far less than it concerns those who hold more inclusive worldviews. The Faithful-level person will often feel the need to try to persuade people with other views to join his camp; he may proselytize and try to convert others to his religion. He does this with extremely good intent; he wants to save other souls. But those at the Faithful level have never heard about spiritual development theory. They are unaware of the levels above their own.

Also, the Faithful-level person is very dependent upon having definite answers about our most important existential questions. He cannot stand to live in doubt. He must know for sure how and why we are here on Earth and what happens after we die. Hence, it should come as no surprise that he is unwilling to question the preset answers his religious authorities provide. And he tolerates very poorly any discrepancies that might arise through new scientific findings. In other words, the Faithful-level person lives in a world of black and white. A given behavior is either right or wrong; a belief is either true or false. He trends toward binary thinking—like the simplest of computers. He has not allowed himself to perceive the full complexities with which our human minds are capable of dealing. Because he divides complex aspects of our existence into simplistic either/or categories, because his sentiments tend to fall on the same side as everyone else in his group, and because he tends to shun critical assessment of the correctness of his group's mindset, we can say that the Faithful-level person is largely *pre-critical.*

ISSUE	FAITHFUL TRAITS
RELIGIOUS ATTITUDE	Needs definite answers; won't question directly
INTERPRETIVE STYLE	Literal
LOCUS OF AUTHORITY	Oracle authority
CIRCLE OF CONCERN	One's own group (ethnocentric)
IDENTITY	Defined by group; divisive against outsiders
RELIGIOUS COMMUNITY	The only "right" one
VALUES	Security, certainty, comfort
VIEW OF "GOD"	External, separate Being
OTHER	Naïve (pre-critical); fear-based

Figure 3. Faithful-stage Traits

(From Margaret Placentra Johnston, *Faith Beyond Belief: Stories of Good People Who Left Their Church Behind* [Wheaton, IL: Quest Books, 2012], 83. Reproduced/adapted by permission of Quest Books (www.questbooks.net])

Our world now calls us to a more comprehensive level of personal responsibility. The newscasts burst with examples of religious leaders guilty of all-too-human foibles. Even our holy books, we now learn, have been altered according to the whims of some human leader in the past, an example being the emperor Constantine, as mentioned in Chapter 2. Uncritical acceptance of conventional teachings and complete dependence upon outer authority bars us from maturity. Attaining personal authority becomes important in the later stages. It is dependent upon a willingness to question, or to analyze critically what has been taught to us. It is because people at the Faithful level are usually not willing or able to undertake such analysis that we say they are pre-critical. The importance of critical thinking to spiritual maturity will be further developed later in this book.

In general, Faithful-level people tend to be good, solid, upright, law-abiding citizens. They will follow the Ten Commandments to the letter and will tend to contribute to society in a largely positive way.

However, because their moral rulebooks were written largely before our society became so multifaceted, they will have difficulty when facing more complex moral issues. Though most of our mainstream culture remains unaware of it, the Faithful-level mindset is poorly disposed to deal with both the complexities and the opportunities our current, postmodern existence presents. Not all elements in our increasingly complex social order are addressed in the Ten Commandments. How do we deal with our heterogeneous society in which people hold innumerable viewpoints? What are the moral implications of stem-cell therapy? Should we permit genetic engineering in the human fetus? What rights should we accord to animals and even to artificial creatures? Where can we turn for answers about postmodern moral dilemmas such as these? Because Faithful-level thinking remains largely unprepared to apply sound creative discernment in current moral dilemmas, it imposes overly simplistic solutions and embodies the very spiritual myopia this book seeks to cure.

Chapter 3

Faith Beyond Belief contains four stories of people addressing the type of cognitive conflict a Faithful-level person might encounter regarding religion in our current society. But a more recent example may be found in a TED Talk recently sent to me by a friend. Megan Phelps-Roper was brought up in Westboro Baptist Church, a small Kansas congregation famous for acts of hate and hate speech directed against people with other religious beliefs and/or differing lifestyles. Megan Phelps-Roper is obviously related to Westboro's founder, Fred Phelps, so we know she grew up very much embedded in the Westboro philosophy. Megan's TED Talk describes an early life wherein "good" and "the clean" were exclusively limited to members of her own church, and "evil" or "the unclean" were defined as "everyone else." Members of her church were constantly at odds with the world and claimed that everyone else was headed for damnation.

In her early years, Megan uncritically espoused the mindset of her surrounding tribe. But eventually, because of that very zeal, she began to post Westboro-type comments on Twitter, a milieu in which she was exposed to messages that often disagreed and conflicted widely with her own. Some grace allowed Megan to consider open-mindedly some of Westboro's inconsistencies that her Twitter friends were pointing out: "How could we claim to love our neighbor while at the same time praying for God to destroy them?" What began as harsh conflict against her Twitter contacts eventually softened into civil conversations, full of genuine curiosity, and over time they engendered mutual respect. Eventually, Megan saw that the people "on the other side were not the demons we had been led to believe." Continuing realizations eventually made it impossible for her to stay in her church.

Spiritual Development Theory: a Key Element...

This was no small move for Megan to make. She realized that her family, "whose thoughts and feelings meant everything to [her]," would never speak to her again. Megan and her younger sister walked out of the Westboro community together around 2012. While it felt as if they were walking into an abyss, it was there that they found light and a way forward. Megan came to feel that "it was a relief and a privilege to let go of the harsh judgments that instinctively had run through [her] mind" in the past. She sorrowfully describes how she now sees mirrored in our public discourses so many of the same destructive impulses that ruled her former church. "We've broken the world into us and them, only emerging from our bunkers long enough to lob rhetorical grenades at the other camp . . . no nuance, no complexity, no humanity." Megan pleads, "I remember this path; it will not take us where we want to go. Escalating disgust and intractable conflict are not what we want for ourselves, or our country, or our next generation." Just before Megan left her family and her church, her mom used the words, "You are just a human being, my dear sweet child," to beg her not to question but to trust God and her elders. But Megan knew her mom was missing the bigger picture: we are all just human beings, and each of our actions contributes to the overall whole of the societies that we make up. Megan ends her TED Talk by pointing out that "the end of this spiral of rage and blame begins with just one person who decides not to engage in these . . . destructive impulses. We just have to decide it is going to start with us."[1]

The Westboro Baptist Church in which Megan grew up can serve as almost a caricature of the Faithful mentality, based as it is on outer authority, black-and-white thinking, ethnocentrism, and literal beliefs. She was banished when she questioned those beliefs. Similar treatment is rendered by many religions. The Amish and Jehovah's Witnesses shun; fundamentalist-type Muslims and Christians scorn and even threaten; Jews censure; Scientologists declare individuals "Suppressive Persons."

The process Megan so boldly engaged in—that of questioning her tribe and seeking for larger, more generally applicable truths outside of it—is the very one that begins the process of growth beyond the Faithful stage. As starkly limited as the Westboro mentality is, it is easy for us to see how Megan grew spiritually in her search for a broader truth. Her story serves as the perfect introduction to the next level of spiritual development, the Rational stage.

The Rational: Stage Three of Four

The next stage—the one through which Megan moved during her process of questioning her Faithful-level beliefs—is the Rational stage, which is the third out of four. I describe it next because it is the second most explicit stage in Western culture after the Faithful stage. I say Megan moved "through" the Rational stage as opposed to "into" it because she expressed things in her TED talk indicating that she may have sailed right through Rational and into the fourth stage all at once, but we will defer that discussion for later in this book.

With all our current global communications and cultural intermixing, it is becoming less and less probable that an open-minded person will limit his religious and spiritual musings to the religious truths dictated by his own tribe. Influences are bound to filter in that contradict the specific religious teachings of the tradition into which a person was born. Only someone who has buried his head underground would not at some point run up against a religious tenet or piece of dogma that fails to jive with information coming in from the larger world.

A person facing such discrepancies, in a process we call *cognitive dissonance*, will, in some cases, decide that his own reasoning process is more valid than the teachings of his religion and will rationally come to reject the religion altogether. Various real-life examples of this process were presented in part 1 of *Faith Beyond Belief* and in the Megan Phelps-Roper example described earlier. This process is the step necessary to progress from the second-level, Faithful stage to the third-level, Rational stage.

People going through the Rational stage may or may not actually reject the religion they are questioning. The important point is that they are critically reflecting on whether they personally can accept the beliefs and the values that were dictated to them by others. If they cannot accept them, then a very bold step is necessary: they must differentiate themselves from the rest of their tribe. They must depart from the comfortable groupthink they were enjoying and wander onto a sometimes-lonely path of disagreeing with their family and friends about important spiritual matters. They must accept personal responsibility for their beliefs or lack thereof—and for their values—as opposed to ceding that responsibility to an outer authority in the way a child cedes responsibility to a parent. Where we can say people at the Faithful level are *pre-critical*, we can say those at the Rational level are *critical* because they do address issues of cognitive dissonance with an open mind and with an energy and drive not found at the Faithful level. (One of my beta readers pointed out how many at the Faithful level do approach their beliefs with great energy and drive, the example she cited being the Westboro Baptist Church. Certainly, we have noted the pathological energy and drive with which such groups defend their beliefs, but they seem not all open to analyzing them critically as an individual with an open mind would do.)

Chapter 3

It goes along with this step that the person's ideas and beliefs begin to be influenced by factors outside her own group. As this happens, she begins to identify with a larger part of humanity. Where we said ethnocentricity is common at the Faithful level, we can say that the Rational-level person tends to be *worldcentric*, seeing herself as part of the group that comprises all humans. Having emerged out of groupthink, people at the Rational level tend to see all humans as equally entitled to everything the universe has to offer. They tend to be very much interested in equal rights, social justice, and other causes that support all people. The idea of any one religious, political, or social group being privileged above others is anathema to their ideals.

Another characteristic of the Rational-level person is that she puts her greatest trust in the powers of human reason. Science and progress bring us greater truth than does religious tradition, she will say. The Rational-level person has no trouble believing in evolution, for example, no matter what the Bible might say about the origins of the earth. She has great confidence that even the greatest mysteries of our existence (e.g., Why are we here? What happens after we die?) will one day be solved through the scientific process. Questions about the meaning of life will be answered in humanistic terms, as opposed to teachings about salvation in some dubious afterlife.

Being the third of the four levels I include in the spiritual development trajectory, the Rational level follows the Faithful level. This order may seem counterintuitive. However, although the Rational level may include nonbelievers, it is characterized by greater spiritual maturity than is found at the Faithful level. It is also more attuned than the Faithful level to the changing realities of our current culture. The Rational-level person has chosen to deal with the complexities of our modern, and possibly even our postmodern, world in a more energetic way. In contrast, a Faithful-level person would rather pretend that these complexities do not exist or may wish for a return to the good old days when everyone a person knew believed the same thing. In this sense, the Rational-level person is better prepared to deal authentically with life in today's world than is the Faithful-level person.

Other traits common at the Rational level include a somewhat more secular attitude, trust in the authority of human reason and the scientific method as means of reaching truth as opposed to divine revelation, and a tendency to feel responsible for discovering truth on one's own as opposed to relying on the outer authority of one's tribe.

In general, the Rational level holds a broader worldview than the Faithful level. Where the Faithful level trends toward ethnocentrism, the Rational level tends to be worldcentric, as mentioned above. They see all humans as equal. They tend to be very much in favor of equal rights for everyone, social justice, etc.

Perhaps because most of religion sounds as if it comes from the Faithful, literal level, the Rational-level person will often seek to distance himself from what sounds like childish nonsense. People seeking comfort from an imaginary Father figure in the sky, people believing that that Father figure will reward or punish them in the afterlife for their behavior in this life, people thinking that that Father figure will grant them personal favors, even in win-lose situations in which one person's prayer being answered must result in someone else's *not* being answered—all these seem like silly expressions of wishful thinking. A Rational-level person will tend to distance herself from such thought patterns.

Chapter 3

ISSUE	FAITHFUL TRAITS	RATIONAL TRAITS
RELIGIOUS ATTITUDE	Needs definite answers; won't question directly	**Skeptical; seeks truth over comfort**
INTERPRETIVE STYLE	Literal	**Reason; science-based**
LOCUS OF AUTHORITY	Oracle authority	**Conscience authority; principled**
CIRCLE OF CONCERN	One's own group (ethnocentric)	**All humans; social justice (worldcentric)**
IDENTITY	Defined by group; divisive against outsiders	**Individuated, but not selfish**
RELIGIOUS COMMUNITY	The only "right" one	**Questioning; may reject**
VALUES	Security, certainty, comfort	**Truth; integrity**
VIEW OF "GOD"	External, separate Being	**Science; reason; truth**
OTHER	Naïve (pre-critical); fear-based	**Critical; seeking; involved in social causes**

Figure 4: Comparison of Faithful- and Rational-stage Traits
(From Margaret Placentra Johnston, *Faith Beyond Belief: Stories of Good People Who Left Their Church Behind* [Wheaton, IL: Quest Books, 2012], 83. Reproduced/adapted by permission of Quest Books [www.questbooks.net])

These two levels—the Faithful and the Rational—are very much at odds with each other. They form the basis for our most ardent culture wars. The reason is that most people have not studied and therefore do not realize that these levels in the trajectory of spiritual development exist. The Faithful are unaware of the Rational level, so they think that everyone who is not religious is from the least developed level, the Lawless (described below). And the Rational think that everyone involved in religion or spirituality of any sort are so because they come from the Faithful level. Those at the Rational level are unaware of the fourth level, which forms much of the crux of this book and will be discussed in detail in chapter 6.

So, the Rational-level person *does* suffer from a visual distortion. The very stance of distancing from traditional belief tends to lead to the complete rejection of anything outside the here-and-now, everyday experience. This can blind the Rational-level person to the appreciation of spiritual elements that connect us all to one another and to the universe. In his devotion to science and reason, he will tend to throw the proverbial baby out with the bathwater.

The fourth and final level of spiritual development this book defines is playing an important role in improving our spiritual vision on a culture-wide basis in the West. I will describe that level after presenting a few other factors.

The Lawless: Stage One of Four

A child developing normally will go through a period in which the whole world is about her. Piaget told us that this stage usually predominates between the ages of two and seven. In it, the child is unable to see a situation from anyone else's point of view. Her world revolves around her; she is naturally egocentric. But normal human development takes an individual beyond this limited perspective, so that by adolescence she will begin to include other people in her understanding and in her circle of concern.

Sometimes, a particularly unfortunate person will reach adulthood having failed to move beyond the egocentrism that had been healthy in his childhood. Egocentrism in an adult is not healthy at all. In spiritual

CHAPTER 3

development theory we use the term *Lawless* to describe this stage. An adult in the Lawless stage is in a state of arrested development. This person displays narcissism and sees any perspective that differs from his own as false. He is guided only by his own will and feels that the laws of society, or of his religion, do not apply to him. He has never internalized the values and rules of his society or religion and is guided merely by self-interest. He may belong to a particular faith or may even be the leader. But he does not authentically submit his own will to the God of his religion or to any other goodness principles. He mainly does things for whatever ways they might advance his own personal agendas. If he belongs to a religion, he will only espouse the most superficial understanding of its creed. We can say that the Lawless person is *pre-religious,* and therefore, godless. Most Faithful-level people see all nonbelievers as godless sinners. They assume that all people who don't follow a religion—that is, all atheists—fall into the Lawless camp, though few would use that term, per se. In general, Lawless individuals have an ill effect on their society, as opposed to contributing to it in a positive way as people at the other stages do. Being egocentric, most Lawless people lead chaotic lives and live in some kind of material misery. Occasionally, though, one will have incredible drive and may rise to levels of immense power—even possibly the presidency. This is because he is not limited by the norms to which most people who are regulated by their tribe *or their conscience* adhere.

The Lawless-level person fails to sense any connection to anything bigger than himself and relates to other people only in a superficial, self-serving, or manipulative way. His sense of self-importance is so great that he assumes ordinary rules do not apply to him. Thankfully, full-fledged Lawless individuals are uncommon in a civilized society, but citizens who are normally law abiding can sometimes sink into

Lawlessness in extenuating circumstances. These people are not so much spiritually myopic as just plain blind. They are spiritually blind to the possibility of connecting with anything larger than their own selves. See chapter 4 for more on spiritual amaurosis, or blindness.

ISSUE	LAWLESS TRAITS	FAITHFUL TRAITS	RATIONAL TRAITS
RELIGIOUS ATTITUDE	Disinterested, or superficial interest only	Needs definite answers; won't question directly	Skeptical; seeks truth over comfort
INTERPRETIVE STYLE	Self-centered	Literal	Reason; science-based
LOCUS OF AUTHORITY	One's own will; unprincipled	Oracle authority	Conscience authority; principled
CIRCLE OF CONCERN	Self (egocentric)	One's own group (ethnocentric)	All humans; social justice (worldcentric)
IDENTITY	Selfish	Defined by group; divisive against outsiders	Individuated but not selfish
RELIGIOUS COMMUNITY	May join for own needs	The only "right" one	Questioning; may reject
VALUES	Personal pleasure	Security; certainty; comfort	Truth; integrity
VIEW OF "GOD"	Self	External, separate Being	Science; reason; truth
OTHER	Undeveloped, manipulative, insincere, chaotic lifestyle	Naïve (pre-critical); fear-based	Critical; seeking; involved in social causes

Figure 5. Lawless-stage traits (far left) compared to those at the Faithful and Rational stages

(From Margaret Placentra Johnston, *Faith Beyond Belief: Stories of Good People Who Left Their Church Behind* [Wheaton, IL: Quest Books, 2012], 87. Reproduced/adapted by permission of Quest Books[(www.questbooks.net)])

Chapter 3

The Lawless-level person is less spiritually advanced than one at the Faithful level. For a Lawless person to move up to the Faithful level, possibly through a born-again experience, is a definite and highly beneficial step in spiritual growth.

All three of the stages described above suffer from some degree of spiritual myopia, but the Lawless are more spiritually myopic than the Faithful. And the Faithful are more spiritually myopic than the Rational. Considering the worldview of each of these stages, we can begin to see how spiritual development progresses:

> The Lawless are EGO-centric: "It's all about me."
>
> The Faithful are ETHNO-centric: "It's all about our group."
>
> The Rational are WORLD-centric: "It's all about humans—our mind, our science, reason, and individuality."

Before we consider the worldview that might arise beyond the Rational level—that is, the Unitive worldview—chapter 4 will address some factors that impair our spiritual vision and hold back spiritual progress.

4
Signs and Symptoms of Spiritual Myopia: A Disease of Insularity

Before we explore what a clearer spiritual vision might consist of, we need to take a hard look at factors that are doomed to reinforce the spiritual myopia from which much of our society suffers. The first three factors below—personification, literalism, and fundamentalism—relate mainly to symptoms of the Faithful level in traditional religion. Spiritual amaurosis applies mostly to the Lawless and the Rational levels, while triumphalism, binary logic, and the need for certainty apply equally to all three stages of spiritual development we have discussed so far.

Personification

Various factions in our society work to restrict a broader spiritual awareness. Some may do so deliberately, while others are motivated

Chapter 4

by fear of (or lack of trust in) the forces of change. Many strong influences still impel some people to hold on to aspects of religious belief that foster continued spiritual myopia. One of the seemingly most innocent but problem-filled of these aspects is personification.

Boats are given names and referred to with feminine pronouns: *she* and *her*. How many people have you known who have given their car a name, at the same time therefore also assigning it a gender? This is *personification*, the act of attributing human qualities to something—an animal, object, or abstraction—that isn't human. It seems to be a normal human tendency to want to personify important elements in our lives.

Often people use personification to describe something so that others can understand it better. When telling a story, for example, personification can add interest. We can say that a certain character in a story personifies a concept. An author may create a certain character, for instance, to be the personification of evil. Most attempts at personification are useful and/or fun. Surely, personifying our car or our boat is a harmless diversion. No one would think we mean to imply that such objects are human. Nor when we say a fictional character is the personification of evil do we mean to imply that evil is an actual being.

In ancient times, there were many important powerful forces in people's lives that they could understand only very poorly. Wind, rain, and fire all had tremendous impact on the quality of life, but ancient people had no idea what caused these forces; they had little notion of when the forces might strike and no way of controlling their impact. So, each ancient society tended to *personify* such forces into a deity of some sort. In their cultural lore there arose the notion of a "god" that embodied each of the powerful forces. The purpose of

Signs and Symptoms of Spiritual Myopia...

this personification was to help people acknowledge their inability to control the force, to better understand it, and to deal with it better in their lives.

As mentioned in chapter 2, despite there being little communication among the various ancient societies, they each tended to envision similar "gods," or at least gods that represented the common forces controlling the lives of their people. The gods that these societies dreamed up did not exist as actual beings, of course, but the *forces* they represented were very real and had tremendous sway over the lives of the people. It is impossible to know what percentage of the population recognized that their gods were not actual beings but instead personifications of natural forces.

In today's world, we know a great deal about what causes wind, rain, and fire. We in the developed world are fairly successful at controlling the impact of these forces on our lives. In fact, we even *employ* them to enhance our lives in many ways. So, no longer is there much need to personify wind, rain, and fire. Yet there are other powerful forces strongly influencing our lives that we still don't fully understand. Love, fear, hope, and hate serve as examples. These forces exert even stronger influence at the unconscious and subconscious levels than at the conscious one, making them even harder to comprehend in their complexity.

One most powerful force in particular still reigns supreme over our existence and yet is rarely discussed. One reason for this oversight is that it acts most strongly below the level of consciousness. Another reason is that finding the words for it is nearly impossible. As I sit here at my computer, my mind runs amok trying to pin it down to one sentence, or one paragraph, or even one book. We could give it many names, but each name would be meaningful only to people

Chapter 4

who have experienced it in that specific way. With that caveat, I will say that this force is *metaphysical*—or dare I say *spiritual*— in kind.

One of my beta readers said I need to acknowledge the similarity of my use of the word *force* here with George Lucas's concept in *Star Wars*: "May the Force be with you." Apparently, Lucas was influenced by a statement made in Arthur Lipsett's short film, *21–87*, by the Canadian filmmaker Roman Kroiter: "Many people feel that in the contemplation of nature and in communication with other living things, they become aware of some kind of force, or something, behind this apparent mask which we see in front of us, and they call it God."[1] Lucas, who has studied religion and has described himself as a Buddhist Methodist,[2] has said that the sentiment underlying this line is universal and that similar phrases have been used extensively by many different people for the last thirteen thousand years. In describing the force during an *Empire Strikes Back* production meeting, Lucas said:

> The act of living generates a force field, an energy. That energy surrounds us; when we die, that energy joins with all the other energy. There is a giant mass of energy in the universe that has a good side and a bad side. We are part of the Force because we generate the power that makes the Force live. When we die, we become part of that Force, so we never really die; we continue as part of the Force.[3]

People from many cultures have given a name to this force. Some people can experience it directly, while others only acquiesce to the way the founder of their religion described it. Many have given it an easy, shorthand name because it is easier to *personify* it than to

Signs and Symptoms of Spiritual Myopia...

contemplate this force in the full extent of its mystery. It is easier to stow it away in a Sunday-only compartment in our minds and leave us free the rest of the week to deal with the practical aspects of our lives. When English-speaking people use the word *God* they are *personifying* this force.

In a way, our religions have cheapened this force. They assign it all sorts of peevish and small-minded human characteristics—anger, punitive-mindedness, and jealousy. They give it a white beard and a throne in the sky. They claim that their specific version of this force is the only right way to describe it, while all others are false. This is the spiritual myopia this book seeks to cure.

All cultures in all parts of the world since the beginning of time have sensed and been influenced by this force. They each have made attempts to name and describe it. Many of these cultures have personified this force into a being so that they could better deal with its presence in their lives. Some have even attempted to control it by making up "rules" this force supposedly "wants" them to follow, thus reducing a person's anxiety about the unknown parts of existence.

As long as not much intermixing among the various cultures took place, people could successfully use whatever name their own society assigned to the force. If they called it *God*, if they ascribed human weaknesses to this God, if they assumed that their founder had discovered a truth that applied only to their people—all these assertions were helpful and useful in their lives. Most were glad to have such easy handles by which to compartmentalize the biggest mystery of life into a formulaic simplicity.

As time went on, people began to ascribe more and more characteristics to the force their society had personified. In one society, they assigned it a gender, claiming that "he" had sent a list of rules

Chapter 4

down from heaven that people must follow and that later he wrote a book dictating everything a person must believe. In some cases, the presence of this being brought great comfort, and so the personification became even stronger. We can see that the personification of the mysterious force in our lives was, and remains in many ways, a good thing. Of course, it also had its unfavorable influences, as well. In other cases, religious leaders have reinforced the personification and used it to threaten people into following their rules, behaving a certain way, and even paying money to the church.

Now that we have huge amounts of cultural intermixing, however, localized and culturally specific personifications of the mysterious force that all people share are creating a big problem. People from diverse cultures who should be learning to live side by side in peace within the same community are instead letting their religion separate them from each other. People sometimes insist that the personification their culture has formed of Divinity is better than the personification other cultures hold. Worse yet, they deny or fail to recognize that it is a personification in the first place. They insist that God is an actual being who favors only their people and that only their religion has the right answers. (What kind of God, one might ask, would ever favor only people from a certain *small* part of his creation? Who would *want* such a God?) Wars are fought over this issue. People are killed in the name of a specific being that began as a figurative representation of a force felt by people of all cultures! Far too few people can see beyond the cultural limitations of their own religion. The conventional world especially promotes this lack of vision. The spiritual myopia of our time is the lack of recognition that what most of our religions call *God* is a culturally determined representation of a universal force.

Signs and Symptoms of Spiritual Myopia...

This force does not have a chosen people; it does not get angry when we don't follow certain rules; it does not require us to believe improbable things; it does not threaten eternal punishment; it does not promise us certain reward. All these aspects of religion are characteristics a certain culture has ascribed to the force their culture has personified into a supposed being.

Literalism

A major factor contributing to spiritual myopia in our society is that so many people lack the understanding that our religious concepts are, in fact, personifications. They read about God in the Bible, and they mistake that personification we call *God* for an actual being. They assume heaven and hell are actual geographical locations and that the rules written hundreds of years ago were meant to apply for all time. They fail to understand that, way back in time, some humans developed belief systems and religions based on a worldview that was subject to far greater cultural limitations than what we have now.

People at the Faithful stage are more prone to literalism than those at the other stages are. They fail to consider that most religious stories were written by minds that had not yet developed the type of critical thinking that arose during the Enlightenment. Acting on divine inspiration—whether it came from God or the gods or something else from the spirit level—the writers of the Bible lacked the ability to scrutinize facts for their literal truth. The stories they told were just that—stories to illustrate various concepts. They probably didn't expect their stories to be analyzed critically or taken literally (see ch. 10, regarding Don Cupitt). So, here we have a reasoning error that has persisted for a few thousand years—"truths" about our existence written by the prescientific minds of people who had no clue about the

Chapter 4

immensity of the universe or about the depths of the human spirit. Inspired or not, their writings were nonscientific, provincial tales written for their own people in their own time and their own location. They never could have anticipated that their imaginative tales would be carried down through the ages; nor could they have understood the need for the tales to hold up to rational and scientific scrutiny.

Another form of literalism contributing to spiritual myopia is that literalists will hold to the letter of *any* laws, as opposed to seeking to honor the basic intent, or the spirit, in which the laws were written in the first place. This attitude results in a narrow and restricted mindset that fails to allow for the use of judgment in exceptional situations and fails to adapt to inevitable societal changes over time.

As an example, let us look at John 14:6: "I am the way, and the truth, and the life. No one comes to the Father except through me." The world in which Jesus made that declaration was very different from the world today. There was no way anyone in those days could predict the astonishing technological advances that would make Jesus's words still accessible two thousand years later. Things change, and our understandings of our truths must change along with it all. Suppose that in 1975 I had made the statement, "We need a telephone booth at least every half mile in all big cities in the United States." In that time and place, of course, that statement would have been true. But is it still true today?

Is it possible that Jesus made the statement, "No one comes to the Father except through me," for the time and the place in which he said it? Could it be that we need a more broadly applicable, more inclusive understanding today? Could it be that something less culturally determined applies when we expand our awareness—as we now can do thanks to technological progress—to all cultures in all times and all places? Could we not now be being called to expand our understanding of "the Father" as a cultural personification of the universal force that connects us all?

Literal interpretations are dangerous because they block recognition of the ways in which we are now being called—thanks to the factors that will be discussed in chapter 5—to expand our spiritual understandings.

Fundamentalism

Fundamentalism is an especially unfortunate form of literalism. Sensing that cultural changes are afoot that threaten the old understandings, some people try to hold back the effects of those changes and react vehemently against them. Such people react from a position of fear, as they are poorly disposed to adapt gracefully to changes that are already in progress. Fundamentalism is a finger-in-the-dike approach that fails to understand or appreciate the enormity of the inevitable changes coming to us in postmodernity or the rich opportunities they present. It is a maladaptation to reality. Unlike what the fundamentalists themselves would like to assert, they are not returning to traditional values; rather, they are a new phenomenon specifically formed in reaction against the current condition.

Whether we are talking about Christian fundamentalism or Muslim fundamentalism (all religions have a fundamentalist faction, even Buddhists[4]), it all arises out of the same mentality: a sense of the exclusive righteousness of one's own group, fear of change, and a sense of threat to the order that is holding certain brittle lives together. Fundamentalists, almost by definition, represent the lower edge of the Faithful level in spiritual development theory—those at the border between Faithful and Lawless. That is, without the rigid worldview offered by their particular religion, fundamentalists are at risk of descending into Lawlessness. They

Chapter 4

are right to try to defend the "old ways" for their own sakes, because they lack appreciation that a broader perspective is available. And they lack the inner moral compass to make valid behavioral decisions outside the rules of their religion. But while they are right to defend their views for their own sake, their influence risks holding the larger society back from progress. Fundamentalists tend to be very vociferous, and the noise they create distracts others from recognizing evolutionary spiritual possibilities available today. It can block recognition of the more advanced spiritual levels that other individuals may have already reached and the more unitive vision of reality that other elements in our culture are trying to offer us.

Taken together, literalism and fundamentalism allow those at the Faithful level (from any religion) to use their religion as a weapon. This weapon can be aimed against anyone and anything that is *other*. Any person who ascribes to a different religion or no religion must either be converted to the literalist's belief system or else discounted as being of lesser value somehow than those whose beliefs agree with the literalist. If the Book of Genesis grants him "dominion over the fish of the sea, and over the birds of the heavens and over every living thing that moves on the earth," (Gen.1:28), the literalist will assume the right to use animals for any purpose he chooses. He will trust that it is his right wantonly to exhaust the natural resources of our earth in attainment of his own needs, with no concern for the needs of the generations that will come after us. He will assume that his purpose is to work toward imposing a Christian understanding of biblical law upon all societies in the world.

As an aside, I recently ran across an interesting commentary on the word *dominion*. Inspired by ruling concepts in the Suzerainty Treaty, in which the ruler is responsible for the well-being of his subjects, Rev.

Signs and Symptoms of Spiritual Myopia...

Carol E. Richardson distinguishes the term *dominion* from *domination*: "Dominion is the ruling over self for self-benefit *as well as ruling over others and land for everyone's benefit together* [emphasis added]." In contrast, she goes on, "Domination is an energy that arises out of fear."[5] I propose that Christian literalists—climate-change deniers and anti-ecologists, as well—have distorted the meaning of the above-mentioned Genesis verse, subverting their *responsibility* toward the earth and its creatures in favor of *domination over* them.

Unfortunately, although large parts of our society are responding favorably to the changing social landscape, remaining fundamentalists (whether they be Muslim extremists or radical, right-wing Christians— they do arise out of the same spiritual level) are becoming increasingly strident and desperate in their efforts to hold back the tides of change. This makes them seem increasingly fanatical, sometimes dangerous, but otherwise irrelevant, and—yes—even ridiculous to those better adapted to the current situation.

If the forces discussed in this book, along with countless other spiritual texts from all ages and all parts of the world, point to *connection* (or what the Buddhists call *oneness*) as the underlying feature defining a clear spiritual vision or maturity, then it is easy to see how literalism and fundamentalism embody the opposite: an exultant *separation* from everything that is *other*, which is a severe expression of spiritual myopia. We need to learn to recognize that anything that separates us from anything or anyone else in creation is the very expression of a lack of spiritual vision. It defines spiritual myopia or spiritual immaturity. (And, yes, I am fully aware that my feeling the need to point all this out is an expression my own lack of oneness. Those "above" me on the spiritual path are most likely shaking their heads in disapproval.)

CHAPTER 4

Triumphalism

Worst of all, a literal, fundamentalist worldview leads to *triumphalism*, meaning a sense of exultation over those who have not bought into the same "truths" as we have, based on our own limited understanding. We assume that what has been valid for us should be valid universally, so we begin to feel superior to anyone who has not yet found our same truth. We triumph over those poor souls who cannot see things our way. This can happen at every spiritual level. A Faithful-level person has accepted the authority of whatever religious superior or holy book she follows. If her authority tells her that everyone who fails to believe the same thing cannot be saved, she believes it in the most literal way. (Note: in this chapter and elsewhere in the book the words *triumphalist, triumphalism,* etc., mean an excessive exultant pride over feeling superior to other people. Please do not confuse this with *Trumpism*; any connection between this concept and the president Donald Trump is unintentional.)

At the Rational level, a person may experience triumphalism by allowing himself to feel superior to all those silly religious people who believe things that seem preposterous to him. Because his process of reasoning has freed him of what seem to be absurd beliefs, he either feels sorry for people who have not done the critical reflection necessary to reach the Rational level, or else he scorns them. What a Rational-level nonbeliever is ignoring is that every civilization since the beginning of time has sought some sort of spiritual connection. Either Rational nonbelievers are unknowingly getting their spiritual fulfillment (though many would not choose to use this term) in some other manner, or they are living radically restricted lives. The section below on spiritual blindness will cover this concept in more depth.

SIGNS AND SYMPTOMS OF SPIRITUAL MYOPIA...

And I suspect that people at the Lawless level believe that all those other people who value love, honesty, peace, kindness, morality, gentleness, self-control, unity, and connection are silly and simply fail to recognize the value in being self-serving.

Spiritual Blindness

Most people understand blindness as the inability to see. But probably few people outside the health field realize that complete physical blindness is fairly rare. We say that a person is legally blind when he cannot see the 20/200 letter on the eye chart, no matter what form of visual correction we give him. So, most blind people have some vision, but what vision they have is just too poor to be useful in completing regular tasks.

Spiritual blindness occurs in two forms. One form is akin to legal blindness. It is characterized by a complete lack of spiritual connection and is very damaging to the person and anyone in his or her path. Spiritual "glasses" do not help. The only cure for this complete form of spiritual blindness—as discussed below—is one that will perhaps surprise the reader. The other form of this condition is more typical of a person who refuses to put her glasses on. She feels no need to connect spiritually or is simply disinclined to do so; and so she suffers a partial blindness that is not very damaging at all. I believe that this form is very poorly understood in our world; rather than an actual blindness, it is more like a refusal to believe in the existence of something the person cannot see and a rejection of any visual aids that would help them see it.

As mentioned, complete spiritual blindness is found in the rare and dreadfully unfortunate individual who has never felt any sense of connection with anyone or anything. This state of being describes the

Chapter 4

Lawless level in spiritual development theory. Such a person is blind to everyone and everything outside of himself, and the only concept controlling his behavior is the fulfillment of his own will. Fortunately, this disability is rather easy to recognize because it occurs mostly in people whose lives are in total chaos: criminals, substance abusers, and so on.

The most dangerous expression of total spiritual blindness is, however, as difficult to recognize as it is rare. Occasionally a very driven person, despite a Lawless lack of connection, manages to use charm, personal drive, and often vastly dishonest means to achieve his highest aspirations (remember, Lawless people feel that the rules of society do not apply to them). Some of our presidents have reportedly had this type of spiritual blindness, as well as some of our most "successful" business leaders.

The Lawless level, constituting a complete form of spiritual blindness, is essentially the same as M. Scott Peck's Spiritual Stage I: the Chaotic, Antisocial Stage.[6] Peck's use of the word *antisocial* does not mean that the person is unpopular or unfriendly. Rather, it means that her actions would promote an unhealthy society. She does not act for the good of anyone but herself. This is the crux of this person's spiritual problem. What the Lawless person fails to understand is that anything she does that would harm society, or promote her own ends over the general good of others, in the long run harms herself, as well.

A very clear caricature of the spiritual blindness of those at the Lawless level is found in Victor Hugo's fictional characters, Monsieur and Madame Thénardier, in *Les Misérables*. The novel portrays the Thénardiers as darker, more serious characters, whereas in the musical they serve as comic relief—but they are Lawless just the same. As the story opens, Monsieur and Madame Thénardier are innkeepers who flagrantly lie, cheat, and steal in any way they can, thinking they are outsmarting the world. For a fee, they agree to take in and care for Cosette, the daughter of a struggling single mother who must turn to prostitution to earn that fee. But the Thénardiers blatantly overwork Cosette; they beat her and give her only rags to wear, all the while spending the money Cosette's mother pays them on their own spoiled and pampered children. When Fantine, Cosette's mother, dies, the Thénardiers extort the protagonist Valjean for more money when he comes to take Cosette away into his care. As the plot continues, the Thénardiers' inn is forced to close, and they change their name to Jondrette, while continuing to take unfair advantage of anyone they can through any possible form of deceit. Much of their trickery is directed against the hero, Valjean, including blackmailing him, robbing him, plotting to kill him, and accusing him of murder. In the musical, at least it is evident that Mme. Thénardier disdains even her husband, all the while plotting out deceitful schemes with him. That both are clueless regarding the effects their behavior has on anyone else, and careless about the impression it creates, at once cements their role as Lawless characters and enriches our understanding of that level in a rich and humorous, though unsettling, way.[7]

So, what is the cure for the form of complete spiritual blindness found among the Lawless? How would a Lawless person begin to gain spiritual vision and move forward spiritually? Since it is not possible to skip a step in the spiritual development trajectory, a Lawless person can move forward only by embracing the very next level: the Faithful level. This would be true in the typical "born-again" experience. A person who formerly lived in chaos will somehow "find the Lord," join a church, and begin living a more meaningful life through the rules, the existential answers, and the sense of community—the *connection*—provided by organized religion.

Chapter 4

If all nonbelievers were at the Lawless stage, then that old-time religion of the Faithful level would be *the* answer to all society's problems! But those at the Faithful level are too myopic to recognize the Rational and the Unitive stages beyond them. They often wind up trying to convert those who have already achieved a more comprehensive level of spiritual maturity.

The less pernicious form of spiritual blindness—the partial form—is much more difficult to understand and even more poorly recognized in our society. It is important to distinguish the complete spiritual blindness described above from the partial form because their effects on society are completely different. While those afflicted with the complete form exert an entirely negative influence on the good of society, individuals with the partial form are well disposed to make huge contributions and have a good track record of doing so.

Basically, it is people at the Rational level of spiritual development who exhibit this partial form of spiritual blindness. Their failure to acknowledge any spiritual reality is—as I have suggested—not so much a blindness as it is a refusal to put on the spiritual glasses that would give them a more complete view of reality. In some cases, the Rational-level person's refusal to acknowledge a spiritual reality is a direct reaction against what seem to be the over-easy personifications, literalisms, and fundamentalisms typical at the Faithful level. Feeling themselves too sophisticated to believe in a personified God for which they have reasoned themselves out of a need, Rational-level people will tend to ignore any signs of spiritual connection. Or, more likely, they are enjoying authentic and satisfying forms of connection in their lives without according them any spiritual basis.

What causes great confusion in the minds of Rational-level people (and much of our society is now at this level) is that they are pretty sure there is no such "being" as the God of traditional religion. And from the way some religious people speak, it sounds as if they believe that the personification they worship is the full extent of what God is. Rational-minded people balk at such simplistic ideas and assume that they can reject everything about religion altogether because it sounds silly. If only they realized that we can't dismiss the forces we don't currently understand as readily as we might dismiss whatever was falsely attributed to God or the gods in the past—such as the ancient divinities that early people believed caused the storms. Those forces that we don't understand today are the invisible *connections* among us, the intuitive hits, the shared expansion of consciousness, characteristic of the evolving global culture of the twenty-first century. These are the spiritual forces with which we wrestle now.

Where the Lawless-level person's blindness stems from an *inability* to see the connections, the Rational-level person's blindness stems from an *unwillingness* (or lack of need) to see them. While the Rational level is a preferable place to be, as opposed to the Lawless or Faithful level, the Rational-level person is limited in her failure to acknowledge that there is much more going on here in the universe than that which meets the eye. If the Rational-level person would only put on her spiritual glasses, she would allow more room for mystery and doubt, and she would begin to appreciate an entire, unseen reality that could add richness and meaning beyond anything she could imagine.

Binary Logic and the Need for Certainty

We can all agree that ours is a complex world. It is becoming more complex by the day. Centuries ago, when at the end of a long life a person was likely to die in largely the same kind of world into which he had been born, simplistic reasoning may have been sufficient. But

Chapter 4

now, the rate of change in our culture is speeding up exponentially. Even our youngest teenagers are living in a world very different from the one into which they were born. This is true at many levels beyond just the obvious technological one. Very few aspects of our existence can be considered to be stable over a lifetime, and even fewer can be discussed in black-and-white, either/or, yes-or-no terms.

K. Helmut Reich studied and described five reasoning levels, the more advanced of which are necessary to deal effectively in today's world, and the simplest of which keep us mired, not just in spiritual myopia, but in a denial of the full complexity of today's reality. Reich's levels are discussed in more detail in chapter 6, but for now we just want to recognize that much of our mainstream society fails to acknowledge the more advanced reasoning levels, and this failure contributes to our spiritual myopia. Reich compared his least advanced form of human reasoning to the binary logic on which our simplest computers were designed: If 1 is true, 0 cannot be true. When applied outside the world of computers, this dichotomy becomes ridiculous. Very few things fall into neat either-or categories. Is rainy weather good or bad? Are taxes a good thing or a bad thing? Yet certain segments in our culture do aim to limit our reasoning choices to Reich's least-advanced Level 1: a yes-or-no, black-or-white simplicity. As an example, certain television news media (you know which ones I mean) dumb down complex issues to the simplicity of binary logic, committing a huge disservice to our society and insulting our human intelligence and reasoning capacities. We humans are capable of much more sophisticated forms of thought.

More advanced forms of reasoning are crucial to dealing effectively with the complex and rapidly changing reality with which we are currently confronted. We now know that while the Bible may hold truths that are "correct" in one sense—as mythic truths—contradictory scientific discoveries about the beginnings of our universe are also correct. And, as will be discussed in chapter 5, more recent discoveries about our expanding universe show that even the scientists are not as definite and as complete in their "correctness" as they once thought they were.

Our challenge in today's world is to resist yearning for the simpler world of the past. That world's simplicity arose only out of humanity's inability to perceive the more complex aspects of our existence. The improved vision afforded us by all the factors that will be discussed in chapter 5—including global communications, cultural intermixing, the perennial philosophy, and the new physics—brings us an increased responsibility to deal effectively with the new levels of complexity that we are only just now uncovering.

In Reich's third-through-fifth reasoning levels, and in the upper levels of the spiritual development stages, a person grows beyond the need for definite black-and-white answers and develops an ability to tolerate paradox. In a similar way, growing beyond the need for certainty is crucial to an understanding of spiritual maturity.

Spiritual maturity requires the ability to live in ambiguity; to live in the questions instead of requiring definite, fixed answers; and to see the excitement and beauty in the mystery behind our deepest existential questions.

The factors discussed in the next chapter call us into a depth of awareness beyond the need for certainty that disallows dumbing down our world to the limits of binary logic. They call us toward a more sophisticated form of reasoning and a broader, more open awareness

Chapter 4

that can be reached only when we challenge ourselves beyond the comforts of pat, existential answers.

Does God exist? A mature form of reasoning will not answer that question with a yes-or-no answer. The answer will be, "It depends."

5
New Lenses for Spiritual Clarity: Indulging in a Bird's-eye View

I have already suggested that we now know the general direction in which spiritual maturity will point us: away from selfish considerations and separation and toward unitive connection, concern for all beings, and making the most of our opportunities to create good in this world, as opposed to focusing on an afterlife. Today, we have many new lenses shedding light on the enlarged spiritual reality toward which spiritual development theory challenges us. All these new lenses arise through scientific progress and improved communications, but they are modified by concerns that surpass modernity's singular materialist, technological focus.

As is true with all forms of change, some of us will gladly don these new lenses and enjoy the clearer vision they afford, but others will insist that their old lenses are just fine. Fear and unwillingness to change will cause them to refuse the greater clarity new lenses would afford. My goal is to allay some of the fears that come naturally when change is afoot and information is limited. These new lenses for spiritual clarity point the way toward trust in the goodness of the bigger spiritual story that is trying to emerge.

Cultural Intermixing

Chapter 2 addressed the fact that centuries ago it was common for people to be born in a certain place, live out their whole lives in that same town or village, and die perhaps without ever having left it. The group with whom people interacted was fairly stable over their lifetime, and they shared that same pool of acquaintances with most everyone they knew. Most people in that pool held largely the same religious beliefs and followed the same cultural traditions. This made for little exposure to conflicting ideas, beliefs, and mores.

In that type of situation, it would be normal for people to hold their beliefs unquestioningly and for those beliefs to remain constant. It was common and acceptable to perceive one's own culture and religion as central—and to see all others as not "counting" quite as much. People were aware that other cultures and religions existed, but it was almost as if those "other" people were not fully real. Holding an insular religious-belief system would have been not just normal and acceptable, but of great value in giving meaning to life, providing community, and establishing guidelines for a good life.

However comforting that type of insular existence may have been, the realities we face in today's world call us to a broader awareness. Global communications and travel are causing extensive intermixing among various cultures. Travel is far quicker and easier now than it was in the past. Planes can carry us to almost anywhere in the world in one day. Few people live out their lives in the town in which they were born, and many even change countries several times. As a result, in metropolitan areas people of all different nationalities and religions are living, working, and worshipping in close proximity to one another. Our neighbors, our coworkers, our doctors, our service people, and even our friends likely as not represent numerous ethnicities and even various religions. Many of us even have people from a completely different culture marrying into our family.

Intermixing of other cultures into ours is inevitable in today's world. Depending on our point of view, we may feel that we are being forced to tolerate the conflicting influences that come from the inevitable contact with these people from foreign cultures, or we may feel that we are being graced with the opportunity to learn from them. We may feel that the conflicting influences they present threaten our worldview, or we may challenge ourselves to expand our understandings and enlarge our worldview to include theirs. Whether we respond defensively or "welcomingly" is our choice, but in the twenty-first century cultural intermixing is a fact of life. Rather than fight against an inevitable tide, healthy people will seek to adjust their worldview to include this new road to a wider truth.

Global communications are another fact of life in the twenty-first century. Like almost anything else, this factor has both positive and negative ramifications. But overall it is making the world a smaller place, and it challenges us to adopt broader perspectives than any civilization before us has ever had to contend with.

The term *globalization* originally applied primarily to the world of finance. According to experts, we are moving toward a global economy in which the different countries increasingly specialize in certain products and transport them to wherever they are needed,

Chapter 5

or they specialize in specific services that can easily be delivered through telecommunications or the Internet. This trend makes all countries both interrelated and interdependent upon one another at the economic level.

Globalization has proceeded rapidly since the 1980s, inviting many arguments as to whether it is a good or a bad thing. People on the political left and the political right both oppose it for different reasons.[1] The left suspects it will perpetuate the inequities and exploitation inherent in capitalism, contribute to poverty in poor nations, and/or reduce the quality of life for women. Some fear that, without proper governance, globalization cannot serve the interests of the people at large, and that it may accelerate deterioration of the environment. Some on the conservative side oppose globalization because they fear it may impose alien values on them, or it may homogenize the globe on secular terms.

In *Thriving in the Crosscurrent: Clarity and Hope in a Time of Cultural Sea Change*, author Jim Kenney applies the term *top-down globalization* to describe the phenomenon of large corporations moving vast amounts of money, goods, and services around the world and the political involvement with same. Often the exchanges tend to move in a one-way direction, with American and European goods, cuisine, and culture overwhelming local patterns. Kenney points out that top-down globalization, having been largely "shaped by free market capitalism and the so-called neo-liberal economic philosophy," has been "exploited by the wealth and power seekers of the late modern age and can readily be seen in a negative light."[2]

Economist Gregory Dahl offers a more inspirational spin. In *One World, One People: How Globalization is Shaping Our Future*, he argues that, because of an arising global economy, a world in which

New Lenses for Spiritual Clarity...

individual nations can do as they please no longer makes sense: "[The system we have today] must inevitably give way to a more rational world order."[3] As the world grows smaller, a higher form of organization among countries is needed, and a new attitude of cooperation is arising. Dahl proposes a new political structure capable of handling the emerging economic interdependence among nations.

Writing in 2007, Dahl could not possibly have predicted the backlash of nationalism that is arising now. Backlash is a phenomenon that arises when broad, sweeping changes—such as the form of globalization Dahl predicts—threaten the established order. Backlash reflects a collective resentment of those changes and an attempt to hold them back. In 1991, Susan Faludi wrote a bestseller called *Backlash: The Undeclared War Against American Women*.[4] This book called out a trend of negative stereotypes against career women that trivialized and demeaned the progress feminists had made since the 1970s. The plight black men face in the streets today is a backlash against the ways in which many African Americans have elevated their education level, sociological status, and contributions to society. Fundamentalism is a backlash phenomenon against the growing tide of spiritual and religious intermixing. And nationalism—"Make America Great Again!"—is a backlash against globalization of the type Dahl describes.

But beyond the more obvious economic changes that globalization is bringing about, and the political changes that it will eventually engender, less obvious changes are also occurring at the cultural and societal level. The Globalization website, set up by some Emory University professors, suggests a broader application of the term. They describe globalization as referring in a broad sense to the expansion of global linkages, the organization of social life on a global scale, and the growth of a global consciousness—hence to the consolidation of a world society.[5]

In a similar vein, Jim Kenney provides both clarification about globalization and appreciation of its more transformative consequences. Over the backdrop of his view of human evolution as currently in a crisis, and in contrast to his *top-down globalization* concept described two paragraphs ago, Kenney offers the term *bottom-up globalization* to describe a "remarkable self-organizing network of committed individuals and groups . . . dedicated to combatting poverty, promoting universal primary education, empowering women," etc.[6] Facilitated by the same new global interconnectedness that allows our global markets, bottom-up globalization is . . . one of the most vital of the new global wellsprings of cultural evolution."[7]

Like it or not, globalization in a cultural sense is a fact of life in the twenty-first century. How are we to respond to this inevitable seeping of "foreign" elements into our culture? Two general possibilities exist.

The initially more comfortable way might be to retreat into our insular worldviews, resisting and resenting the intrusion of these strangers' concepts into our awareness. We can dig in our heels and insist that our own ways are more real, more right, and more valid than all the others. This attitude has brought on the rise of nationalism worldwide, (backlash) insular political movements that attempt to defend a particular culture and society from foreigners and from foreign influences.

On the religious front, some of our religious leaders encourage this type of response by still insisting that their particular belief system holds universal and eternal answers. Every religion has a literal level, described as the Faithful level in chapter 3, at which all its beliefs and practices are specific to that faith. From within this literal level, one's own creed appears very different from—and superior to—all the others. Preaching a literal and exclusive type of faith leaves us mired in discord and allows no consideration of alternate possibilities. Choosing to see only the differences and retreating in fear from those who hold other creeds, we reinforce our own provincialism. If we accept the authority of this type of religious leader, we are called to admit that we are limiting our own growth as well as that of our children and of everyone with whom we have contact. We exclude a part of reality from our awareness.

But another way of looking at the issue of foreign influences on the culture is emerging to the forefront in several camps. There is a second, more vigorous and more truthful way to respond to the confusion that results: we can reach out and seek to understand these other people, societies, and religions. In religion, people are beginning to see beyond the literal level.

A recent report released by the Barna Group seems to bear this understanding out: "We live in a world of competing ideas and worldviews. In an increasingly globalized and interconnected world, Christians are more aware of (and influenced by) disparate views than ever. . . . Millennials and Gen-Xers, who came of age in a less Christianized context, are, in some cases, up to eight times more likely to accept [nonbiblical] views than Boomers and Elders. . . . Americans who live in cities, often melting pots of ideas and cultures, are more accepting of [nonbiblical] views than those in either suburban or rural areas."[8]

Now, just what nonbiblical views are younger, more urban dwelling Christians beginning to incorporate into their beliefs? Barna breaks them up into four categories: New Spirituality (61 percent of practicing Christians in the United States in 2017 agree with at least one idea rooted in this worldview); postmodernist views (54 percent of practicing Christians resonate with at least one of these views); Marxism (33 percent of practicing Christians accept at least one of these ideas); and secularism (22 percent of practicing Christians believe at least one idea based on it). Because New Spirituality aligns more closely with the topic of this book, I will consider it in more detail.

While the term "New Spirituality" may not be in wide use at this time, the titles of various recent books have contained the term. Some authors lament the onset of this phenomenon as a sign of the downfall of institutional religion, while others herald it as a positive evolutionary shift in our culture's understanding of what religion and spirituality are about. Chapter 10 describes a book of the latter type.

I like to think of the New Spirituality as the "New Age All Grown Up." The New Age developed in the Western world around the 1970s and could loosely be summarized as a mindset based on radical individualism and highly eclectic beliefs. Many of these beliefs seemed superficial and born out of wishful thinking and were largely looked down upon by most of mainstream society. But over time, three subtle shifts have taken place. Out of the original New Age concepts has evolved an ethic that extends far beyond self-interest and includes concern for the welfare of—*and responsibility toward*—everyone and everything in the universe. If we all are One, we must treat all with the same respect we would accord to ourselves. Secondly, the more authentic and believable aspects of this mentality have crept quietly into the mainstream consciousness, as described on the following page. Third, the term *New Age* has largely fallen out of common usage with the effect that its concepts cannot be as effectively refuted by the conventional world. For those who have heard of it, *New Spirituality* may be used as a catchall term for the worldview and form of spirituality that has replaced New Age.

The Barna Group polled practicing Christians about their affinity with what Barna considers the three main ideas of the New Spirituality:

1. "All people pray to the same god [sic] or spirit, no matter what name they use for that spiritual being." Forty-five percent of practicing Christians under the age of forty-five agreed with this, along with 26 percent of those over forty-five as well as 39 percent of city dwellers.

2. "Meaning and purpose come from becoming one with all that is." Thirty-eight percent of practicing Christians under forty-five, 22 percent of those over forty-five, and 37 percent of city dwellers agreed.

3. "If you do good, you will receive good. If you do bad, you will receive bad." Fifty percent of practicing Christians under forty-five, 24 percent of those over forty-five, and 43 percent of city dwellers agreed with this statement. (Personally though, I disagree that this is a tenet of the New Spirituality. I wonder if it is a misinterpretation of the New Age "create your own reality" mantra on the part of a conservative organization, as Barna purports to be. Instead, I see the New Spirituality as embodying a greater level of acceptance that one's personal story is not of great concern in the overall scheme of the universe; that, while to some extent we do "choose" our personal experiences, hardships will happen despite one's own efforts, and one should maintain a level of acceptance, equanimity, and universal love despite these hardships.)

Chapter 5

The Barna results are just one indicator that people are beginning to see through the specific symbols of their religion to emerge with a far more general understanding based on metaphorical rather than literal interpretation. They come to realize the allegorical nature of the stories in their religious texts. Then when they are faced with comparing those stories with stories from other faiths, they can see that all religions are not so very different in intent. Chapter 6 will further explore this concept.

Choosing a similar approach regarding the general culture, we will seek out commonalities with those who are different from us. We can forge relationships with the strangers and seek to understand the differences. We can try the strangers' foods, listen to their music, and even engage in conversations about their contrasting religious beliefs. People choosing this more openhearted approach will find themselves seeing commonalities with these strangers. They will likely come to see that there is good and bad, truth and falseness, in all cultures—and all religions. This approach most likely will loosen the stronghold of religious exclusivity and weaken the fences between people with different beliefs. It will broaden our worldview so that we come to *include* these "others" and accept them into *our common humanity*. It will expand our horizons and will lead us to recognize a more complete understanding about our existence.

We do not want to water down the richness of our various religious traditions. But we do want to stop interpreting them literally. The only way religions will survive into the future will be not as rigid belief systems making exclusive truth claims and expressing the need to convert others, but as rich cultural traditions to be celebrated for their diversity and their ability to foster meaning and connection in people's lives.

The Perennial Philosophy

The perennial philosophy is far from new. It has roots going back as far as the fifteenth century (with Marsilio Ficino and Pico della Mirandola), the sixteenth century (with Agostino Steuco), or the seventeenth century (with Gottfried Wilhelm Leibnitz,) depending on which source one consults. It was brought to popular attention by Aldous Huxley's 1945 title, *The Perennial Philosophy*.[9] A short description tells us that certain themes or truths can be found to run through all the learned writings from all parts of the world and written at all different times. Presumably, what shows up in every one of these writings—what endures over the centuries—is that which can be counted on to bring us closer to the truth about life. The differences in religious beliefs and practices that seem so crucial to people in a given culture at a given time, but which come and go over the centuries, can be considered merely localized interpretations specific to a given culture but lacking universal qualities.

Understanding the perennial philosophy in this way can lead to the assumption that all the world's religions are based upon a single universal truth and to the dismissal of the vast differences among them as merely local cultural interpretations. This thought pattern makes it easy for adherents of any religious tradition to dismiss the perennial philosophy out of hand. It negates the sense of uniqueness that drew those people to their particular tradition in the first place and that keeps them loyal to it. "*Our* truths have been divinely revealed," they say. "God himself sent his Son down here to save us. Our religion is the only *true* religion."

Despite such arguments, however, on closer inspection the perennial philosophy does afford some perspectives that are useful in expanding

Chapter 5

our spiritual understanding. Just as one example, Huxley points out how human language, in almost any culture, suffers from inadequate specificity in its spiritual vocabulary. Consider the word *love*. Huxley complains, "'Love' unfortunately stands for everything from what happens when, on the screen, two close-ups rapturously collide to what happens when [an abolitionist] feels a concern about Negro slaves, because they are temples of the holy spirit—from what happens when crowds shout and sing and wave flags . . . to what happens when a solitary contemplative becomes absorbed in the prayer of simple regard."[10]

We can easily think of other examples of sloppy uses of the word *love*. Do we love ice cream in the same way we love specific members of our family? Is our love of sports or music the same as our romantic attachments, or love for our possessions, or for our community or our church? Huxley claims, and rightly so, that such ambiguity in our vocabulary, which extends far beyond just our use of the word *love*, leads to confusion in thought. And even worse than causing confusion, our sloppy use of spiritual vocabulary prevents sophisticated spiritual realizations from ever forming and retards the average person's progression to advanced spiritual levels.

Still working with the word *love*, Huxley explains that spiritual masters from every tradition have delineated a type of love (or charity) that far supersedes our conventional understandings. One characteristic of this type of love is that it is *disinterested*—meaning that the one who expresses it seeks no reward, no return, no benefit whatsoever. Huxley says that, here, "God is to be loved for Himself, not for his gifts, and persons and things are to be loved for God's sake, because they are temples of the Holy Ghost."[11] Choosing to view Huxley's use of religious language as metaphorical, we see that not only is this kind of love disinterested, it also includes love for everyone and everything. It extends to people of other faiths, people from the other political party, and people whose lifestyle differs from ours. It extends to animals and to all of nature. It is universal. Hear how this perspective differs from traditional religious language, which often encourages the believer toward self-interest, (e.g., "If you pray, God will grant your wishes in this life. If you follow the rules God will reward you in the next life.")

Besides being disinterested, another characteristic of this "highest" form of love is that it is not an emotion. It is an act of the will, and, as Huxley points out, "an immediate spiritual intuition by which the 'knower, known and knowledge are made one.'"[12]

How a person grows in spiritual depth to the degree that this kind of disinterested, charitable love is experienced, or even understandable, is a complex topic I make no claim to be able to explain. But the perennial philosophy affords a perspective that allows us at least to recognize *the possibility* of such love. Hindered by our culture's sloppy and self-focused uses of the word *love*, and the self-interest promoted by our well-meaning but limited conventional clergy, how can we expect ever to find our way clear to a selfless, dispassionate love for all of humanity, or all of creation?

The need for more specificity in vocabulary is only one small part of the kind of perspective afforded by the perennial philosophy. Huxley distinguishes between what he calls time-dependent philosophies (or religions, such as Christianity, early Judaism, and Islam) and eternity-based philosophies (including Buddhism, Quakerism, and Hinduism, among others): Those philosophies that take the concept of time seriously—that is, they are dependent upon historical figures or events for their truths; they prescribe particularities for the present; and they claim to predict the future, even into eternity—have been able to justify large-scale violence in the name of promoting their specific beliefs.

Chapter 5

In contrast, eternity-based philosophies are not dependent upon an exclusive revelation at one sole instant of time. Rather, they view time as without beginning and the universe as supporting "sentient beings of every possible variety who are born, evolve, decay and die, only to repeat the same cycle—again and again, until [all have reached] eternal Suchness or Buddhahood."[13] These philosophies tend to be generally more tolerant, more humane, and less violent. Not obsessed with promoting their own theological imperialism, they focus instead on a kind of ultimate good. You cannot get this kind of perspective by listening to a literalist-type preacher from a certain tradition on Sunday mornings, or from reading the Bible. No wonder the conventional mind rebels against an overarching phenomenon such as the perennial philosophy. It calls us to stretch our minds and hearts to something larger than the everyday reality that so many people feel is holding their lives together.

Arthur Versluis's *Perennial Philosophy*, a much more recent title than Huxley's, sheds additional light. Versluis focuses more on the concept of transcendence: "Perennial philosophy holds that there is a central path to transcendence, and that we find this path reflected in different religious traditions."[14]

"Why *transcendence*?" we may well ask. According to Versluis, transcendence is synonymous with spiritual ascent, or the highest assertion of human potential. It is a path to realizing truth through the emancipation of consciousness in which self-focus is replaced by a more expanded sense of unity. The sense of one's self as a separate being is replaced by the sense that *we are all One*. This experience occurs naturally in predisposed individuals whenever conditions are ripe for it. (Many of our traditional religions have been based on the transcendent experiences of the founder.) In whatever culture transcendence and contemplative ascent may arise, they always bring the person to this sense of unity. This is similar to the mystical path described by most religions.

But the term *mysticism* has often been confused with an unfocused and undisciplined "emotional furor," to the extent that the concept now alienates many people. Versluis is careful to point out that his use of the term *mysticism* concerns "the contemplative ascent above emotional attachment and aversion, into the imaginal realm, and beyond that" and is just about synonymous with perennial philosophy.[15] "Perennial philosophy," he says, "is as much a set of guidelines as it is a model for beginning to understand consciousness in more profound ways."[16] Versluis suggests that, like mysticism, the term *perennial philosophy* itself may no longer hold appeal in the light of the currently emerging "science of consciousness," to which it fully corresponds. He suggests we replace *perennial philosophy* with the updated name *contemplative science.*

Among adherents of perennial philosophy, no one is saying that all religions are the same. Yet, if we are open to it, the perennial philosophy offers truths that take us beyond the realizations that our mainstream society and conventional understandings of religion can afford us.

The Westar Institute

The Westar Institute is a much newer and less broad-ranging phenomenon; but, like the perennial philosophy, it serves to add perspective to our understanding of at least the Christian religion. Founded in 1986, this organization is dedicated to fostering cutting-edge scholarship on the history and evolution of the Christian tradition. Westar conducts collaborative, cumulative research in the academic study of religion and addresses issues, questions, and controversies that are important both to the academic community and to the public.

CHAPTER 5

Westar lists some stringent criteria for its scholars who are held to the requirement of being "critical." That means that, in addition to holding a PhD in theology, religious studies, or a related discipline from an accredited university, the two-hundred-plus Westar Fellows must be willing to make empirical, factual evidence—evidence open to confirmation by independent, neutral observers—the controlling factor in historical judgments.[17] A page entitled "Ethos and Protocols" for their fellows includes an injunction against "learning merely to reinforce old dogmas or confirm one's biases."[18] The same page demands that their fellows be "ruthlessly honest," "radically inclusive," conduct their research in a cumulative manner, and agree to operate according to a consensus. Whether these activities bring them to confirm or deny specific aspects of their own belief system, the overall guiding criterion is truth—truth as opposed to dogma. Critical, open-ended, peer-reviewed research is the controlling element, as opposed to religious conviction. A list of Westar scholars includes such notable names as Karen Armstrong, John Shelby Spong, and the late Marcus Borg.

Westar scholars meet semiannually to share and formally discuss the results of their research on specific predetermined topics. Statements are generated, and a vote is held on each to determine whether to adopt that statement into the consensus of the group.

The first and best known of the Westar seminars was the Jesus Seminar. Conducted between 1985 and 1998, its purpose was to discover and report a scholarly consensus on the historical authenticity of the sayings and deeds attributed to Jesus in the Gospels. In the judgment of the seminar, only 18 percent of the sayings and 16 percent of the deeds attributed to Jesus in the Gospels are authentic.[19]

New Lenses for Spiritual Clarity...

Once the scholars make determinations regarding the accuracy of specific "truths," they set out to share their findings with the public. This is in keeping with a second aspect of their mission, which is to "communicate the results of its research in nontechnical terms, [so as to equip] the general public with tools to critically evaluate competing claims in the public discussion of religion."[20] Toward this end, Westar invites the public to topical programs all over the United States, wherein they share their findings. Even though Westar scholars concluded their structured discussions in the Jesus Seminar in 1998, the resulting *Jesus Seminar on the Road* programs continue to be presented to the public around the country to this day. The scholars themselves are now discussing concepts that are somewhat less amenable to concrete historical study. They are currently working on what they call the "God Seminar."

We may ask what Westar's work might have to do with a cure for spiritual myopia. As we know, people at the Faithful level of spiritual development refuse, or are afraid, to think critically about key aspects of their belief system. In a similar way, "evangelical" scholars reportedly tend to conduct their research in such a way as to confirm their preexisting biases regarding biblical truths. They behave closer to the Faithful level in spiritual development.

Westar distinguishes itself from these more conventional scholars by demanding open-ended critical analysis. So, Westar, as an institution, can be said to represent the Rational level, which is all about critical reflection and courageous, open-ended questioning. In this sense, Westar challenges the traditional (Faithful) way Christianity is represented in our culture. It offers any willing listeners a road out of the spiritual myopia of insular and stagnant religious beliefs.

Chapter 5

Though Westar, as an institution, represents the Rational level, having attended a few of its seminars I can assert that some or many of its scholars probably incline toward the next level in spiritual development that I call the Unitive level—discussed below. (But the Westar mission, together with its academic professionalism, precludes its publicly espousing anything that cannot be proven scientifically.) As an example, I recently attended a Jesus on the Road seminar entitled "Christianity before Christianity."[21] As its title implied, this session presented discoveries scholars are making now about early Christianity that might differ from popular assumptions. One point was how, before the fourth century, beliefs differed among all the various Christian groups. Only in the fourth century was the Nicene Creed set down to "clarify" just what all Christians were supposed to believe. The Nicene Creed, a doctrinal statement of what constitutes "correct" Christian belief, exists today in various forms, but it goes something like this:

> I believe in one God, the Father Almighty, Maker of heaven and earth, and of all things visible and invisible.
>
> And in one Lord Jesus Christ, the only-begotten Son of God, begotten of the Father before all worlds; God of God, Light of Light, very God of very God; begotten, not made, being of one substance with the Father, by whom all things were made.
>
> Who, for us men for our salvation, came down from heaven, and was incarnate by the Holy Spirit of the virgin Mary, and was made man; and was crucified also for us under Pontius Pilate; He suffered and was buried; and the third day He rose again, according to the Scriptures; and ascended into heaven, and sits on

the right hand of the Father; and He shall come again, with glory, to judge the quick and the dead; whose kingdom shall have no end.

And I believe in the Holy Ghost, the Lord and Giver of Life; who proceeds from the Father [and the Son]; who with the Father and the Son together is worshipped and glorified; who spoke by the prophets.

And I believe one holy catholic and apostolic Church. I acknowledge one baptism for the remission of sins; and I look for the resurrection of the dead, and the life of the world to come.   Amen.[22]

The Nicene Creed imposed ecclesial (i.e., relating to church structure) restrictions on what had been a more fluid and less authoritarian type of faith typical of earlier Christianity. Westar scholar Stephen J. Patterson suggested that the general idea behind early Christian faith was something less stark and less literal than the Nicene Creed would have us believe. Scholars are now considering that St. Paul's letter to the Galatians may provide us with what may be considered a "first creed" of Christianity.[23] Paul is sometimes called an apostle, though he was not one of the original twelve. His epistle to the Galatians, written around CE 49 or 54, reads:

> Now before faith came, we were confined under the law, kept under restraint until faith should be revealed. So that the law was our custodian until Christ came, that we might be justified by faith. But now that faith has come, we are no longer under a custodian; for in

Chapter 5

Christ Jesus you are all sons of God, through faith. For as many of you as were baptized into Christ have put on Christ. There is neither Jew nor Greek, there is neither slave nor free, there is neither male nor female; for you are all one in Christ Jesus. And if you are Christ's, then you are Abraham's offspring, heirs according to promise.[24]

Patterson explained that "removing the Pauline language" renders this text more accessible to people of today and allows us to discern the far more poignant intent underlying this message:

You are all sons of God ("in the Spirit"[25]);
There is neither Jew or Greek;
There is neither slave nor free;
There is no longer male and female:
For you all are one.[26]

Unfortunately, the understanding of Paul's letter as a unitive and inclusive message disappeared over the following centuries. Only now are we able once again to appreciate it as such—now that we can recognize that unity and inclusiveness are characteristic in spiritual emmetropia. Note how starkly Paul's language differs from the more divisive and triumphalist messages that come from some later Christian authorities.

Westar scholars are people who find religion a topic sufficiently compelling to have devoted their professional lives to it, and these scholars have minds capable of the critical analysis that the early Christian leaders lacked. (See more about this under the work of

Don Cupitt in chapter 10.) Finally, Westar scholars well-schooled in modernity's approved methods of critical analysis, and having committed to freeing themselves of any predetermined biases to which they might be emotionally inclined, are holding themselves to the mission of carrying out what the early Church leaders failed to do. We are wise to thank them for the light they are shedding on Christian history, regardless of the effect that their findings may have on our predetermined biases.

We will now turn our attention to a few other elements that begin to transcend modernity and point us toward broader spiritual appreciations.

The New Physics

The term *new physics* was originated, I believe, by the English scientist Paul Davies in his 1984 title, *God and the New Physics*. Throughout several of his books, Davies attempts to explain how more recent discoveries in physics are giving insights into what were once considered solely religious or philosophical questions. While it may not be in common use today in the scientific community itself, the term *new physics* does appear in a handful of recent articles that discuss possible religious and spiritual implications relating to quantum theory (and to more recent scientific findings such as the Higgs boson, which I make no attempt to do here).[27]

In taking up this topic, I first want to refer to an aspect of cultural history we have already mentioned; namely, that in antiquity people perceived the world to be animated by divine presences. Early religions assigned the names of different "gods" to refer to the sun, the wind, the rain, etc. This custom showed a certain humility, a kind of submission to the forces that dramatically impacted their lives. Early people never expected to be able to appreciate the scientific principles behind these forces; their only possible response to them was awe.

The eighteenth-century Enlightenment and the modern age changed all that. Humanity began to discover a lot about the scientific basis behind many such natural forces—what controlled the tides and the weather, for example. While in earlier times the world was seen as enchanted, with the Enlightenment a purely scientific view arose. The world was reduced in concept to an inert matter mechanized by static scientific laws. In their hubris, people began to feel that they could learn to control these forces and employ all the world's resources for the sake of their own comfort.

In *Restoring the Soul of the World*, David Fideler explains that we are living in a transitional time.[28] Thanks to recent scientific findings—and to global connections that allow us easily to incorporate information from all different fields and cultures into our understandings—modern science's purely mechanistic view of reality can now be seen as a radical oversimplification. What were once considered hard, fast scientific truths are clearly giving way to something new. Fideler makes a passionate plea for a re-recognition of the "soul," or the animate aspects of our living universe.

Among Fideler's arguments are the implications of the new physics or quantum science. While I have read many explanations of quantum science, Fideler, holding a PhD in philosophy and the history of science, has provided the one that I best understand; and it is the only one I know of that satisfactorily links what happens at the subatomic level with what may be happening in our larger, observable macro world.

Without going into detail on a topic far outside my own expertise, let me just summarize two of Fideler's main premises: 1) At the subatomic level, particles do not behave as fixed, inanimate matter

New Lenses for Spiritual Clarity...

that obeys preset "scientific" rules. Rather, they display some degree of aliveness; they "know" and behave differently depending on whether they are being observed. 2) As Fideler puts it, "Any two particles which once originate from a common system will continue to be entangled and function as a common system instantaneously, regardless of physical distance."[29]

Fideler uses these premises to suggest that consciousness is *always giving birth* to reality in a participatory, cocreative way within our deeply living, knowing, and intelligent universe. Also, if the cosmological Big Bang was a real event, we can say that, before it, all elements in the universe were once connected. Would that not mean, according to the above second premise, that we all originated from a common system and therefore remain "entangled," or at least connected, forever? Does this not fit into our unity theme as part of the cure for spiritual myopia? Could it not be that our increasing scientific knowledge is pointing to new levels of awareness about how we are all connected?

Big History

The word *history* normally suggests a specific time frame and events within the limits of *recorded* human experience. An exciting, new academic arena is emerging that deals with a far larger perspective. Drawing on the field of cosmology, some are calling it "Big History." It examines the time frame from the proposed, but ever more credible, "Big Bang" that started the universe up to the present day. That is, Big History covers a 13.7 billion-year span.

Now taught in universities and secondary schools, this project was originally the brainchild of Australia's David Christian from Macquarie University. Unlike conventional history, which is considered to be its own discipline, Big History draws upon resources from the hard

Chapter 5

sciences as well as the social sciences. It considers perspectives from the fields of anthropology, archeology, astronomy, biology, climatology, cosmology, environmental studies, economics, evolutionary biology, geology, natural history, prehistory, and population studies.

Where conventional history focuses on humankind alone, Big History goes back to the formation of the universe, stars, and galaxies and considers how human beings fit into this larger story. Big History acknowledges the existence of our sun as just one star in a bevy of about one hundred billion stars in our galaxy alone—the Milky Way—and our galaxy being just one out of about two *trillion* galaxies that scientists now know make up the universe. What is more, these galaxies are constantly speeding away from us, such that space itself is constantly expanding among the galaxies in every direction. The universe is not just constantly expanding; it is itself creating new space as it expands.

Big History humbly acknowledges that, not only is the universe much larger than we originally thought and still continually expanding, but also that human knowledge of such things continues to expand, as well. When our knowledge expands, we must adjust our understandings to incorporate new data. This raises the question of toward what new recognitions we are headed and suggests an appreciation of our existence as one of increasing complexity.

Such a perspective calls us to reconsider the static and limited understandings of the specific creation myths held by our various religions. While it may be comforting to believe that our world was created in seven days because it says so in a holy book that *one* culture holds as inviolable, we would be burying our head in the sand like the proverbial ostrich to limit our understanding thereby. Whether held literally or otherwise, such beliefs are simply too provincial to

New Lenses for Spiritual Clarity...

explain our presence in what Big History tells us is a vast and *continually expanding* universe.

Because Big History or cosmology has not yet reached mainstream consciousness, a large part of our population still operates out of limited and outmoded paradigms based on awareness only of *this* earth or *this* solar system and of a "story" that applies only to one culture. Big History calls us to wonder if we don't need a bigger kind of God to account for a universe that has trillions of galaxies and that is still growing.

In discussing the new physics, Fideler introduces us to another voice that adds spiritual perspective, this one from the 1950s: Harow Shapley, in an article entitled "Man's Fourth Adjustment,"[30] suggests that the earliest humans saw themselves as the center of the universe but at some point came to the humbling realization that the earth itself had to be included in their view of what made up their physical reality. This realization can be called the First Adjustment—humanity's first cultural step away from anthropocentrism. The Second Adjustment occurred when the Copernican revolution forced people finally to accept that the earth revolved around the sun. They initially resisted this information because, once again, it seemed to further diminish humankind's place as the center of the universe. However, of course the science was irrefutable. Once again humans were forced to expand their worldview even wider—further diminishing the impact of their own existence within it. Then, in the last century, a Third Adjustment became necessary when it was discovered that the total of galaxies numbered in the millions (now *trillions*) and that our own galaxy contains billions of stars. Shapley explains, "Man becomes peripheral among the billions of stars of his own Milky Way; and, according to the revelations of paleontology and geochemistry, *he is recent and apparently ephemeral in the unrolling of cosmic time.*"[31]

Now, Shapley mused back in 1956, a "need for a further jolting adjustment appears."[32] Planets must exist in at least some of these other solar systems. Astrophysicists tell us that our kinds of chemistry and physics are not unique to our earth. "We can no longer doubt but that whenever physics, chemistry, and climates are right on a planet's surface, life will emerge and persist."[33] Accepting the premise that life on Earth is most likely not unique but part of the larger life pattern of the living universe, humankind will advance to the Fourth Adjustment in a series that has continually brought the human race out of its own egocentrism toward a much grander perspective. It should cause any thinking person to question the staid existential proclamations of religious founders whose understandings arose in an age when none of this was known. In this context, could we not begin to see Jesus's claim that "no one gets to the Father except through me" in a different light? How exactly would sentient beings elsewhere in the universe ever hear about Jesus?

The Interfaith Movement

The interfaith movement aims for mutual acceptance and understanding among people of different religions. This is engendered through respectful and constructive dialog and at times through cooperative projects in service of a common social goal.

Occasional interfaith efforts have been recorded for many centuries, but actual interfaith dialog among the Abrahamic faiths began in the early twentieth century and gained momentum around the 1960s. In 1965, the Catholic Church issued a document called *Nostra Aetate* as an outcome of the Second Vatican Council.[34] This document begins with the words, "In our time, when day by day mankind is being drawn closer together, and the ties between different peoples

New Lenses for Spiritual Clarity...

are becoming stronger, the Church examines more closely her relationship to non-Christian religions."[35] It goes on to acknowledge, as I have been saying in this book, that "from ancient times down to the present, there is found among various peoples a certain perception of that hidden power which hovers over the course of things... [and] this perception and recognition penetrates their lives with a profound religious sense."[36] It goes on to mention ways in which a few different cultures have dealt with their quest for meaning and their existential questions by forming specific religions. Nostra Aetate ends with the conclusion that "the Catholic Church rejects nothing that is true and holy in these religions... [which] often reflect a ray of that Truth which enlightens all men."[37] This document was a huge step forward beyond the prior exclusivist position of the Catholic Church (which formerly had discouraged Catholics from even interacting with adherents of other religions) and a milestone in the interfaith concept.

By the late 1960s, a few interfaith groups had formed, and some of these pooled their efforts around social issues of the day—civil rights and the war in Vietnam. In 1970, an organization called Religions for Peace was formed under the motto, "Different Faith, Common Action." This organization fosters efforts among various world religions to stop war, end poverty, and protect the earth by working together toward the common goal of peace. In 1978, the Interfaith Conference of Metropolitan Washington brought together eleven faith communities to promote dialog and understanding.

While most interfaith efforts involved organizations working together, a bolder interfaith concept involved dialog among actual individuals. One such example is described by Gustav Niebuhr, author of *Beyond Tolerance: Searching for Interfaith Understanding in America*.[38] In 1991, Rabbi Jerome Davidson at Temple Beth-El in

CHAPTER 5

Nassau County, New York, invited selected members of his congregation to begin conversations with members of an Islamic mosque several miles away. Reportedly, they started off modestly, discussing wedding and birth ceremonies, but eventually moved on to discussing theological principles in their sacred texts. Finally, they broached a dangerous divide when they began comparing their differences over the Middle East.[39]

In the 2000s, the interfaith movement gained even more momentum, possibly because of the events of September 11, 2001. Committees and think tanks were formed, programs were designed, and conferences were held, all to promote interfaith acceptance and understanding. One notable example is the work of Eboo Patel, a proclaimed Muslim. In 2002, he founded the Interfaith Youth Core (IFYC), a Chicago-based nonprofit organization working on college campuses toward the goal of making interfaith cooperation a social norm. IFYC works to develop religious pluralism, characterized by respect for people's diverse religious and nonreligious identities. It mutually inspires relationships among people of different backgrounds and common action for the common good.[40]

Inherent to the interfaith concept is the need to foster pluralism, which should be distinguished from the goal of creating unity. In pluralism, separate beliefs, rites, and rituals among the religions are maintained; adherents of the various religions coexist peacefully, despite their religious differences. The goal of pluralism is truly to accept the inherent differences among them and to enhance mutual respect and understanding despite the differences. In pluralism and in the interfaith movement, no attempt is made to downplay the differences among the religions. The term *interfaith* implies that the inherent differences among

New Lenses for Spiritual Clarity . . .

the religions involved are being respected and maintained. There is no intent or effort to synthesize the various beliefs.

By now, a few people are suggesting the need for an update in the interfaith concept. Reverend Donald Heckman, then the executive director of Religions for Peace (USA), addressed this problem in a 2013 Huffington Post article, "Why the Interfaith Movement Must Rebrand."[41] He describes a labeling confusion between the original interfaith mission of respectful coexistence among people of different religions and what has morphed into a mixture of loose connections among people who affiliate with multiple religious or spiritual institutions. Further, there are those who try to downplay religious differences in an attempt to amalgamate all religions into a common entity. This confusion could be addressed if the word *interfaith* could be accorded its original connotation, and then those wishing to mix religions together would use the term *interspirituality* instead of interfaith. Interspirituality will be further discussed in chapter 8.

6
The Unitive Level in Spiritual Development: Even Clearer Vision

Because an understanding of the fourth and final spiritual development level is crucial in the treatment of spiritual myopia, and essential to our goal of peace among the religions, I have given it its own chapter. The Unitive orientation is not explicitly recognized in our society. Generally, it is poorly understood and underappreciated. Only when we consider it among the larger perspectives presented in this book can we grasp its depth and importance in enhancing spiritual vision.

In *Faith Beyond Belief*, I use the term *mystic* for this fourth stage; but in this work, I will instead use the term *unitive* for several reasons. For one thing, the word *mystic* can lead people astray because it sounds too woo-woo. For another, *mystic* makes the level sound like one that very few of us could ever reach and even fewer could see as a goal. On

CHAPTER 6

the other hand, in today's world, being unitive or inclusive does sound like a laudable value to aim for. In fact, despite all the outward chaos in our culture, in Western society today many people are attaining or at least approaching unitive values.

How Does One Get There?

So how does a person reach the Unitive level? You will remember that the most advanced level we discussed, in chapter 3, was the Rational level. At this Rational level, a person has chosen freely to evaluate the beliefs of the religion into which he was born and may likely have chosen not to limit his understandings to the precepts of his given religious tradition. He is a free thinker and a seeker of truth. Once he emerges past the group-think of traditional religious belief, he has two choices: He can dissolve into a triumphalist swagger for having been so smart as to reason himself beyond the Faithful level. Or, if he is sufficiently open-minded, he will *continue seeking*. In this case, he is bound eventually to run up against connections he cannot explain according to the rules of human reason or science. Issues will occur to him that do not fall into the black-and-white categories that basic human reasoning allows. He will come to appreciate the paradoxes in life and learn to deal with a more complex and more comprehensive reasoning style.

I want to go into this matter of reasoning in some depth, because one serious symptom of the spiritual myopia found in our mainstream culture is drastically oversimplified reasoning. We can thank a researcher named K. Helmut Reich for having studied levels of sophistication in reasoning skill.[1]

Our simplest computers are designed according to a concept called binary logic. A system is either on or off for a given function. When humans reason this way, we can call it yes-or-no logic, black-and-white logic, either/or logic, or binary logic. So, using binary logic, the weather is either nice today or it is awful. A person is either smart or stupid. A law is either good or bad. Some of our media outlets are very much into reducing complex issues to binary logic; thus, a president is either all good or all bad, a new law is either great or the worst thing that ever happened. But very few things in our complex, multidimensional reality are well represented by such drastic oversimplifications. Weather that may be good for picnickers may be bad for a farmer needing rain. People are smart in some ways and less gifted in others. Our laws may favor one group of people while disadvantaging others. Nearly every person we know has some good features and some bad ones and makes some good decisions and some bad ones.

K. Helmut Reich interviewed people to assess their capacity for complex reasoning and came up with five reasoning levels.[2] At the simplest level, the person saw the world only in either/or terms and was capable only of binary logic. So, if one description or explanation or model or theory or interpretation was correct, all others must be wrong. At the next level, the person would concede that, for most issues, there may be something valid to both or all the descriptions, explanations, models, theories, or interpretations. At the third level, a person could see that both or all the possible descriptions, explanations, and so on are definitely needed to account fully for the phenomenon under question. At the fourth level, a person could explain how all the descriptions, explanations, models, theories, or interpretations are related to one another. And, at the fifth and final, most sophisticated level of reasoning, a person was able to supply an overarching synopsis of the entire situation under question.

Chapter 6

When we apply these reasoning levels to how we arrive at decisions about our most confounding social issues and our deepest existential questions, we can see that a mature understanding involves more than one way of looking at things. Most importantly, those who have reached the more sophisticated reasoning styles are called upon to understand—hopefully, with some degree of kindness—the position of those who cannot see beyond the level of binary logic.

In terms of religious belief, the more sophisticated reasoner will understand that religious and spiritual motivations are vastly multifactorial and that spiritual truths cannot be reduced to simplistic black-and-white distinctions. A person with well-developed spiritual reasoning skills will not assume that the entirety of religious or spiritual truth can be loaded into any single holy book written thousands of years ago or that questions about the existence of God can be answered in black-and-white terms. It bears noting that a person can enjoy complex reasoning skills in other areas and still restrict his spiritual reasoning to the more simplistic black-and-white levels. This characteristic may be due to many factors outside the scope of this discussion, but suffice it to say that spiritual instincts are informed by many other factors beyond just reason—emotions, general life events, and individual spiritual experiences, for example.

Often individual spiritual experiences will lead a person to conclude that the God he envisions up in the heavens is an exact representation of the Ultimate Reality because a prayer he had uttered was "answered." While this may be very appealing at the emotional level, and may suffice to spark a lifelong religious commitment, applying a few advanced reasoning skills should make it evident that a "bigger" truth must be in play, since people from all traditions seem to be convinced that their prayers "work" just as well.

The Unitive Level in Spiritual Development...

Another reason a person might limit their spiritual-reasoning skills to simplistic black-and-white levels is that certain factors in our society deliberately work to discourage complex thought. For example, some religions discourage advanced education out of fear that if people learn too much, they will find reasons to leave the religion. And, as mentioned elsewhere in this book, certain news media intentionally "dumb down" their message. In a 2015 talk on his then-upcoming book, *The Market as God*, Harvey Cox went into some detail about how certain television entities intentionally design their messages to bypass the cognitive grid and go directly to the emotional core. This allows the media to control the audience's purchasing choices *and their political decisions.*[3]

Returning to the question of how our Rational-level person might progress to the Unitive or Universal level, it is when that person keeps questioning with an open mind that she may notice complexities that allow her to open to a broader worldview. Her reasoning skills expand to recognize ways in which her reality is not limited to that which may be investigated scientifically and is not adequately described in black-and-white, either/or terms. This broader perspective allows recognition of elements that defy conventional logic and will include information that does not protect the person's current worldview. A more comprehensive reasoning style is one feature a person will attain on the road to spiritual maturity.

Of course, a person does not reach the Unitive level by reasoning alone. Volumes could be written about this stage and would still only make the tiniest dent in what this stage is about. Indeed, many volumes have been written, although few refer to it as the Unitive level. One of the volumes that best helped me begin to understand it was Evelyn Underhill's *Practical Mysticism*.[4] (More about Underhill later.)

Chapter 6

It seems that mystical or spiritual experiences, or connection with the universe, can lead a person toward the Unitive level. Abraham Maslow helps us to understand this. He claims that nearly everyone has transcendent personal experiences, but many fail to take conscious note of them; and he calls such people "non-peakers." Maslow says the "non-peaker" is someone who "is afraid of [his or her transcendent personal experiences,] who suppresses them, who denies them or "forgets" them."[5] In contrast, the "peaker" is one who acknowledges and welcomes these experiences and allows them to inform his or her worldview. Historically, the peakers who enjoyed the most dramatic experiences have wound up as founders of our major religions, the wisdom they received during the experience being the foundation upon which each religion was formed. But between the maximum peakers who formed our religions and the non-peakers who are often left to run them are the many ordinary people who enjoy direct spiritual experience in a less dramatic way.

Such experiences are not necessarily related to religion per se. They could run anywhere from dramatic transcendent feelings of the self being dissolved into the universe, such as may occur to advanced meditators, to something as banal as just suddenly coming to "know" or hear, taste, smell, or see something for which there is no corresponding evidence in the outer world—no objective way others could know, hear, taste, smell, or see the same thing. Despite the variety of ways in which such events are experienced, the main thing they have in common is that they involve connection with something beyond the everyday reality. They imply that something else is going on in the universe beyond what is perceived by our five senses, and beyond that which may be subjected to study through our normal scientific methods.

The Unitive Level in Spiritual Development...

Trust in such experiences has been highly suspect in most of the conventional modern world. The Rational mindset tends to scorn anything that suggests the supernatural in any way and to reject everything that does not submit to the scrutiny of our scientific methods. But this is another feature of the spiritual myopia that was discussed in chapter 4. Repeated or dramatic experiences of direct and personal feelings of connection may cause a person to be disposed toward the Unitive level. Allowing such experiences to inform one's own personal truth, despite the lack of validation from their tribe, may factor into the likelihood of moving beyond the Rational level and toward more universal understandings.

Here, a certain distinction may be of use. Much of the Rational world sees everything not subject to consensus validation as suspect. Indeed, many who call themselves "spiritual" deliberately seek to escape the everyday reality and dwell in realms that others can't see. They assume that mere access to these realms qualifies their spirituality as elevated above the ordinary. But, in fact, the mere search for otherworldly experience can distract from its real value and purpose. If experiences outside everyday reality don't lead to a greater sense of connectedness with a universal Reality, then they are mere diversions and contribute nothing to overall goodness in the world. If they don't lead a person toward greater compassion, acceptance, inclusiveness, forgiveness, and love, then they are mere diversions. They may be harmless to the people seeking them, but they do damage the larger picture in that they serve further to alienate the Rational world, which can easily see through their superficiality. They add to the spiritual blindness of all those not inclined to validate the existence of other realms.

Spiritual experiences from outside our consensus reality are just one type of connection that can encourage spiritual growth. Some

Chapter 6

forms of connection are far more mundane, have nothing to do with religion or spirituality per se, and can very easily be missed by those not prone to notice them. There are many ways to connect to something greater than ourselves. Religion is only one of them.

As far as what the Unitive level actually looks like, again, volumes have been written, and a full study would take a lifetime. But Evelyn Underhill, one of the clearest interpreters I know, defines it this way: "Mysticism is the art of union with Reality. The mystic is a person who has attained that union in greater or less degree; or who aims at and believes in such attainment."[6] The chief ingredients of a mystical character are "courage, singleness of heart, and self-control."[7] Growth to this level involves diminution of the importance of the self as a separate individual. The seven common forms of egotism—pride, anger, envy, avarice, sloth, gluttony, and lust—"constitute absolute barriers to . . . attainment of Reality. So long as these dispositions govern character we can never see or feel things as they are; but only as they affect ourselves, our family, our party, our business, our church, our empire—the I, the Me, the Mine."[8] They must be overcome for spiritual growth to happen. Therefore, "Selfhood must be killed before Reality can be attained."[9] Further, "An ever more profound harmonization of the self's life with the greater and inclusive rhythms of existence . . . [demands that you expand your view of reality beyond] your family group, your class, your city, party, country, or religion [to include] the whole race, till you feel yourself utterly part of it, moving with it, suffering with it, and partake of its whole conscious life. . . . Self-mergence is . . . dependent on a progressive unlimiting of personality . . . [until you] enlarge your boundaries and become the citizen of a greater, more joyous, more poignant world, the partaker of a more abundant life."[10]

THE UNITIVE LEVEL IN SPIRITUAL DEVELOPMENT...

A Few Characteristics

We could go on and on about this Unitive level; for now, though, let us just list a few common characteristics. For instance, we could say that, at the Unitive level, a person may hold her religious and spiritual beliefs in a metaphorical, rather than a literal, way. Again, this would be because she has already passed through the other prior stages. She no longer holds literal beliefs as she did as a Faithful, and she also no longer entirely rejects them as she did as a Rational.

We could also say that the Unitive-level person has overcome his own ego and thus exhibits a deeper sense of humility than others. He has experienced the ego diminution that Evelyn Underhill identifies as summarized above.

We could say that the Unitive-level person is in less need of existential certainty than is characteristic at the other levels. Having dared to employ one of Reich's more sophisticated reasoning levels described above, she knows that complex reality cannot be submitted to black-and-white distinctions. Rather than grasp at ready-made religious, spiritual, and existential answers supplied by others, she is comfortable leaving such questions unanswered and will enjoy basking in the mystery of the unknown.

We might say that, rather than be ruled by some outer authority, as are those at the Faithful level, or by human reason, as are those at the Rational level, the Unitive-level person is ruled by a spirit authority—something that he feels from within but that is deeper and more authentic than his mind or his conscience.

The most definitive concept that characterizes levels of spiritual development is the extent of the person's worldview. Indeed, the spiritual development trajectory may be characterized simply as a continually expanding worldview. Let's review the perspective of each stage so that we can appreciate how each one represents a broader, more inclusive worldview than the one before it:

We have discussed that the Lawless person's world is all about himself, so that we can say his worldview is *egocentric*.

<blockquote>Lawless = egocentric: *"It's all about **me**!"*</blockquote>

The Faithful-level person, on the other hand, identifies mainly with something larger than himself. He enjoys a very strong sense of being part of his particular group—his religious group, his political party, his neighborhood, his favorite team—in a worldview that is mainly *ethnocentric*.

<blockquote>Faithful = ethnocentric: *"It's all about our **group**!"*</blockquote>

At the Rational level, a person's worldview tends to be wider yet. The Rational-level person likely identifies with, or feels herself part of, all of humankind. Thus, we can say that the Rational-level person enjoys a broader and more inclusive worldview than those at the Lawless or the Faithful level. Not only does she include all people, but to varying degrees she may be more likely to concern herself with animal welfare and environmental concerns. We can say that the Rational-level person includes all the *seen* universe in her worldview. Her worldview is *worldcentric*.

<blockquote>Rational = worldcentric: *"It's about **all humans**—our mind, our science, our reason, our individuality!"*</blockquote>

Following this logic, we can see that the worldview at the Unitive level must be something broader than worldcentric. What could a

The Unitive Level in Spiritual Development...

Unitive-level person include that the Rational level one does not? We could say that the more elements of the visible world a person includes in his circle of concern, the closer he is to the Universal level. He who extends his circle to include animals, nature, and ecology is enjoying a worldview that goes beyond just humans. Often the Rational level includes some or all these concerns, so the Unitive level must include something beyond even these. If the connections that Rational-level humans sense are based on the intellect, on human reason, then the Unitive level must be based on something beyond mere reason and intellect.

So, the Unitive level tends to include something the Rational level rejects; namely, the elements that come to us from the nonvisible world, the invisible connections among us that send us intuitive hits, creative inspiration, and the drive to put our own lives on the line in the hope of creating a better world for everyone else. It could be said that the worldview of the Unitive level is all-inclusive—or Universal.

At the Unitive level, a person is informed by, or rather inspired by, *unseen* connections that people at the other levels mostly fail to notice. Perhaps instead of just feeling sorry for people less fortunate than she, the Unitive-level person actually experiences pain at seeing a maimed person begging on the street, feels that person's agony from within herself. Maybe instead of just *thinking* animals deserve certain rights, the Unitive-level person senses that animals are more than what they appear to be and senses a deeper connection with them than anything that can be appreciated objectively. Instead of simply knowing intellectually that we need to preserve our environment for future generations, perhaps the Unitive-level person feels actual pain at the sight of smoke rising from factory smokestacks or at the very thought of melting glaciers. Perhaps the Unitive-level person experiences overwhelming awe at the vastness of a starry sky at night.

Chapter 6

Whereas people from all levels can see the same sky, the same animals, and the same smokestack, the Unitive-level person is drawn outside of her little personal self to experience her connection to these things in a more visceral way. She allows them to inspire her to humility in recognizing how small her little self is in the overarching scheme of all that the universe comprises.

At the Unitive level, a person feels himself part of, and connected to, everything everywhere—all people, of course, but also all animals and all of nature to include the stars and planets and other galaxies. Further, he recognizes an "unseen consciousness" connecting all elements in the universe. He is connected to the universe in an intuitive way.

Because such a person allows himself to "know" things that come to him from this unseen consciousness, his awareness is not limited to consensus reality—meaning the things that other people can test scientifically, read on paper, or figure out using standard reasoning skills. Having already passed from the Faithful to the Rational stage, he does not care if others in his "tribe" don't see the same things he does. He does not depend on having others authenticate his conclusions. And, having moved beyond the Rational stage as well, he has the humility to trust knowledge that comes to him from the unseen consciousness, even if his rational mind might not be able to verify it.

Being able to sense this connection to an unseen reality is a "skill" that is unfortunately not valued in our society, and lack of appreciation for the value of this skill holds people back from reaching the Unitive level. Without this sense, without acknowledging this unseen reality that connects us all, we are limited to spiritual myopia.

Oneness with all things is not just a Buddhist concept. It typifies the most spiritually evolved individuals from any culture and is one

The Unitive Level in Spiritual Development...

way of describing the Unitive level. At the Unitive level, the person's worldview is all-inclusive. We can say that her worldview is *universal*.

Unitive = universal: *"We are all **One**!"*

The unseen consciousness connecting all elements in the universe that the Unitive-level person *feels and directly experiences* is the entity that our religions have personified and simplified into a being they call *God*. Because the Unitive-level person connects to this entity directly, she has little need of the rules and comforts provided by the outward elements of traditional religion. If she participates in organized religion, it is because a given tradition affords a simplified, easy way for her to enhance the spiritual connections that for her arise from within. For this reason, at the Unitive level a person may choose a certain religion as the most comfortable way in which to express her spirituality and to experience it as part of a community. But she will tend to see that religion as one acceptable way among many, as opposed to the literalist who insists his religion is the only answer.

Spiritual development theory probably never comes as good news the first time a person learns of it, because it suggests that, no matter where we may be on the spiritual development trajectory, we can never say we have arrived at full spiritual maturity. We always have more to learn and further growth to undergo.

To summarize, we could characterize the four stages of religious consciousness with a mantra for each level:

The Lawless: "It's me against the world."
The Faithful: "It's us against the world."

Chapter 6

(Those who have studied spiritual development will recognize the immaturity in the previous two statements in that they are grounded in being *against* something. Spirituality joins; it does not separate.)

The Rational: "We *are* the world."

The Unitive: "The universe and I are One."

In a postmodern world, we are called to recognize that oneness is not just for Buddhists anymore. The ability to view unity as a goal of all forms of spirituality is a crucial factor in the cure for spiritual myopia.

ISSUE	LAWLESS TRAITS	FAITHFUL TRAITS	RATIONAL TRAITS	**UNIVERSAL TRAITS**
RELIGIOUS ATTITUDE	Disinterested or superficial interest only	Needs definite answers; won't question directly	Skeptical; seeks truth over comfort	**Prefers the Mystery; seeks unity over truth**
INTERPRETIVE STYLE	Self-centered	Literal	Reason; science-based	**Metaphorical**
LOCUS OF AUTHORITY	One's own will; unprincipled	Oracle authority	Conscience authority; principled	**Spirit authority; (will of God; order of the universe)**
CIRCLE OF CONCERN	Self (egocentric)	One's own group (ethnocentric)	All humans; social justice (worldcentric)	**All that exists, incl. animals, nature, and the unseen (universal; unitive)**
IDENTITY	Selfish	Defined by group; divisive against outsiders	Individuated, but not selfish	**Seeks community with those at all levels**
RELIGIOUS COMMUNITY	May join for own needs	The only "right" one	Questioning; may reject	**Chooses one (or more) from among many acceptable possibilities**

ISSUE	LAWLESS TRAITS	FAITHFUL TRAITS	RATIONAL TRAITS	UNIVERSAL TRAITS
VALUES	Personal pleasure	Security; certainty comfort	Truth, integrity	**Unity**
VIEW OF "GOD"	Self	External, separate	Science; reason; truth	**Universal principle; inner light; love; goodness; ALL**
OTHER	Undeveloped; manipulative; insincere; chaotic lifestyle	Naïve (pre-critical); fear-based	Critical; seeking; involved in social causes	**Second naïveté**[11] **(post-critical) humility; forgiveness; gratitude; acceptance; compassion**

Figure 6: Universal-stage traits (Mystic, far right) compared to those at the Lawless, Faithful, and Rational stages

(From Margaret Placentra Johnston, *Faith Beyond Belief: Stories of Good People Who Left Their Church Behind* [Wheaton, IL: Quest Books, 2012], 89. Reproduced/adapted by permission of Quest Books [www.questbooks.net])

---

[11] Second naïveté is a term used by French philosopher, Paul Ricoeur. What he called the "First Naïveté" and the "Critical Distance" correspond roughly to our Faithful and Rational stages, respectively. His Second Naïveté corresponds roughly to our Universal stage. It denotes a returned openness to spirituality, a deeper form of faith than that which occurs in the Faithful (First naïveté) stage. This was explained in much greater detail in *Faith Beyond Belief*. Ricoeur, From Paul. "Religion, Atheism, and Faith." In *The Conflict of Interpretations*, 467.

By Their Fruits Ye Shall Know Them

It was back in the early 1990s that I first learned about what I am calling the Unitive level, originally through M. Scott Peck's book *The Different Drum,* where he uses the corresponding term "Mystic/Communal stage." At the time, I was stunned. Nothing in my experience to that point had ever suggested that people at such a level of consciousness exist. This is because these spiritual levels were not then—as, to a lesser extent, they are still not—explicit in our society, much to our detriment. Having now spent many years studying this subject, it is so clear to me that if only the spiritual development stages I describe were understood by a larger contingent, less mature "values" could not continue to be promoted by the many various factions in our society that serve only to hold us back.

Soon after first reading about Peck's Mystic/Communal stage, I remember describing it to a friend with the words, "And I am quite sure I have never met anyone at this level!" But he knew immediately what I meant and told me about two people of his acquaintance who clearly fit the description. Despite their status as Catholic nuns, these two ladies did not just blanketly accept every teaching of the Catholic Church. They had challenged what they had been taught and had their own ideas about everything. For example, they offered sound arguments for why women should be priests. They had studied many other spiritual traditions and were incorporating a lot of Eastern spiritual thought and vocabulary into their Christianity.

Clinical psychologists by training, their actual work centered around helping Catholic clergy work through the ways in which they were suffering under—or their psychological health was being limited by—some of the less evolved teachings of the Church. They helped these clergy move past their preoccupation with a supposed afterlife, refocusing their energies toward wholeness in this life, both to improve their physical health and to reconnect with present-day concerns.

The Unitive Level in Spiritual Development...

These two nuns dedicated themselves to spreading a more healing view of spirituality than that which fell directly within the limits of their religious training; yet, according to my friend, they were joyful in their mission of being of service to their peers and exhibited a profound humility. They were supportive of each other's talents and were inspiring and delightful to be around.

The spiritual position of these two nuns could undoubtedly be attributed at least in part to some clairvoyant experiences or unitive encounters they reported having had with the spiritual realms when they were young. (Experiences of unitive consciousness are considered to be one of the factors that can inspire people forward spiritually; see chapter 8 for more.)

When I first began studying this subject, and unschooled in what unitive-level people are about, I missed the fact that not everyone connected to traditional religion is at the Faithful level—just as the two nuns were not. Now that I know what traits are typical of a unitive worldview, I can discern at least a few of them in almost everyone I know, which only goes to show that we are all a mix of traits from each of the stages. As a reminder, we don't use these levels to judge individual people, but rather to help us know which way is forward, what characteristics are typical in spiritual maturity. Much of conventional society lacks this knowledge, so our mainstream messages typically direct us away from clear spiritual vision, rather than support it. Far too many of the dominant messages still serve to keep people mired in spiritual myopia, blinded to spiritual truth. The value in knowing about spiritual development theory is that it helps us to resist the influence of those elements that block

Chapter 6

our spiritual vision, and to choose instead messages and guidance that might help us move forward.

The primary trait that we know is typical in spiritual maturity is a unitive or universal worldview. In it, we see ourselves as part of everything we know of in the universe. We see ourselves as connected to all people, not just our family, our religious group, our political party, or even our nation. Anything that separates us from others in a triumphalist way shows our lack of connection.

I can use myself as an example here. I make no claim to being especially unitive myself, despite clearly recognizing it as a goal. Even though I am well aware of the harm in divisiveness, I have not managed to rid myself of some divisive habits. I grew up in a family that could care less about sports, and I went to a college where the football team had been suspended for the whole time I attended, so I missed out on the slavish devotion much of the mainstream lavishes upon their favorite sports team. Then, in the midst of a weekend reunion at my husband's college a few years ago, I felt quite isolated as almost the only person not flaunting the school colors everywhere possible, including orange or purple hair and even body paint. A conversation I was having with a very nice woman took a sudden downturn when she asked me (as a matter of course) whether I would be attending the game the next day, and I blurted out, "No. Personally, I cannot begin to understand why they all care so much which side of the field that stupid ball lands on!" Obviously, I felt the need to distance myself from the group obsession because I could not share the zeal, could not feel I was a part of it. Because it is not important to me, I sometimes cannot resist the urge to point out what I see as shallow, tribal values. I can't help focusing on the cost in terms of time, money, and primarily the energy that so many people freely expend on something the outcome of which matters so very little in the overall scheme of things. What if all that energy and time and money spent on football were directed instead toward doing good in the world? Because I know my attitude toward sports is triumphalist and divisive, I usually manage to squelch negative comments, but that day at my husband's college, I was so overwhelmed by the mania that I just could not help stomping on that very nice woman's enthusiasm for her team. That was *mean*. It was a spiritually myopic thing to do.

On the other hand, many others are successfully promoting unitive values. If you look up Sister Joan Chittister, a Benedictine nun, you will find a shining example of someone who has spent a lifetime working to cure the spiritual myopia so prevalent in the rest of the religious hierarchy, as it is commonly understood. Her TED talks, her books, and everything about her life bespeak a spirituality that is free of the exclusive claims, the triumphalism, and the literalist chains that so detract from the validity of most religions. Over the years she has worked tirelessly on behalf of peace, women's issues, and church renewal. Theologian Chung Hyun Kyung has said: "Joan Chittister showed us how a woman with integrity could reconcile faith and feminism and thrive in one's own religious tradition no matter how oppressive it is. She taught us how to own our power and act from that power for greater justice, peace, and democracy."[12]

Some notable quotes from Sister Joan:

> Beware the religion that turns you against another one. It's unlikely that it's really religion at all.[13]
>
> A religion that does not nurture its weakest does not know God the birthing mother. A world that does not

preserve the planet does not know God the creator. A world that does not honor the spirit of compassion does not know God the spirit. God the lawgiver, God the judge, God the omnipotent being have consumed Western spirituality and, in the end, shriveled its heart.[14]

An authentic spirituality does not cater to culture; it calls culture to accountability.[15]

It is in community that we come to see God in the other. It is in community that we see our own emptiness filled up. It is community that calls me beyond the pinched horizons of my own life, my own country, my own race, and gives me the gifts I do not have within me.[16]

A Few More Characteristics

Other characteristics that help us recognize and understand the Unitive level have been mentioned briefly throughout this book, but I describe them again here to reinforce the view of the Unitive level as I understand it. These characteristics include:

Metaphorical interpretation: In contrast to the literalism described in chapter 4 as a symptom of spiritual myopia, at the Unitive level a person is more likely to interpret the particulars in his holy texts and belief system as metaphors for intangible truths. Heaven and hell are not viewed as actual geographical locations. Perhaps they are viewed as a state of mind experienced in this life or in the afterlife, if the person believes in that. Biblical propositions are considered to teach a concept anecdotally rather than state actual fact. Prayer may be just one more way of connecting with the wider Reality as opposed to a way of asking for favors from or worshipping an actual separate

The Unitive Level in Spiritual Development...

Supreme Entity. The Unitive-level person may or may not use the word *God*, but the more she has emerged beyond literalism, the less anthropomorphically she perceives that Entity.

Tolerance of paradox: Whereas people at the Faithful and Rational levels tend to evaluate reality in black-and-white terms and to demand solid, existential answers—based on the authority of either religious tradition or science and reason, respectively—at the Unitive level the person has come to live without solid answers. He is not only comfortable without such answers but may actually enjoy living in the questions and find the mysteries of life exciting. Rather than reject new information if it doesn't jibe with his current understandings, he is more likely to suspend judgment until and unless he can figure out where the new information fits in.

Spirit authority: Because the Unitive-level person has moved beyond having reality dictated by traditional outer authorities and has perceived weaknesses in the answers that human reason and science can supply, she becomes readier to "listen" to the voices that speak to her alone. James Fowler, considered the father of faith development, in his definitive work *Stages of Faith*, tells us that the person ready for transition (to what he calls "Conjunctive Faith," which is roughly equivalent to the beginning of our Unitive stage) "finds him- or herself attending to what may feel like anarchic and disturbing inner voices[17] . . . the person opens up to unconscious factors, the voices of one's deeper self."[18] This deeper self is the spirit authority that a person comes to trust as his or her most important source of truth.

Acceptance vs. despair: Evelyn Underhill tells us that the mystic or Unitive-level person has expanded her boundaries beyond the physical self. This helps the person understand that Reality is so much bigger than her own little story. When something unfavorable happens, this understanding allows the perspective that our own setbacks may not be that important in the overall scheme of the universe. It allows the person to appreciate that she is not in control of circumstances. This mindset is evident when a person says about a recent unfavorable event in their life, "I am sure this happened for a reason."

Forgiveness vs. blame: Unitive-level people tend to be able to rise above the tendency to blame others for ills that have occurred. It may be because they perceive that the perpetrator was doing the best he could, or because they can perceive circumstances that led him to commit the harm. In any case, Unitive-level people hold a more generous attitude and are more inclined to forgive than to blame.

Gratitude vs. "I want more": At the Unitive level, a person is more likely to accept whatever graces are in her life with gratitude. She is less likely to search for ever more money, more fame, more excitement, etc.

Community vs. solitude: Many people equate spirituality with the view of some lonely hermit meditating alone all day on a solitary mountaintop. Whatever that signifies, it seems more of an escape than the active engagement with the world Evelyn Underhill describes, along with many others who have studied the spiritual development trajectory. The desire to escape reality may be a means of accessing more intense spiritual experiences for oneself, but it cannot lead to inclusion of all of Reality into one's level of concern. It cannot call a person to dispense with his or her own concerns and bravely face the world with all its evils and all its problems, in hope of mitigating the suffering of others. Fowler tells us that in his most advanced stage—which he calls "Universalizing Faith" and which in the days when he did his research was exceedingly rare—exemplars begin to exhibit a trans-narcissistic love that not only transcends their own ego but leaves them ready to "spend and be spent"[19] in making their view of transcendent Reality come alive for others. Such people are often seen as subversive by those at more conformist levels and are likely to be more honored and appreciated after death. Typical examples include, to some extent or other, Mahatma Gandhi, Martin Luther King Jr., and Mother Teresa. Regardless of the importance one may place on the now historically known personal limitations of these three individuals, we can see that each of them dedicated and sacrificed their lives in the profound service of something greater than their own selves. Each of them must have felt connected to—or a part of—something greater, a connection to something ultimate to the particulars of their own lives.

Humility vs. ego: We have already discussed to some extent how spiritual development leads to the diminution of ego. The individual self is sensed as less and less important in the overall scheme of things and dissolves into a greater whole. In extreme cases, this shift may allow the person to subject him- or herself to extreme discomfort and suffering in service to some greater good.

Focus on this world vs. salvation: In keeping with the above traits, we come to see how spiritual advancement directs our focus sharply on the here and now and promotes active engagement with the very real problems of the world. While some spiritual adepts insist that our experience of this world is not real, the more advanced among them will still work to improve the way the least among us experience it. Perhaps this serves as one example of the paradoxes that the Unitive level permits? In any case, spiritual maturity shifts focus away from the insistence of some religions that the afterlife is the only aspect of life that really counts.

Competition: In view of the spiritual development trajectory, it should be dawning on us that competition also promotes spiritual

Chapter 6

immaturity. The very need to be better than someone else, or to do better or to have more, is both rooted in spiritual myopia and creates more of it. If everyone's goal—or every company's goal—is to outdo the next one, that makes for a dog-eat-dog world in which it is every man for himself and care for the other has no place. The very need to be better than someone else is also rooted in insecurity. If a person feels fulfilled and comfortable herself, she would not care if someone else did better in any particular skill or type of accomplishment. A goal in spiritual maturity would be to do well enough and accomplish enough and have enough to feel good about and please ourselves. Only then can we feel such an abundance of personal blessings that it spills over to share with others.

Generosity: Generosity arises out of a sense of having enough. I would guess that most of you with the time and mental energy to read a book like this do have enough, but many of you may be unaware of the extent to which that is true. For instance, your home and car are either paid for or are being paid out of a steady income stream from your job, your pension, or your investments. You have a closet full of clothes and are not too worried about where your next meal will come from. You have a pantry full of food, cash to replenish it, and sufficient disposable income that you eat out more than one meal a week. This is a standard of living far, far above those in many parts of the world and even many in the United States. Okay, so maybe you can't fund your dream vacation, or you wish you could eat out every day. In the overall scheme of things, though, you are comfortable; you do have enough.

Yet, I would safely bet that most of us have responded uncritically to some influence telling us that we *don't* have enough; we have felt some pressure to desire and acquire more. All it takes is for someone else to have a bigger house, a fancier car, or an airplane, and conventional

The Unitive Level in Spiritual Development...

values lead us to feel we have failed. Too many of our mainstream messages are purposefully crafted to play on our fears that we lack something essential and to keep us ever wanting more. These are selfish, manipulative messages, designed to motivate us to buy more stuff. In the process, they make us feel paranoid about getting more and getting ahead.

And then there are the political messages designed to keep us fearing that someone is going to take away what we already do have, or that someone is getting something for free in a way that somehow diminishes our own sense of well-being.

In other words, our dominant societal messages—from our politicians, most of our media, and even some of our churches—promote and perpetuate spiritual myopia. Instead of leading us toward spiritually mature values of acceptance, gratitude, compassion, generosity, humility, and oneness, they blind us to our blessings and prevent us, if we fail to examine them critically, from consciously experiencing and expressing abundance. And they squelch any tendencies we might otherwise have toward generosity, acceptance, and compassion toward others.

When a person feels personally satisfied, it spills over into wanting to share one's blessings, especially with those less fortunate. Yet society tries to make such people feel like Pollyannas—silly folks blatantly ignoring all the evils in the world, all the ways others may be scheming to take something away from them. Those not critically reflecting on the deception involved in our dominant societal messages will find themselves allowing needless risk factors to cloud their spiritual vision.

So many elements in today's world are calling us to awareness of a spiritual reality far more broad, diverse, and open ended than what

Chapter 6

our traditional religions will typically admit. Spiritual development theory describes how individual people might find their way beyond spiritual myopia. It is really only the Lawless and the Faithful levels that contribute to strife among the religions. At the Rational level, people are more focused on their own personal story in life and don't attach too strongly to specific religious teachings. At the Unitive level, the differences among the religions may be seen as rich cultural legacies, valued mainly as points of entry into an almost totally inclusive and universal type of spirituality. It happens that whole cultures can traverse a similar trajectory, which brings us to the topic of human cultural evolution.

7
Human Cultural Evolution: A Hopeful Outlook

As chapter 2 outlined, spiritual and religious understandings have been evolving throughout recorded human history. The general trend of cultural movements has been toward broader and more complete spiritual understandings, and in this sense they have represented progress. But human cultural and spiritual understandings are continuing to evolve. This chapter will show that, despite the tremendous chaos that appears outwardly these days, the changes emerging now may be seen in a largely favorable light and predict hope for the future.

Ontogeny Recapitulates Phylogeny

"Ontogeny recapitulates phylogeny" is a fancy phrase used to describe an obsolete theory in biology that an organism's growth as a fetus repeats the same developmental stages as its species did as the species evolved over time. *Ontogeny* is the course of development of an individual organism from fertilized egg to adult. *Phylogeny* is the course of development of a group of organisms over time. Hence, the theory suggests that, before a human embryo emerges at birth as a human infant, in utero it has displayed traits similar to all the stages humans have gone through in their evolution from their ape-like ancestors.

While this is an interesting idea, it is no longer considered correct from a strict biological standpoint. But a related concept does seem to hold up when considering cultural evolution, and many authors are emerging from different camps to describe this process, though I do not believe any of them use the terminology of spiritual development theory as I describe it.

Chapter 2 of this book describes how every form of civilization throughout the ages has sought meaning, mostly through some form of spiritual connection. What becomes important to our study of the causes and cure for spiritual myopia is to acknowledge that the way each culture has met that need for meaning has been evolving *in a forward direction*. In a very general sense, the trajectory of human cultural evolution can be seen to mirror that of individual spiritual development. While this statement may seem surprising in this age of mass shootings and political and religious divisiveness, I will summarize below a trajectory that other, more scholarly authors have covered in much greater depth. (The bibliography lists many of these authors.)

Whereas earliest humans had only the vaguest notion of the concept that something might exist beyond our here-and-now reality, later ones have become ever more sophisticated in this respect. At first, in antiquity (spanning from the seventh century BCE to the fourth or sixth century CE), people attributed physical forces they did not understand to various "gods." Over time, into premodernity, the

Human Cultural Evolution: A Hopeful Outlook

understanding evolved that there was only one God, in the sense of a singular being who created the universe and ruled over it.

Most of our traditional religions were formed prior to the modern era, meaning sometime before the seventeenth century. As chapter 2 discusses, they were formed by people who were likely to be born, live their whole lives, and die in the same location. Such people had little or no access to anyone or anything outside their own culture. So, the religious stories they told themselves were just about *their* people and showed little concern for other people from other countries or other cultures. The existential explanations they offered featured their people prominently over others; their God offered salvation only for *their* people. Religious beliefs were dispensed by the outer authorities to the people to control their behavior, quell doubt, and keep them from questioning too much.

The culture of premodernity espoused values that are typical of an individual at the Faithful level—conformity of belief, submission to an outer authority, fear and mistrust of our human nature, and focus on the afterlife. Religions formed in premodern times reflect this mentality.

Early modernity, beginning around the seventeenth century, brought scientific realizations that much of what was earlier attributed to the various "gods" was explainable by physical laws. When science shed doubt on the creation myths in certain holy books, for example, some factions dug in their heels ever more forcefully, insisting that their founder had revealed the only factual truths and that only their creation myths held any validity.

Researchers have since shed even more doubt on the factuality of those "revealed" truths, finding, for example, that the original books of the Bible were altered during the Council of Nicea under

Chapter 7

the influence of the emperor Constantine (as mentioned in chapter 2), and that the emphasis in Christianity on belief and salvation was advanced only in the third or fourth century. Also important was the discovery that many ancient cultures contained similar creation myths, important dates, and similar key figures.

For example, even if the details of the stories differ, many of these myths involve a creator who lives in the heavens and an original pair of humans—a man and a woman. In many of the stories, man was created first and woman later. And often the original humans were formed from some other material: the flesh of a god, in the case of the Babylonians; trees in the Norwegian tradition; clay in Chinese lore; and red, white, black, and yellow earth according to the Lakota Sioux. Most of these myths include a flood, humans doing something to displease God or the gods, or people developing "punishable" traits such as envy and greed.[1]

Also, we now know that Jesus was not actually born on December 25. The choice to celebrate on that date originated in an ancient Roman celebration called "Saturnalia," when people indulged in all sorts of depraved behavior, and with the pagan celebration of the winter solstice, the "Nativity of the Sun," because that is the date on which daylight begins to lengthen. In addition, the ancient Babylonians believed that the queen of heaven was born on December 25, the Egyptians celebrated the birth of the son of the fertility goddess Isis on December 25, and ancient Arabs claimed that the moon was born on December 25.[2] Zoroastrians commemorate December 26 as the death anniversary of their founder, Zoroaster; Jews celebrate Hanukkah around that time of year as well; Buddhists celebrate Bodhi Day on December 8, or the Sunday immediately preceding it.

Human Cultural Evolution: A Hopeful Outlook

Wiccans and other pagans continue to celebrate the winter solstice on December 22 to this day.

In *Creative Faith*, Don Cupitt opines that, until about the year 1600, human minds were literally "pre-critical," meaning that they were simply not capable of the type of intellectual scrutiny we apply today in science and medicine. Early Christianity was "simply an untidy, accumulated cultural tradition. . . . It knew nothing of our modern intellectual standards, and never expected to be required to meet them. It had not yet even invented our ideas of research, and of a large, organized, tested body of knowledge."[3] Cupitt goes on, "By our modern intellectual standards, [early church leaders and even early theologians such as Augustine of Hippo and John of Damascus] had no method [of serious apologetics] at all, because they could not countenance the idea of critically sifting the evidence and discarding material that did not stand up."[4] The stories shared by the early Christians were just that—stories in which they felt free to play fast and loose with the facts, exaggerating a bit here to make a point, embellishing a bit there to add interest. They had no concept of having to back up their words logically, factually, or scientifically.

People at the Faithful level today differ from early Christians in that, in most cases, the minds of contemporary believers are capable of critical analysis. Some of them may be accomplished scientists or mathematicians who apply complex levels of critical analysis every day in their professions, but they have simply chosen not to apply the same standards to the literal authenticity of their religious beliefs. They choose not to analyze their beliefs in a completely open-ended way. Often people will say they have analyzed their religious beliefs for validity. But it is one thing to analyze a concept while *looking for*

Chapter 7

proof of a conclusion one has already reached, and quite another to do so in a totally open-minded manner. And spiritual development is not at all a matter of intelligence, per se. Standard measures of IQ and degree of accomplishment in the world have nothing to do with a person's level of spiritual maturity or spiritual intelligence. It is not a matter of being *able* to analyze and figure out complex concepts. Rather, it is a matter of being *willing*—or having the *courage*—to see through the myopia of provincial, conventional, but comforting outer-based "information" and learn to "see" with one's heart.

With the advent of modernity around the sixteenth or seventeenth century CE, people began to see through the logical and scientific limitations of the early Christian stories. Not willing to be duped by doubtful "revealed" explanations, they began to distance themselves from religion and spirituality as the main source of their truths. They prioritized reason and science over anything supernatural; hence, modernity came to be known as a secular age.

Secular modernity caused us to distance ourselves in a critical manner from all things supernatural. In a rather triumphal way, we came to suspect the validity of anything that could not be measured or proven by scientific methods. When evolution came to be seen as a foregone conclusion, we inferred that the story of Genesis lacked factual accuracy. When astronomy and geology defined the contents of the known universe, no evidence of heaven and hell were found, so doubt set in about the existence of those places.

Modernity accorded more importance to life in this world and the rights of the individual. It favored science and reason as better sources of truth about reality than it did the accounts revealed in holy books. Instead of seeing the world as ruled and inhabited by supernatural beings, modernity saw it as dead material that obeyed strict

Human Cultural Evolution: A Hopeful Outlook

scientific laws; the belief was that most elements in our world could be controlled through scientific means. In this sense, modernity at the cultural level was like the Rational stage for the individual.

Modernity began to fade as a mindset around the middle or end of the twentieth century. The strictly materialist view of the universe began to weaken with the discovery of quantum science and other factors discussed in chapter 5. People began to see ways in which the modern mindset left something missing. It had taken the soul out of the world, and we are only now gaining perspective on how erroneous and how damaging that mindset was. We must now seek to understand just what it is that is emerging in our current, twenty-first century.

The word *postmodernity* may bring up negative connotations for many of us. We may think of crazy, unfocused fragmentation of our culture in which marketing efforts are directed toward anything but the merits of the product being advertised; the concept of authority has almost no meaning at all; and, in terms of behavior, just about anything goes.

Whereas, say, back in the fifties, there were all sorts of rules about proper behavior and etiquette, most of them are no longer recognizable today. There aren't even any dominant fashion trends that can be identified; and, while fashion may seem a trivial matter, it is a strong indicator of cultural attitudes and mores.

For example, once when I was a child my cousin and I needed to go somewhere on the trolley car with my aunt. I was wearing normal play clothes—not torn jeans or a T-shirt with an offensive saying—just a nice, matched set of shorts and a top. Yet my aunt told me I could not get on the trolley dressed like that! In contrast, today people board an airplane wearing any sort of "disrespectful" attire. At this point

Chapter 7

in the first draft of this manuscript, my editor noted that she didn't think fashion trends are the best example of behavior changes. But I experience the relaxing of strict guidelines regarding acceptable personal appearance as emblematic of an overall easing of societal strictures that dominated my early years. I remember the days when a woman who appeared on the street without gloves was considered not a lady. When fashion hemlines were short, anyone wearing a longer skirt would be looked down on, and vice-versa. While I believe young school-aged kids today still go through a period of desiring to "fit in" in this way, the diversity of styles seen on the street now herald a tremendous lack of sartorial conformity. Compare the variety of hairstyles and length at which men wear their hair today with the 1960s, when a guy who let his hair touch his collar was considered subversive and dangerous! Personal expression has taken on an entire new meaning, symbolic of the more tolerant approach toward diverse lifestyles in our current society in general.

Once in graduate school, I was casually dating a guy who drove an old, beat-up Volkswagen "Bug" while I was enjoying the late model Oldsmobile Cutlass that had been my college graduation present from my parents. It actually occurred to me to wonder whether I could "be seen" dating a guy who had a "lesser" car than mine. What adult would even consider such things these days? I see this overall trend as indicative of a shift from undue concern with outer conformity and appearances—a concern that is largely at the expense of the inner reality—toward a focus on more authentic values.

Further, much of what appears as confusion and cultural fragmentation in our times actually results from influences coming in from outside our provincial environments, in terms of the global connections and cultural intermixing as discussed in chapter 5. Even if we don't travel much or live in a multicultural community, we can hardly avoid exposure to ever more varied elements from other cultures. We can find products from all different countries in our stores, and terminology and practices from all different other cultures are finding their way into common usage. Is there anyone reading this book who has never tried a yoga class, or who doesn't know what the word *guru* means? Our perspectives are expanding to include truths from other cultures as well as truths that are discovered individually.

Services today are often delivered internationally. Who among us has not phoned for some type of computer assistance, only to find ourselves in conversation with someone in India? I have read that these days a single product is often made up from various parts that each come from different countries. A simple Google search tells me that the iPhone 6 is made up of five parts that come from China, one part from California, two parts from Korea, and three parts from Japan.[5] This intermingling requires an uncommon amount of cooperation among all the countries involved and an unavoidable interplay among their economies. And as the economies intermix, so, inevitably, do the cultures.

For the most part, this cultural expansion is a good thing. It brings us closer to an overall truth, as opposed to a limited and provincial truth that applies only to one isolated culture. But for people who do not understand the trend, it can be very scary. To them, it looks like our society is falling apart. They see the straight-laced times of the 1950s and early '60s (before Woodstock, that is) as the good old days, even though they may have been good only on the surface.

A Bigger Story

In short, we are no longer an isolated country unto ourselves. We are part of a huge interconnected network in a globalized world, and we

Chapter 7

are being forced to include increasingly broadened appreciation of what should be included in our worldview. The way forward culturally is not to establish dominance of our nation over the rest. Yes, readers, "America First!" is a spiritually *immature* mantra. Nor is the way forward naively to insist that our religion is the only right one, or to promote the idea that those of a certain nationality must be cast out from our shores. These are all notions that come out of a provincial, premodern mindset and a fear of accepting even the advances that modernity has brought to us. The mindset that is forming now in postmodernity calls us to a bigger story!

Just as individual humans can grow spiritually throughout their lifetimes, societies can evolve over time, as well. An individual at the cutting edge of a new understanding may sound crazy to those in the mainstream and be cast as a misfit. But over time, more and more people come to acknowledge the worth of that "crazy" understanding, and it becomes more mainstream.

The bigger story toward which we are being called in postmodernity includes a strong resurgence of interest in religion and spirituality. Modern-minded people may see this trend as a regression in cultural progress. But as we seek to understand the phenomenon, we can begin to recognize it as a forward evolutionary shift. Just as we are now becoming aware of the Unitive level in individual spiritual development, a little investigation suggests hope that our overall culture is evolving toward more universal understandings, as well.

Because our society is only at the threshold of this type of understanding, many people cannot see what I have called the Unitive stage of individual spiritual development as an advance over most of conventional religion and the Rational mindset of secular modernity. But just consider the reaction a person in Constantine's time would have had to an explanation of the Rational stage. To say that an individual human could question the authority of his king or his spiritual leader and to believe that people could rely upon their own conscience to guide their actions would have sounded anarchic, blasphemous, and frightening. Consider next the reaction a person in the 1950s would have had to an explanation of the Unitive stage. To say that we are all One or that the various versions of truth held by many different religious traditions could all be valid at the same time would have sounded, as it very well may still sound to some today, chaotic, fanciful, and licentious. Even today, talk of equal rights and universal values based on interconnection strikes fear in the hearts of some who mainly identify with smaller, more provincial segments of the universe—their religion or political party, for example.

Despite the widespread chaos that appears at the surface in our postmodern times, it seems that spirituality is evolving to a deeper level, representing yet another cultural advancement. Many voices are beginning to describe this bigger story, exemplified by the entries in the bibliography of this book. The ethos that is emerging in postmodernity benefits from an enlarged understanding that comes to us through globalization and other factors, as discussed in chapter 5.

Also, in postmodernity new ways of creating meaning are emerging, but under vastly different circumstances than those under which our organized religions were formed. The type of spiritual focus emerging now respects the findings of science and includes the "this-life" focus of secular modernity. But, unlike in modernity, it recognizes our universal spiritual yearnings for meaning and connection, and it acknowledges the mysteries of our existence that caused the traditional religions to form in the first place.

Chapter 7

Thanks to an enlarged perspective from globalization, the emerging spiritual focus acknowledges that our reality is much bigger than one nation, or one religion, or one ethic. Leading-edge philosophers and open-minded theologians perceive a shift toward broader, more comprehensive existential understandings than those put forth by our traditional religions. Provincial and insular supernatural beliefs no longer satisfy the Rational modern mind and leave the emerging postmodern Unitive spirit looking for something more. Broader, more inclusive realizations are emerging, based on the core values shared by all the world religions; they are too multifactorial and too diverse to be captured by any one religious organization. This adds an *evolutionary* element to this change—again because it brings us closer to an overall truth, as opposed to the limited and provincial truths put forth by our traditional religions.

This is Not Relativism

One accusation often hurled at any attempts to unify spiritual messages is to say that they merely represent "relativism." In philosophical texts, the word *relativism* refers to several related but different concepts, most of which are so abstract as to have little place in our discussion here. Other texts, which emanate largely from the Faithful-level mindset, use the term to refute the pluralistic ideologies now surfacing in our culture. I will address only this latter concept here.

Defenders of the Faithful mentality patently reject anything that smells like relativism in the hope of preserving their worldview. A reminder that the Faithful level derives its sense of order from a stable, unchanging reality, an outwardly imposed structure, conformity, outer authority, and definite rules helps us understand this perspective. The Faithful need these elements to hold their world together,

Human Cultural Evolution: A Hopeful Outlook

but in Western culture many of these elements are unraveling at a very fast pace.

The fear that the Faithful tend to blame on *relativism* stems from two crucial connotations of the word. The first is *moral relativism*: Today's loosening of societal norms about appropriate clothing, gender identification, and premarital sex are all mixed up in the Faithful-level mind with absolute societal ills such as killing, stealing, and sexual predation. The Faithful cannot imagine how anyone could adequately govern himself without absolute standards about what is right and what is wrong. They fear that without black-and-white rules about everything, people would not be able to resist killing, stealing, and so on. One wonders how Faithful-level religious leaders have managed to inspire in their congregants this abject lack of faith in human nature. I suppose growing up being told you are a sinner may have something to do with it. Unless everyone conforms to the same rules, the only result the Faithful can conceive of is chaos. But a distinction between rules and values may clear up this confusion.

Standards of personal appearance are not a moral issue. I have already reminded readers that in the 1960s a man whose hair merely touched his collar was considered subversive. Now I doubt that even the most ardent defenders of the conservative worldview would notice the variety of lengths to which today's men allow their hair to grow. This is only a trivial example of how cultural standards change over time.

Similarly, societal injunctions against premarital sex are intended to avoid situations in which 1) people in general, but especially girls, are taken advantage of by partners not willing to make a long-term commitment; and 2) unwanted pregnancies resulting in children not being properly cared for. These restrictions were all necessary in a world that included few self-governing individuals and no scientific

Chapter 7

means of avoiding pregnancy. Today, however, all that is required to avoid pregnancy is the discipline to use proper birth-control measures. While not everyone is sufficiently disciplined to do this, we can be confident that large numbers of today's young people are. And, given that many Millennials are delaying marriage ever further beyond the first bloom of their fertility, expecting them to abstain from sex until their thirties or later becomes increasingly unrealistic. Rather than rail against premarital sex, why not instead trust that educated and sophisticated young people have the wherewithal to protect themselves against the risks involved? Why not be sure that their upbringing includes awareness about those who would take advantage of them sexually, about the importance of not taking advantage of others, about sexually transmitted disease, and about how to avoid unwanted pregnancy? Such training would impart crucial *values* about reproductive responsibility that would serve the purpose, even when the conventional *rules* no longer work.

Homosexuality—or, more broadly, the entire current gender revolution—is another issue that would take volumes to discuss. Here, I will offer only the observation that much of the Faithful level's rejection of homosexuality (and dread about gender ambiguity) results more from fear than from conviction that it involves moral offense. Few in the grips of such dread, however, would admit it. If the value of human dignity is to be upheld, the rules about gender distinctions must give way when an unstoppable cultural shift brings the two into conflict.

The second connotation of the word *relativism* that causes fear in the Faithful level is *cognitive relativism*. I am not sure this is the best term; I found it on a Christian apologetics website in an article deploring relativism.[6] Since I can't think of a better term, I will continue to use it. *Cognitive relativism* concerns the claim that all truth exists in relation to culture, society, or historical context—that no absolute truths exist. One can see how this definition would unbalance those at the Faithful level of spiritual development who trust that the set of propositions they hold to be "absolute" truth have been divinely and exclusively revealed to them by a (hopefully) unchanging authority. Allowing elements from other such authorities (i.e., holy books from "competing" religions) would detract from the validity of theirs. In this light, pluralistic spiritual stances like interspirituality appear rudderless and scary. But when your religious and spiritual truth is limited to the revelations of *one* holy book—from *one* age, from *one* part of this world and from this planet only, from just our *one* solar system and our *one* galaxy out of trillions in a continually expanding universe—you've got to admit your point of reference is too small.

The Absolute Truth, if it exists, has got to include that whole picture. It's got to apply to more than one infinitesimally small portion of creation. The bigger spiritual story is a necessary derivation from the scientific and intercultural discoveries that have come to us since the original religions were founded. The bigger spiritual story is not relativism; it is an all-comprehensive inclusivism.

The Age of the Spirit

Call it religion, call it spiritual connection, or call it simply a sense of enchantment with the universe and our existence within it: there is a definite swing away from modernity's strictly rational and materialist worldview. The rise of religious fundamentalism might make it seem as if our culture is reverting to a premodern mentality. But there is a way to look at this phenomenon, not as a step backward, but rather as an advancement, a way in which our society is evolving in a forward direction spiritually.

Chapter 7

In chapter 2, I referred to Harvard theologian Harvey Cox's prediction that, after having moved beyond early Christianity's "Age of Faith" and beyond the "Age of Belief" that began in premodernity, we are now moving into an "Age of the Spirit." (As an aside, Cox makes no link between his Age of Belief and modernity's secular focus. That every author's perspective does not line up exactly with every other one does not invalidate any one of them; nor does it disallow us from gaining understanding from their descriptions.) Cox tells us that what he calls the emerging Age of the Spirit includes a more egalitarian and less hierarchical view of religion, as well as openness and dialogue with those from other faith traditions. We can hardly avoid noticing how this represents a significant spiritual advancement over the Age of Belief that began in the time of Constantine. But the Age of the Spirit is also more comprehensive than modernity's singular devotion to constant technological progress, unmoderated by ecological considerations or inclusive values. Evidence of Cox's Age of the Spirit abounds if one is prepared to recognize and welcome it.

Personally, I see the Catholic Church's naming of Pope Francis in 2013 as one such sign. Whereas the prior pope, Benedict XVI, was all about the hierarchy, tradition, and unchanging beliefs, Francis embodies a much more open and less dogmatic form of faith. His reign so far has been marked by a stunning humility. He has rejected the luxurious Vatican papal quarters in favor of a more modest suite in the Vatican guesthouse, where he can enjoy community with others. His papacy has been characterized by outspoken support of the world's poor. He has shown commitment to interfaith dialogue and environmental concerns. And he has even suggested a relaxing of the traditional ban that forbids divorced and remarried Catholics to receive the sacrament of Holy Communion (considered a privilege available only to those in good standing with the Church and free of serious sin at the time.) The interfaith and interspiritual movements discussed in chapters 5 and 8 represent other examples of (and basically the rest of this book is about) our culture's movement away from the Age of Belief and toward the Age of the Spirit.

The New Spirituality

Related to the Age of the Spirit, though perhaps espoused by a somewhat different demographic, we will now consider more fully a phenomenon we can call the New Spirituality. Even though leading-edge spiritual seekers are surpassing traditional religiosity in scope and secular modernity in perspective, the new spirituality is a movement barely yet recognized by most of our mainstream society. In place of rigid rules and superficial, fixed existential answers, the new spirituality takes the person *out of his or herself* toward concern with the greater good of all *in this world*. In this sense, our society as a whole is connecting with something greater than itself! So, in terms of spirituality, good things are happening in postmodernity. But, just as other kinds of changes in the overall culture, they can be frightening to people not prone to see the bigger picture.

Another factor that keeps the greater society from recognizing the new spirituality is the often superficial and immature nature of how it is expressed. In this respect, it is like any other emerging movement or perspective, be it religious or secular. As mentioned earlier, the new spirituality I am trying to describe was born out of the New Age movement prominent in the 1960s and '70s. Most of those concepts sounded far too superficial, too woo-woo, and too silly to garner much respect in any rational corner. But in the ensuing forty years, it seems, a few of those early, New Age practitioners have grown up.

Chapter 7

The early culture of the New Age was characterized by crystals and incense, loose associations (e.g., assigning meaning to a random bird we happen to see outside our window), and magical thinking (e.g., thinking we can influence the likelihood of rain or snow in our entire region through our own personal thoughts or actions). But what has now evolved out of it is a spiritual focus that is deeper, more authentic, more demanding in many ways than what most of our traditional religions teach, and more comprehensive than secular modernity's strictly materialist worldview. Although examples abound—including an emphasis on interconnectedness, ecumenism, and service (see ch.10 for more detail)—a pervasive spiritual myopia blinds most of the conventional world to this new spiritual development.

The new spirituality is a move in the same general direction as Harvey Cox's Age of the Spirit. Along with many others, Cox tells us that this age represents a significant spiritual advancement over the prior Age of Belief begun in the time of Constantine. But it is also more comprehensive than modernity's singular devotion to constant technological progress, unmoderated by ecological considerations and values of inclusiveness. In its most mature and most authentic expressions, the new emerging spirituality represents a learning opportunity that it behooves most of us to learn more about. In particular, the system of ethics it proposes involves a sharply honed sense of interpersonal responsibility, a view of a morality that is far more demanding than the Ten Commandments.

To be sure, there seems to be a correlation between how individual humans evolve and how societies evolve. Individual spiritual development takes a person from a Lawless childhood through the adolescent/adult Faithful stage of conformity (which unfortunately often endures throughout an entire conventional adulthood,) and then

Human Cultural Evolution: A Hopeful Outlook

into the questioning Rational stage of individualism, ideally occurring in young adulthood, before reaching the fully mature Unitive stage of universal connection that is possible in later adulthood. Huge, sweeping cultural changes over millennia of recorded human history disclose a similar trajectory. The generally Lawless cultures of antiquity gave way to a Faithful-type authoritarian conformity in premodernity. Modernity brought on Rational-level questioning and the importance of the individual. Chapter 5 describes postmodern factors that offer us a chance of bringing about a truly unitive and universal human community. Indeed, in cultural development, ontogeny *can* recapitulate phylogeny.

And phylogeny *can* echo ontogeny, ushering humanity toward the next step forward. If only more of us will cooperate, if more of us can recognize which way is forward, we can each seek out our own personal cures for the spiritual myopia of outmoded worldviews and obsolete belief systems. The more that individuals come to recognize the new understandings, the greater a part of the society they live in is influenced by their thought, with the eventual result that those understandings become ever more mainstream. This creates a circular pattern in which a culture can constantly evolve. When more of us have contributed to the understandings driving the current pattern, postmodernity will be clear of what seems now to be an insurmountable chaos and can usher us into a totally inclusive, completely Unitive, and entirely universal human community.

At all times, certain factions lead human cultural evolution, a critical mass of folks follow them, and a small minority remain behind the evolutionary curve. Because those at the tail end of an evolutionary change fail to or refuse to understand the progress, they will fight back, sometimes very loudly, trying to restore what they have romanticized

Chapter 7

into an ideal past. "Make America Great Again" is but one example of this kind of myopia. To what exact period of American history are proponents of "Make America Great Again" harking back? The 1950s, when only white American males could hold positions of power and minorities (including the "minority" of half the population, namely women) took a back seat to white male authority? The days when a couple could not safely walk down the street holding hands if they were not of the same race? The days when gays had to hide in closets their whole lives? Even the days when the United States was the clear world power in just about every field of endeavor are not something to yearn for when you consider the obvious value of approaching the world with more humility and a spirit of collaboration over that of dominance. So, no, making America Great Again is not a spiritually mature goal. It promotes separation and divisiveness, which we now know are typical at the least mature spiritual levels. Proponents of this mantra represent the very tail end of the evolution of our culture. They may hold power for a while but only as harbingers of better days to come. This evolutionary tail end that they represent is the very spiritual myopia this book has sought to correct.

8
More Universal Perspectives: Further Vision-Opening Opportunities

A few additional concepts will further help expand our understanding of how a clearer spiritual vision would play out in a more evolved society. While some of these ideas may sound shocking to the conventional mind, taken together they make a compelling argument for a larger rendition of what religion and spirituality are all about.

Interspirituality

The term *interspirituality* was coined by the late Brother Wayne Teasdale, author of *The Mystic Heart*.[1] He used it to refer to the increasingly common understanding that all the world's religious traditions share the same essential purpose. Leaders and practitioners of different religions are coming to appreciate and share the spiritual treasures that come from various traditions. They are coming to recognize

Chapter 8

that, despite the huge degree of *outer* diversity displayed among the beliefs and rites and rituals of our various religions, an *inner* core of common values can be seen by those awakened to this unitive worldview. This is like the view of the perennial philosophy (see chapter 5) that each of our religions represents a localized effort on the part of a certain culture to respond to the common need all humans share: that is, to answer our deepest existential questions. Interspirituality recognizes that all spiritual paths arise out of the universal human need for meaning and for a sense of connection to some force greater than ourselves. They all lead to a common endpoint—a sense of inner peace and compassionate love for all of creation, and a recognition of a universal force (or higher power, energy, ultimate reality, divinity, ether, god, or God) that connects us all. In the most authentic cases, this stance will compel the person with a sense of personal responsibility to assist in the attempt to transform the culture in the direction of universal love and inclusiveness. Teasdale optimistically claimed that, in the third millennium, interspirituality will become more and more the norm in humankind's inner evolution.[2]

Authors Kurt Johnson and David Robert Ord have taken the interspirituality concept to a new height in their book, *The Coming Interspiritual Age*.[3] They posit that our civilization is slowly coming to recognize the commonalities that drive the world's religions and that lie behind our spiritual yearnings. They claim that interspiritual awareness is a *necessary effect* of globalization in a postmodern world and predict that this realization is part of an overall *leap in human evolution*.

Bearing a 2012 copyright, and therefore written before the dreaded end-of-the-world scenario predicted for December 21, 2012, *The Coming Interspiritual Age* claims that the year 2012 would, indeed, be an apocalyptic time, even though it would only be recognized as such decades afterward. They describe a compelling thread running through all the source materials (the Mayan calendar, the I-Ching, Nostradamus, et al.) that predict a more hopeful interpretation of religion/spirituality compatible with the modern mind.[4] They point out that in the 1960s and '70s many Christian seminaries began to treat the Bible more as a historical document and less as a sacred text revealing the divine "word of God." They point out that Judaism has already made this transition beyond a literalist approach to their sacred texts and predict that Islam will be the next major religion to do so. They see this as a developmental *advance*, "essential to any future view of 'truth' that could be universally compatible with globalization."[5] What they imply is that once the "revealed-truth" aspects of a given sacred text are eased, the contents may be seen simply as one culture's way of approaching ultimate truth. The characters and the existential declarations may be recognized metaphorically, and suddenly the differences from the truths of other cultures may appear less dramatic—a step toward unity consciousness. This transition will serve as a benchmark in the evolution of human consciousness, a step in the direction of higher awareness and advanced skill sets that herald a more interconnected future.

Isn't the Bible the Inspired Word of God?

Readers still holding to the belief that the Bible is the directly inspired word of God may benefit from the following perspective. Anyone who has ever done creative work of any sort—music, art, literature, even architecture—will admit, provided they have a shred of humility, that their work did not arise entirely out of their own conscious mind. Here is my own personal story about that: After the publication of

Chapter 8

Faith Beyond Belief in 2012, I began musing on what my next book would be. I had two very different concepts in mind, but for several years I could not seem to make any progress. The first book had taken up so much of my time and so much of my energy, and I began to question whether I was even up for pursuing this topic further with either concept.

Then in the summer of 2015 I was invited by Sister Jenna of the America Meditating Radio Show to Peace Village, a retreat center in New York. Participants included about thirty authors, coaches, and clergy, all of whom work in one way or another toward the vision of a unitive worldview. The program consisted of meditation, discussions, and various "clearing exercises."

When the formal retreat had ended, I had a few hours to "kill" before leaving for the airport, so I decided to visit the labyrinth on the Peace Village property. Some fellow program participants offered to show me where the labyrinth was, and, on the way there, a man said to me in a particularly direct and specific way, "Now, Margie, when you go to a labyrinth, you are supposed to *ask a question!*" Of course, I knew that, as I had walked other labyrinths before, but in deciding to walk the labyrinth that day I had no specific question in mind. Because of his directive, however, just before beginning to walk I took a moment at the labyrinth entry point to formulate a question that had been rolling around in my head throughout the retreat: "Should I try to write another book, or should I forget all about this spiritual development topic and focus on my optometry work instead? And, if I should write another book, which of the two concepts I have been considering should I pursue?" Well, I had not walked five feet into that labyrinth before the entire concept and a complete outline for this book you are now reading simply

More Universal Perspectives...

"downloaded" into my head. While the title—*Overcoming Spiritual Myopia*—was almost the same as one of the other book concepts I had been considering, the content was *entirely* different. It felt as if magic had occurred. It was a good thing that I happened to have my purse with me, as I had a pen and just enough paper to scribble out the new outline and a few tentative paragraphs that came to me at that time. Moreover, a few yards farther along, a plan arose in my mind for how I might write this book in a far more efficient manner than the way I had written my first book.

So, where did all those new ideas come from? Obviously, they were "my" ideas, but surely they were inspired by something beyond my conscious mind. If they came from my subconscious, who is to say that this subconscious mind is not a part of the collective consciousness or the higher transpersonal consciousness, which, various philosophers have claimed, connects us all? I am not about to say that this book was channeled. No, it took countless hours of conscious effort on my part, wording, rewording, adding and deleting whole paragraphs, and getting collaborative feedback from several beta readers and a very skillful editor.

But, as a result of my experience at the labyrinth, I can easily see how someone whose "download" from the "ether" came to them in more complete form might say that their work was channeled or dictated by the Divine. Neale Donald Walsch is one current-day author who insists that at least his early works—the *Conversations with God* series and subsequent titles—were dictated to him directly by God. Sure enough, his works do seem to present an "updated" message that could be construed as coming from a literal sky God. It was only many years after I first encountered Walsch's work that I came across an article in which he admitted that the God he referred to in his work is not a literal being. So, if it was not a being that dictated Walsch's works, who or what was it? How different is that from my receiving the outline for this book from "the ether"?

When it is said that the Bible is the inspired word of God, could it not be that its writers "received" messages from the same source that inspired Walsch's writings and perhaps even that dictated the outline of this book to me? Walsch has been careful to point out that his interpretation of the messages he received may be distorted by the limitations of his very human mind. Could it not be that the Bible may have been inspired in a similar way, but that it, too, suffers from a lack of astrophysical and cosmological knowledge in the minds of those who received it? Given this possibility, should we not be taking that limitation into account when deciding how to interpret the Bible?

Reports of Direct Spiritual Experience

We can theorize about interspirituality all we want, but the most reliable sources of this understanding are those who know it by direct experience. They may insist that Jesus spoke to them, or that God told them to do this or that. But these experiences come to selected people from all religions and all cultures, so their source must be something far broader than just the Christian God. The common place from which such experiences arise—the underlying spiritual Reality—is not limited to any one group.

Some people will try to use such experiences to justify the validity of their own tradition. When they say Jesus appeared and spoke to them, they assert it as proof that Christianity is the only true religion. Author and philosopher Ken Wilber lends perspective here: He has said that while a person from any tradition may have a spiritual experience, people will tend to interpret their spiritual experiences in the

More Universal Perspectives...

language of the religious tradition that is familiar to them. Christians will see Jesus, but people from other religions will see figures from their own tradition.[6] Even people who claim a direct, personal relationship with God or Jesus or any religious figure from any religion are likely to be participating in this phenomenon. They are interpreting their connection with a universal Divine in culturally specific terms from their own tradition—it's just human nature to relate experiences to that with which we are familiar. And surely a direct relationship with a simplified, personified figure is more comforting than trying to relate to a vast universal force we cannot even picture.

Some people have had spiritual experiences not limited to any religious understanding. They tend to be those who have engaged most deeply in a meditation practice, or even those who have undergone profound life changes, such as a near-death experience. Many will report having directly experienced unity consciousness. They will have experienced a temporary state of feeling connected to everyone and everything in the universe. If we are going to see interspirituality as a good, we must grant respect to those who have enjoyed the most vibrant and direct experiences. We must recognize that our brains are very prone to mistaking the general for the particular. That spiritual experiences are common among people of all religions and all cultures proves only one thing: spiritual experiences occur. To insist they prove the validity of our particular spiritual beliefs is a logical error that only deepens our spiritual myopia.

Near-Death Experiences

Sometimes when a person almost dies, or dies and is revived, they will report having experienced a series of profound images and emotions while they hovered between life and death. Such reports are called

Chapter 8

near-death experiences, or NDEs. Reports of such experiences date back to the time of Plato, but they began to be taken more seriously around the 1970s after Dr. Raymond Moody published a book called *Life After Life*.[7] In 1981, an organization called the International Association for Near-Death Studies (IANDS) was formed to study reports of this phenomenon formally and to consider the relationship of NDEs to human consciousness.

Comparing NDE reports from various cultures, common factors were found: a sense that the person had glimpsed the afterlife; a profound sense of peace; a sense of being in an otherworldly realm; a sense of meeting deceased relatives and/or spiritual or religious figures; and, to a lesser extent, a sense of experiencing some type of life review.[8] An important consideration here is that the person would tend to "meet" with a spiritual or religious figure who was in keeping with his or her own religious or cultural background. This makes sense, because, as mentioned above, those who study states outside everyday consciousness say that people will tend to interpret any such encounters in terms of the religious or spiritual language or imagery with which they are familiar.

In the strictly scientific community, NDE's have historically been attributed merely to sensory deprivation or oxygen deprivation in the brain and are, therefore, distrusted. More recently though, a few scientists and medical doctors have described an NDE that happened to them personally. Eben Alexander's *Proof of Heaven: A Neurosurgeon's Journey into the Afterlife* is one example.[9] Mary C. Neal's *To Heaven and Back: A Doctor's Extraordinary Account of Her Death, Heaven, Angels, and Life Again: A True Story* is another.[10] These authors, along with others recounting after death revival or near-death events, tend to trust that the experience was beyond anything that could have a mere physical cause.

For purposes of this book, the most important thing to consider about NDEs is the effect they tend to have on the survivor. While a very small number of people have reported negative experiences (views of hell, encounters with cruel beings, feelings of anxiety), most NDEs are experienced as positive events that cause uplifting emotions and often have lasting beneficial influence on the experiencer's values and attitudes. The most common effect of an NDE is that the person no longer fears death, to the extent that some even express a longing to return to the peaceful, calm state they experienced during the NDE. Another common feature in NDEs is an encounter with beings that express a deep love and acceptance toward the experiencer. Often the experiencer will carry that feeling back into their everyday life; and, going forward, they will exhibit a more loving attitude toward humanity and a strong increase in their concern for others. They may be motivated to begin working toward social goals in service to the good of all people.

Regarding spirituality, many NDE experiencers will be graced with an increased sense of meaning or purpose. Some report a new trust in some kind of Higher Power that they may or may not call God. Interestingly, this does not particularly translate into any stronger tendencies toward a church-going religiosity.[11]

Unless one particularly looks for it, it is easy to miss the similarity between the values that a near-death experience tends to engender and the values that arise during spiritual growth. However, once those similarities are pointed out, it becomes hard to miss that both experiences do lead a person in a similar direction—toward a more universal and more connected spiritual stance. Thus, it can be said that an encounter with the spiritual realms does, in fact, tend to lead a person toward greater spiritual maturity.

Taken together, all these factors are leading us to a new type of realization. It is one that can only be appreciated in the light of the larger message offered to us by spiritual development theory:

- That religion and spirituality are more about the universal human search for meaning and connection and less a source of pat, existential "answers."
- That each of our religions is but one culture's way of answering the universal human need for connection, and the differences among them may be attributed to local customs and the direct individual experience of the original founder(s) of each system.
- That, as one matures spiritually, he or she will become less attached to the thought that his religion is the "right" one and will become more open to wisdom offered by other traditions.
- That, in this process of spiritual maturing, he or she will become more universal, less provincial, more accepting of people with different beliefs and different lifestyles, and more inclusive toward those who are "other."

What about Prayer?

Many kinds of prayer exist. Some religions have preset prayers that people memorize and say in a ritualistic way. Other peoples' prayers take the form of personal conversations directly with their God or a special saint, or some other nonlocal entity viewed as having desirable powers. Sometimes a person will pray in hope of having

More Universal Perspectives...

a specific request granted for something they want or need. This is called petitionary prayer. Sometimes a person will pray that something good will happen for someone else. That is called intercessory prayer. There are prayers of praise and worship, prayers to help a person decide between two alternative courses of action, contemplative prayer, and probably hundreds of other types. Most people will say that their prayers "work," which implies that the particular entity to whom they are praying—God or a particular saint—is actually "up there" listening and will deliberately act to help them. But people of all faiths pray, and they *all* feel their prayers work. Otherwise, why would they keep doing it?

A bit of perspective may be gained here if we return to the idea of *emmetropia*, which in optometry refers to perfect focus and I am using in a spiritual sense to mean a state of being in which one can appreciate concepts universally. Spiritual emmetropia involves recognizing all our personifications as particular names we have assigned to the general concept of a universal force that connects us all. Those who think they are praying to their particular understanding of God are actually invoking a more universal entity that the various cultures have envisioned in different ways. Spiritual emmetropia calls us consciously to recognize that all these different personifications are equally valid and that not all of them refer to an actual, separate, anthropomorphic being like the Christian God.

A personal example may be useful here. Long after having left behind the Catholic beliefs in which I had been brought up, I was introduced by a friend to a type of energy work called Reiki. Reiki, a healing technique that originated in Japan, is based on the idea of an unseen "life force energy" that flows through our being. It can be enhanced when a Reiki practitioner either lays their hands on you or

Chapter 8

"sends" you Reiki over a distance. In the 1990s, this sounded like the most ridiculous thing I had ever heard, but I agreed to receive a treatment just to go along with the friend who was offering it. Finding the treatment pleasant, and trying to keep an open mind, I also agreed to a temporary "attunement" that allowed me to "do" Reiki myself for a period of time. Eventually, I signed up for a class where I would be permanently attuned at the most basic level—where it was necessary to lay hands over the person you were "Reikiing." Thanks to various experiences, my appreciation for the power of Reiki increased over time, and eventually I signed up for more advanced levels in which the Reiki could be sent over distances to people far away and to general situations needing resolution. When I later explained all this to a different friend, she stunned me with the question, "And how exactly does that differ from prayer?"

By that point, I had come to have utmost respect for the powers of Reiki. We had been taught that Reiki always goes to "the highest good," meaning that you may "send" with a specific intention, but if some other "need" is greater, the intelligent energy of Reiki will direct itself to that other situation. Similarly, if you are "sending" to help someone through a problem, your particular idea of how things should go may not represent the greater good, and your efforts could result in the effect opposite from the one you hope for. For example, say you sent Reiki to a couple having marital problems in the hope that they would stay together. If they really didn't belong together, if greater good would result from their being apart, your efforts could result in them splitting up quicker and with less strife. I had had a few humbling experiences of just this sort of intelligent energy healing, and I knew it worked. Why would this second friend suggest it was the same as prayer? To whom exactly would the Reiki I sent be directed? Surely not to the same "God" all those religious people prayed to! But . . . over time I began to realize that if the God of others was a personification of some universal force, then the Reiki I sent was, indeed, a prayer to that same force. The only difference was that I was comfortable directing Reiki to "an unseen life force," whereas I would have felt silly "praying" to an old bearded "father" God in the sky.

So, what if all forms of prayer "work," not because the particular personification to which they are directed "exists" in a literal sense, but because all those personifications to whom the various people of the world direct their prayer represent the same *universal* life force that connects us all?

What about Miracles?

A miracle is an occurrence or phenomenon that cannot be explained by natural scientific laws. Spontaneous disappearance of a malignant tumor, for example. Or, as in one case I saw on the Internet, a person with a lifelong limp went to a prayer service where the minister prayed directly for her leg and, before their very eyes, it grew out to normal length and the limp was suddenly, miraculously gone. Another case described a person whose car broke down in a snowstorm early on Easter morning about three hours from Grandma's house. The family laid hands on the car and prayed. The car started and ran just long enough to conk out once again in Grandma's driveway.[12] Occurrences like this are often described as miracles and are usually attributed to God's grace. After all, if one were praying to his or her "God" and the wish were granted, wouldn't that "prove" that God exists? Well, how about all the other miracles that happen when people pray to "other" gods from other religions? What would they prove? Could it be—once again—that miracles happen, not due to the personification to which

CHAPTER 8

the prayer is directed, but rather thanks to the existence of a universal miraculous force equally available to people in all traditions?

What about Revelation?

Christianity insists that its truths were divinely revealed. It is this very fact that gives solid authority to Christian teachings. Other religions also claim that their truths are based on divine revelation. Judaism holds that Moses received the Ten Commandments directly from God on Mount Sinai. In Islam, Mohammad received messages from the Angel Gabriel, and these messages formed the basis for the Qur'an. Mormonism holds that Joseph Smith translated the Book of Mormon into English by divine inspiration.

The Hindus also believe that their Vedas are eternal truths revealed by God to the great Rishis (or seers) of India.[13] And the Bahá'ís believe in progressive revelation.[14] They believe that each prophet to come along revealed valid truths, but that each set of truths builds upon all the prior revelations and adds some further new information. They believe that their prophet, Bahá'u'lláh, is the most recent prophet and that therefore Bahá'ís have the most complete set of truths available today.

While I personally have not studied Bahá'í, I do think its followers are onto something—and that would be that we must consider more than one set of "revelations" if we are to appreciate the fullness of spiritual potential. What if every set of revelations was valid for the time and the place in which it was revealed? What if each set of revelations had been custom designed for the cultural and social mindset of the people to whom it was revealed? Would that not imply that, as cultures changed, the limitations of a given set of revelations would become evident and new revelations would become needed? Could the reason that the Rational mindset of secular modernity came to

More Universal Perspectives...

dominate our culture be that our scientific findings have outgrown the "Christian" teachings at their literal level? Could it not be the case that limiting ourselves to the teachings of just one religion keeps us mired in spiritual myopia? Could it not be true that opportunities offered in today's globalized world call us to broader, clearer, and deeper spiritual appreciations? The remaining two chapters further make the case for moving beyond the spiritual myopia of our current culture and finding ways to appreciate a more Unitive and universal form of spiritual emmetropia. Such realizations are necessary if ever we are to enjoy peace among the religions.

9
Overcoming Spiritual Myopia: The Prescription

In the light of all the concepts presented so far in this book, we can see that most of our conventional understandings do suffer from a spiritually myopic worldview. Elements arising in our postmodern world call us to a broader perspective.

At this point I want to invite readers to recognize two important points. First, spiritual inclinations arise because of many varied factors. Vastly numerous and exceedingly complex as these factors are, I make no claim at being able to characterize any of them to their fullest extent. For the sake of simplicity, we could group these factors into three main points of origin. Those factors that are born out of a person's religious heritage and individual life circumstances result from that person's *history*. Those factors arising from direct personal experiences of the Divine and capacity for spiritual development emanate from the person's *heart*. And those that result from reasoning or

Chapter 9

an intellectual wrestling with cognitive aspects of belief arise from the person's *head*. This book limits itself to just one of these factors—it presents facts and reasoning aimed at the reader's cognitive grid. Reasoning is the only gift I personally am able to deliver to the spiritual equation. Progress in the other areas must come from other sources. But opening one's mind should allow other spiritual growth factors to filter in more easily.

Allowing that other sources are necessary to enrich our spiritual understandings brings me to the second point I invite readers to consider: In no way does *Overcoming Spiritual Myopia* recommend alienating ourselves from our current religious heritage. The concepts presented here are meant to inspire readers to expand their spiritual understandings—not to throw away their current religious affiliations, but to begin to incorporate them into a larger, more comprehensive perspective, a bigger story.

After a brief review of what has been presented so far below, I shall address ways in which spiritual myopia may be corrected and present a hopeful prognosis for a better world.

Treatment

Recalling chapter 2, "Looking Back through Time," we face three important ideas:

1. Every society down through the ages in every part of the world has developed religious or spiritual beliefs and practices. Obviously, something very basic to human nature causes people to want to connect with the spiritual realm, whatever they may perceive that realm to be. From Harvey Cox: "All

Overcoming Spiritual Myopia: The Prescription

religions and cultures are responses to the same fundamental mystery, but each perceives and responds in its own way."[1]

2. Looking at the way Christianity has developed over time, we can see how the multifaceted-belief system we call Christianity today differs greatly from the intent of its original founder.

3. We can see that, as humanity develops more advanced technology, insular "truths" tend to widen into broader, more comprehensive perspectives. A courageous approach to reality and truth will challenge us to incorporate these concepts into our spiritual understandings.

Chapter 3, "Spiritual Development Theory," shed light on how a spiritual path may develop for an individual and pointed out how holding fixed, insular religious beliefs cannot be the endpoint. Similarly, complete rejection of all things beyond our everyday reality shuts us off from the connection humans seem to desire. Chapter 7, "Human Cultural Evolution," showed how entire cultures tend to pass through developmental stages like the ones that individuals experience. Comparing spiritual development theory with human cultural evolution, we can see that both trajectories point in the same direction. In short, higher spiritual maturity equates with an ever more inclusive worldview, unity as the major value, and diminution of self as a prime trait, although each of these will play out in different ways for different people, in different cultures and different places.

Chapter 4, "Signs and Symptoms of Spiritual Myopia," described some spiritually myopic but all-too-human tendencies a person must move beyond if she seeks to overcome spiritual myopia. It showed how many values of the conventional world hold people to spiritually

Chapter 9

immature understandings and limit people's growth. Conservative worldviews, attempting to hold back the inevitable cultural shifts, are particularly limiting and restrict growth that would otherwise proceed to the benefit of all. This happens specifically because those with a conservative mindset tend to choose an almost *willed* blindness to the beauty of the larger process. They lack hope for humanity and, in fact, lack trust. Our mainstream society lacks the very kind of trust that is most prominent in those who are spiritually mature. While the latter can see that the larger picture is much grander and more comprehensive than their own little personal story, those with a conservative mindset still feel that everything is all about themselves—*their* next tax break, *their* well-being over that of others, *their* success at someone else's expense.

Being focused more on self than others, the conservative mindset is the prime example of spiritual myopia. Failing to appreciate ways in which we are all connected—all One—the conservative mentality retards progress and limits its own growth. All the elements discussed in chapter 4 can be seen to retard spiritual maturity in that they each focus on exclusivity and self-importance, precluding the unitive worldview that we now know is basic to spiritual maturity. They each cause people to focus more sharply on the self—on their own salvation in the next world, for example—affording believers no access to the diminution of self that we now know best respects the human need to connect to something larger than the self.

Chapter 5, "New Lenses for Spiritual Clarity," suggested some new lenses a person may try on to help her gain better vision. It spells out various elements in today's society that call us to a larger perspective culturally, religiously, and spiritually. Taken together, these elements demand that we move beyond the insular and provincial

Overcoming Spiritual Myopia: The Prescription

understandings of most of today's organized religions and most of our conventional society.

The world is changing rapidly. Technology is bringing what had once been siloed information down to the level of the average person. In using the term *siloed*, I mean that all the real information was once confined to the religious hierarchy, such that the average person only ever learned what the religious authorities wanted him to hear. In contrast, today we can say that information of all sorts has become democratized, including religious and spiritual wisdom. Anyone can study whatever they want on the Internet, and some parts of society are doing just that. The more we learn about comparative religion, the less we can view any religion exclusively.

To be an adherent of popular religion, without recognizing its position as one choice among many valid ones, is like being so involved in the trees that one fails to notice the forest. An old tale found in Sufi, Buddhist, Jain, Hindu, and Bahá'í lore shares ancient wisdom that illustrates this point. Typically attributed to the Sufis, the tale involves a number of blind men investigating an elephant by touching it. Depending what part of the elephant they happen to touch, the elephant feels like a completely different entity. The blind man who happens to touch the elephant's trunk declares that an elephant is like a waterspout. The man who touches the elephant's leg declares it to be like a pillar. The one touching its tail claims that an elephant is like a rope, etc. Each of these men has partial knowledge; each of them is right in terms of their own experience, but each is blind to knowledge of the whole.

In the same way, each of our religions is right in that each holds a partial view of the truth but is blinded to the overall whole of religion/spirituality/connection/God. When purporting to deliver exclusive

Chapter 9

truth, each religion is as closed to the larger truth as the blind men with access to only one part of the elephant.

Various similar analogies are cropping up to describe the same concept. In 2004, Matthew Fox, formerly a Catholic priest and currently an Episcopal priest, wrote a book entitled *One River, Many Wells*. The title implies that the source of our spirituality (or God) is like one river running underground that pops up in many different little wells in the form of our various religious traditions. Fox shows how various traditions all seek to address four categories of common human inquiry—how we relate to creation, how we relate to Divinity, how we relate to ourselves, and how we relate to the future. His book shares the very deep ecumenism for which Fox is known and reinforces the idea that ultimate truth is far bigger than any one religion.

Another analogy that surfaces occasionally is that of a mountaintop. There are many paths up the mountain, and each one looks very different along the way. Some paths are more arduous than others, some are rocky and steep, and others are smooth and winding. The scenery and even the climate may vary along the different paths. But once you get to the top, you can look around and see that, though each path originated in a very different place, they all lead to a common endpoint—that being our encounter with ultimate Reality.

An online article entitled "What's Wrong with the Perennial Philosophy?" explores a few more analogies in a critical way.[2] The blogger, Jules Evans, discusses a book written by Jorge N. Ferrer that offers the analogy of one ocean, many shores. Much like Fox's one river, many wells, here the ocean is the common spirituality we all share: the quest to connect to an expanded reality and liberate ourselves from our ego. And in the light of the huge variety in individual spiritual experiences, and the religious expressions that emerge from

Overcoming Spiritual Myopia: The Prescription

that one common reality, that great ocean appears differently at the many shores it touches.

Evans criticizes Ferrer's use of an ocean as a metaphor and suggests replacing it with that of a rocket launch pad, symbolizing the various spiritual traditions and ethical practices that take a person beyond the ego. From that launch pad, a rocket may reach many different destinations, (i.e., the variety of religious and spiritual traditions). In support of religious pluralism, the end of Evans's blog post suggests the idea of a grand symphony wherein all spiritual "universes, . . . some singing bass, some singing alto, and [some] on kazoo," interconnect in a way that not only completes but also enhances the overall work of art that is our larger spiritual reality.

That all these analogies are entering our consciousness implies that we, as a whole, are becoming ready for a larger understanding about religion. Our revealed religions can be seen in a different light. They were revealed, and certain to that people, for that time. Now, though, our revelations come from an enlarged perspective brought to us in a globalized world, with scientific, religious, sociological, and psychological resources that any reasonably intelligent person can access.

Together these factors call us *to responsibility* to work toward an enhanced sense of peace, justice, and love that extends to all. We aren't making full use of our faculties, we aren't fully mature until we emerge from the shallow values our conventional world seeks to inspire in us and come to see beyond the spiritual myopia that keeps us convinced that only one religion among the thousands that exist has the truth.

In a very general sense, all these factors in today's world tend to point people in the direction of the upper stages of spiritual development. What needs to emerge now is a way for people to recognize

Chapter 9

how exactly current cultural changes—and the chaos that accompany them—do offer us opportunities for greater, deeper meaning and greater spiritual maturity than the homogenous and outwardly law-abiding culture that dominated the United States in the fifties and early sixties.

The good news is that, thanks to all these factors, we learn that it is possible to find spiritual meaning in life without having to believe literally in improbable things (virgin births, talking snakes, a pitchfork-carrying devil hiding under the earth in hope of tormenting sinners into eternity). And that a healthy, coherent society is possible without demand for conformity in belief systems, political views, or lifestyle choices. This perspective calls us instead to cooperate with a timeless and universal human search for connection with something greater than the self. It leads us to a more unitive, more inclusive appreciation of what life on Earth is about.

Of course, some people remain unready for this enhanced perspective. In the light of overwhelming opportunities to expand our understandings, some insist on maintaining insular and provincial beliefs set down by men who had no access to the information we have now. This very human tendency to want to remain within our comfort zone has produced the spiritual myopia that is creating great harm in our society today.

However, I claim that, over time, the evidence will overcome the provincialism that still blinds some of us. The information currently accessible offers great opportunity to expand our vision beyond the spiritual myopia from which we now suffer. There is little excuse for refusing to don the vision-expanding glasses of knowledge. Thoughtful people cannot be excused for continuing to hold a willed ignorance of the larger truths—the grander spiritual reality that lies behind the

Overcoming Spiritual Myopia: The Prescription

limitations of each separate religion and the steps necessary to its recognition—available to us now.

To benefit from the eye-opening elements now so numerous in today's world, we must be willing to let go of time-honored "truisms" and think critically about the authority sources we have been honoring. We must trust that greater information will bring us closer to ultimate truth than provincial belief systems can ever do. We must remain open to changing aspects in our society and larger perspectives afforded by scientific research as well as by the knowledge that sharing our current technologies affords us. We must be willing to expose ourselves to the full forces of the initially painful, but eventually freeing, truths and not give in to self-protective small-mindedness.

In short, the prescription for overcoming spiritual myopia at the individual level is to develop a mind that stands open to new scientific and cultural findings as they unfold. But as the mind is not the only factor influencing our spirituality, people will also want to develop a heart that stands open to personal wisdom as it comes from the collective consciousness. If they are involved in an organized religion, they will want to filter its teachings through that open mind and the individual experiences of that open heart. They will know the value of not settling on a fixed interpretation unless they find one that reconciles all available factors.

Whether involved in a specific tradition or not, people will need to develop some type of practice that helps open the heart and the spirit. As this is somewhat outside my particular area of expertise, I will share the advice Dr. Larry Culliford has included in his most recent book, *Seeking Wisdom: A Spiritual Manifesto*. A noted theorist on the kind of spiritual development discussed in this book, Culliford says advancement along the spiritual path—meaning the move from

Chapter 9

self-centered egocentricity (our Lawless stage) through the middle stages and on to what he calls selfless universality (our Universal stage)—comes about "largely through letting go, releasing both attachments and aversions."[3] Toward the latter stages, it becomes increasingly crucial to adopt what Culliford calls a "Spiritual Development Programme" (SDP).[4] This is a series of practices that improve harmony and balance among the various aspects of our nature. Often including regular sessions of quiet time, prayerful meditations, or nonreligious practices, an effective SDP can be either religious or secular in nature, or perhaps even a combination of both. In addition to the typically religious activities of retreats, pilgrimages, and worship, Culliford lists some secular equivalents: folk traditions and rituals, contemplative reading or engagement with music and the arts, and regular acts of kindness and compassion.[5]

Whether through the use of reason (the mind), or practices of the heart and the spirit, a person overcoming spiritual myopia will eventually develop an unshakable trust that the big story in the universe is Goodness, even when our own little story may contain imperfections and some unfortunate people's stories may contain horrors.

At the cultural level, the prescription for overcoming spiritual myopia is that our society outwardly acknowledge and encourage the traits of spiritual emmetropia and to distinguish them from elements that only encourage further spiritual myopia. People wise to the spiritual development process will know how to embrace that which enhances love, inclusivity, selflessness, and connection (which is really all our religions were meant to teach in the first place, before they were corrupted by "ecclesial" elements that have done much to blur our spiritual vision). People wise to the spiritual development process will resist the urge to embrace those elements

Overcoming Spiritual Myopia: The Prescription

that encourage hate, exclusivity, selfishness, and separation. They will refuse to grant authority to societal elements (literalist, exclusivist preachers, talk radio shows spreading hate and divisiveness, news outlets aimed at dumbing down their message to discourage critical thought in their audience, despite a motto of being "fair and balanced") that encourage hate, exclusivity, selfishness, and separation. The spiritual myopia in which we now live has arisen specifically from the lack of this wisdom.

Prevention

If we are to cooperate with the hoped-for transformation to a more spiritually aware society, we must begin with not indoctrinating our youth into insular religious beliefs. But how are we to do so when our religions purport solely to teach the values necessary to goodness?

We can begin by teaching our children that the particulars of our religion are *examples* of goodness and that other religions can also be consulted as sources of additional wisdom as the child grows up.

Parents, teachers, school administrators, and religious educators would all have to see the bigger picture in order to teach it. At a minimum, they would have to have considered the concepts discussed in this book. They would probably have to have studied these concepts in much greater detail than this book can afford. They would have to start separating values concerning goodness from religious dogma—those values not being dependent upon a single source of dogma but rather on the larger, more comprehensive overarching study of spiritual development. Such people would have to be clear on unity, inclusiveness, and connection as absolute spiritual values. And they would have to understand how a truly unitive and inclusive worldview would play out in making everyday-life decisions.

Chapter 9

Clergy, as well, would have to stop preaching divisiveness and exclusivity and would have to have the humility to spread the idea that theirs is only one of many valid avenues to truth.

Welcome New Wisdoms

The world is changing rapidly. Technology is bringing what had once been siloed information down to the level of the average person. The more we learn about comparative religion, the less we are able to view any religion as exclusively true.

Popular religion is not the same thing as mature theology. Yet less educated preachers—or those under pressure from the hierarchy to increase donations from their congregants—continue to put forth their literalist proclamations as absolute truth. The answer to this problem is knowledge—knowledge that provides a way out of the willed ignorance that Huxley claims befalls so many.

With today's resources, there is no excuse for fully mature people to shut the door on broader understandings. Maslow's hierarchy of needs says that once our basic needs have been achieved, a healthy person will direct his energies toward higher-level needs. Most people finding the time and energy to read this book will be those who live in a certain level of physical comfort. They should have the energy to expand their vision beyond the provincialism of exclusivist religion.

Today many avenues abound to enlarge understanding of what spirituality is all about. This book barely scratches the surface. The prescription I offer to overcome spiritual myopia is to open one's eyes to greater truth. This means not turning one's back on any opportunity to learn more. Knowledge leads to truth. Since today we can hardly avoid access to increased knowledge, we have a responsibility to acknowledge these broader truths.

Overcoming Spiritual Myopia: The Prescription

And I emphasize that all the increased knowledge in the world will not lead to spiritual emmetropia unless the reference point is larger than that person him- or herself. As we have seen, it is travel through the spiritual development stages that inspires this expanded worldview beyond the self toward universal connection. A person must approach his studies and considerations with an evolutionary perspective in mind, lest he fail to recognize the overall trajectory.

Mainstream society is accustomed to thinking of evolution in terms of physical changes. But numerous authors have already described the process of cultural evolution, as discussed in chapter 7. This process includes the idea that we are moving toward a more sophisticated form of consciousness that recognizes how we are all part of the same whole. "We are all One," to use the language of the Buddhists, who mean the statement, not in the literal sense that we are all one being, but in recognition that anything we might do to harm another person harms ourselves, as well. Conversely, anything we do for the *good* of others also benefits *us*.

Conclusions So Far

If we fully embrace an evolutionary worldview, we are forced to face the fact that what is truth one day will be superseded by a larger truth the next. However, today, at the dawn of postmodernity, in considering the various factors this book discusses we may conclude at least these following things:

- It is time to update conventional views on religion and spirituality. We are challenged to rise to a broader perspective that is more complete, more inclusive, and more loving.
- Perhaps Darwin was right in his theory of survival of the fittest. Those most adaptable to our changing environment will

Chapter 9

thrive far better than those who attempt to hold back change. The challenge is to seek understanding of inevitable change so as to adapt more readily.

Having evolved beyond modernity's overall rejection of a spiritual universe, and still recognizing people's need to connect with the same while also acknowledging the beauty and richness of some of our long-standing religions, we need to develop appropriate terminology. Many on the spiritual path have already replaced the word *religion* with the word *tradition*. Where the word *religion* calls to mind an exclusive, fixed belief system, the word *tradition* is more open-ended. Religion says, "My group has the right answers." Tradition merely says, "The group I happen to relate to connects with the spiritual reality in this way."

- Having recognized that conventional religious beliefs are mostly culturally determined and will be left behind as newer, incoming scientific, sociological, psychological, and historic discoveries are made, we should look to diminish the "belief" aspect of our religious organizations. By now we should recognize that whatever the claim of a given religious founder, it was based on his own individual spiritual experiences. But the religious structures and beliefs that later followers imposed regarding divine exclusivity suffered from a provincial lack of perspective from which we need no longer suffer now. In place of exclusive and divisive belief systems, our religious traditions would do well to focus instead on "faith." Some people equate the word *faith* with ascribing intellectual assent regarding the truth of specific existential propositions that cannot be objectively proven, but there are other definitions

Overcoming Spiritual Myopia: The Prescription

as well. Consulting a Merriam Webster dictionary, I find three definitions of the word *faith*:

1. allegiance to (or trust in) someone or something;
2. a belief in God; and
3. a firm belief in something for which there is no proof.

While an author is free to ascribe any commonly accepted connotation to any word they use, they are also free to clarify the connotation they *intend* in any given work (see more about this in ch. 10). I want to make it clear that in this work I am limiting my use of the word *faith* to the first definition: allegiance to (or trust in) someone or something, namely connectedness among all elements (people, animals, plants, rocks, planets, solar systems, galaxies) of the universe. I intend no connotation relating to belief. And *trust* in the sense that I intend it connotes no form of intellectual assent. Rather, it specifically connotes a *lack* of intellectual assent. The faith that I would like to see our churches emphasize is the trust that those at the Unitive level hold. This trust is characterized by the lack of need for assurance about what happens after death; it is the trust that no divine Presence would demand that people here on Earth give intellectual assent to existential propositions that fly in the face of discoveries made through the intellectual gifts with which we are endowed. And it is the trust that the specifics of our little individual lives are far less consequential than the overall good of the whole.

- Further, we must trust that the inevitable societal changes we are experiencing now represent positive growth. Surely, we can see that humanity has evolved since the days of antiquity. While the upheaval of each step in human cultural evolution must have been frightening to those on the ground at the time, in retrospect we can see how, as a group, humans have become more civilized down through the ages. Why would our current cultural shifts not represent a continuation of that growth? If we truly trust in the goodness of a universal, divine Presence, would it not follow that we are meant to trust what it calls into existence?

- Lastly, use of the word *God* is so rife with controversy! People at the Faithful level see their Creator as a glorified man in the sky, while those approaching the Unitive level each have their own understanding of the ultimate reality; and very few of them understand it as that bearded old guy in the sky. Yet no one dares to distinguish one group's (external, separate, judgmental) God from the other's (internal, unitive, inclusive) god. Many of us who say that we don't believe in God may do so because we are put off by the idea of an actual supreme being in the sky. In this way, the word *God* itself may be a metaphor that is holding many of us back.

The loud proclamations of the religiously assured cause unnecessary and spiritually immature divisions among people of different religions, as well as among people who believe in the force represented by religion and those who don't. It should be becoming evident that while the force may be real, the personifications that each religion has assigned to this force are just that—personifications.

I propose that we leave the word *God* to the literalists and that the rest of us replace it with any metaphor that feels comfortable.

Overcoming Spiritual Myopia: The Prescription

Retired United Church of Christ pastor Jack Good, in *The Dishonest Church,* accuses our churches of deliberately confusing the public with insistence on literal connotations and suggests that people in today's world no longer relate well to the metaphor of God as a father. He recommends that we consider replacing that metaphor with something more current and offers three replacements:

1. *God is Music.* I can easily understand how music moves some of us toward feelings of universal connection, but I don't think that it is quite universal enough to qualify as a new metaphor for God. Some people who have never been exposed to music, and some of us not trained to recognize the order and discipline involved, may not connect easily with this concept. Moreover, who is to say that music is more moving than inspired art or the beauty of nature?

2. *God is Light.* As someone who has spent an entire career manipulating the focus of light to help people see better, this metaphor does speak to me. But, as with music, I do not feel that light is universal enough to bring large numbers to their metaphorical knees.

3. *God is Love.* The English word *love* is very confusing because it refers to many kinds of feelings. As mentioned in chapter 5, God may be hard to see in the way we love ice cream or love a certain sport. The way we love romantically may be closer, and the love of a parent toward their child may be closer yet.[6]

The ancient Greeks used at least six different words (some texts list up to thirty) for what we in English call *love*. Romantic love was

Chapter 9

called *eros* in honor of the Greed god of fertility. Deep friendship or brotherly love was called *philia*. This was also used to describe the love we feel when working side by side with others toward a shared goal. *Storge* denoted family love, the bond held by parents toward their children, and vice versa. *Pragma* is an interesting word, little discussed in our culture. The root of our word *pragmatic*, it referred to a love based on making compromises to help a relationship work over time, showing patience and tolerance, such as what may develop between partners in long-married couples.[7] *Ludus* referred to playful love, as in the affection between children or young lovers. *Philautia* was love of self. This could occur in a negative way, as in narcissism, or in a healthy way. If we feel secure in ourselves and like ourselves, we can extend a more genuine love toward others. That would be the healthy form of philautia.

Finally, *agape* was the most elevated form of love. This term referred to a selfless, unconditional love—a radical, boundless, and all-inclusive love for everyone and everything in the universe. It is similar to the kind of love Huxley (see chapter 5) described as typical of spiritual masters. This is the love that the Unitive level in spiritual development is all about.

If only we, like the Greeks, used different vocabulary to distinguish among the many forms of love, the metaphor of God as Love (in the sense of *agape*) would be perfect. But to consider love as the metaphor for a universal divine Presence, we have to understand and appreciate it as the kind of selfless love that goes beyond our little particular selves and applies to everyone.

10

Prognosis: A Transformed Society

To many who have read this far, it may seem that I live in some fairyland of unrealistic dreams. Saying that our culture is evolving in a forward direction may sound crazy at a time when every day brings us news of a mass shooting somewhere and when politicians and other public figures display complete lack of morality, diplomacy, and dignity—saying ever more hateful and divisive things about their competitors and even starting wars or dropping bombs for motives many of us find questionable at best. Some encourage us to disdain groups outside our own religious or political faction and blanketly to target people from a different race or culture as our enemy.

But looking at the long view over centuries, we can certainly agree that the life of the average person has improved since the days when only the aristocracy was considered of any importance. Peasants could be killed at will, with about the same degree of compassion that many

Chapter 10

today show toward an unwanted insect that has found its way into the home. For a far more developed version of this concept, see Steven Pinker's book, *The Better Angels of Our Nature: How Violence Has Declined.* In seven hundred pages, Pinker provides detailed graphs and scientific studies to describe in painstaking detail how what he calls the better angels of our nature—empathy, self-control, reason, morality, and taboo—are prevailing over the demons, which he identifies as dominance, revenge, ideology, sadism, and the evil that held more sway over people in the past.[1]

Indeed, considering merely the span of my own life, I also sense improvement just since the days of my youth, when people who were "different" in any way could be openly discriminated against. Not only were there no handicapped spaces in parking lots back then, but I recall an incident when my mother called a popular restaurant to make reservations for a dinner with some friends, one of whom was confined to a wheelchair. When my mother asked how this friend would be seated, the owner rather haughtily, and with a full sense of his own justification, informed my mother: "Ma'am, we don't serve the handicapped here!" It is easy to forget how the rationale has shifted over perhaps fifty years from one in which "normal" people didn't want to be reminded of the existence of the less fortunate, and the less fortunate were expected to remain hidden so as not to disturb the contentment of the more fortunate.

Compare that situation with today, when the best three or four spots in any parking lot are reserved for the handicapped, public doorways and bathrooms must be designed with adequate space for wheelchair access, and we even have laws that attempt to quell outright discrimination against certain minority or disadvantaged groups. Since the 1960s, at least we as a nation in the United States

Prognosis: A Transformed Society

have become more inclusive. We have evolved to recognize that those with physical or even mental disabilities are no less human and no less deserving of rights.

But the 1950s were influenced by a rigidity in behavior rules that made it appear as if we, as a society, had it all together. Specific roles were assigned according to one's position. The husband was the breadwinner and made all the important decisions for the family. A proper wife obeyed her husband, stayed home and cooked and kept the house clean. The kids were to be "seen and not heard." Boys were never allowed to play with dolls, express any form of emotion, and, especially, ever, ever cry. Girls never played with trucks and were discouraged from engaging much in sports.

Blind obedience to supposed "authorities" was a given sign of a person's "goodness." The authorities merited obedience based on being seen as morally superior to ordinary people. Such authorities included the boss, the preacher, the teacher, and the president. The word *sex* could not be mentioned in public. On TV, a couple could never be seen in bed together; in any necessary bedroom scene a husband and wife would always be found in separate twin beds. Great importance was allocated to fitting in with the group. Those exhibiting any form of individuality were viewed as eccentric and were to be shunned.

In the decades since the 1950s, the rules of behavior have become far more nuanced and complex. Whereas once we were shocked to see two humans of the same gender showing public displays of romantic affection, now we cannot even be sure of the original gender of some of the people we see on the street. Some of our more enlightened public places already label their restroom doors to allow people to select a restroom according to their preferred gender identity, regardless of their gender at birth.

Chapter 10

At the surface, these changing mores may appear random and even licentious to some. Some of us may feel they represent a turbulent breakdown in the order of our society, leading to an intensified sense of chaos. Those unaware of the larger trajectory will naturally respond with more fear-based drastic reactions, creating even more chaos for a downward spiral into complete lawlessness.

The Pains of Healing

But a different interpretation is possible. Whereas at the surface these changes may appear random, chaotic, and even licentious to some, they actually represent greater opportunity for individual truth and a deeper form of authenticity for those who do not fit the conventional mold. For anyone not focused on fear of the other, today's greater diversity in lifestyles, dress, and forms of spiritual expression, may be celebrated as more individuals are permitted to live openly in a truth they had been forced to suppress in the past. While many have described how all these changes—greater choice in lifestyles, fewer rigid roles imposed by society, diversity and freedom of expression, acceptance of gender multiplicity, etc.—herald an evolutionary leap forward, I have found most comfort in Jim Kenney's book, *Thriving in the Crosscurrent*. In this 2010 title, Kenney uses the metaphor of a sea change to describe what we were experiencing in our culture at that time. He describes modernity as a powerful wave that crested half a century ago. Modernity's values were power, wealth, order, competition, and an exclusivist approach to other cultures, religions, and value systems. Modernity profoundly shaped every culture in the world, but its values are slowly beginning to subside; that wave is dying out.

Kenney goes on to explain that, while it may appear on the surface that we suffer from immense chaos, the confusion we all

Prognosis: A Transformed Society

perceive these days can be compared to what happens with waves in the ocean. When an earlier wave begins to wane and a new one is beginning to form, there is a point of maximum turbulence between the two. Eddies and whirlpools form that confuse the appearance of the water's surface and make it difficult to determine the overall direction in which things are moving.[2] If the societal chaos corresponding to this metaphor was notable in 2010, it has become ever more intense since then. Today, we are hopefully at that point of maximum turbulence. The waters here are in complete chaos; on the surface, it appears that there is no forward direction. Even though modernity's outmoded values are slowly waning, their ugliest sides keep rearing up in a last gasp of a hopefully dying swell. Despite outward appearance, beneath the surface a new wave of more evolved values is gaining strength.

Kenney tells us: "Cultures evolve to facilitate a better fit between their guiding values and the real world."[3] In response to improved perspective from cultural intermixing and globalization, the incoming values include egalitarian ideals grounded in fairness, interdependence, and cooperation, and an inclusivist or pluralist stance with respect to other cultures and religions.[4] Readers of this book, now schooled in diagnosing spiritual myopia, will be able to perceive how these values align with a clearer spiritual vision.

Note how most of the declining modern values as Kenney defines them—power, extreme wealth, competition, and so on—line up with the Rational stage of spiritual development. Values still stuck in what he calls the crosscurrent and swirling around in ever more vociferous eddies—such as patriarchy, the legitimacy of war, ecological exploitation, pollution, racism, injustice, and religious exclusivism—arise out of the Faithful stage that was more typical of premodernity. The new

Chapter 10

more evolved and more inclusive values Kenney sees trying to arise in postmodernity include nonviolent conflict resolution, universal human rights, social and economic justice, ecological sustainability, and interreligious harmony. These are the values of spiritual maturity to the extent that we can conceive of it today.

Kenney is cautious to warn us that no sooner will the new values become commonplace than another wave of even newer values will begin to supplant them. This is the way cultures move, not always in a forward direction. But considering the overall trajectory throughout the centuries, an analogy given to me by someone in a discussion group I once led may be helpful. A pendulum is something heavy—like a metal ball—attached to a chain or a string. The whole structure is supported by a point above it called the fulcrum.

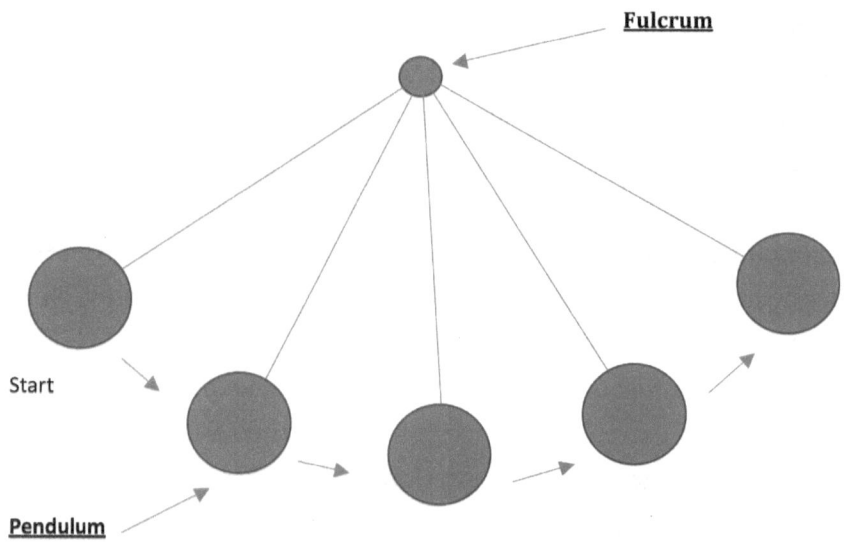

Figure 7. A pendulum and its fulcrum

Prognosis: A Transformed Society

Remember Martin Luther King Jr.'s statement, "The arc of the universe is long, but it bends toward justice"?[5] If we can trust that human culture evolves in a forward direction over time, then we can say that, although the pendulum of cultural change may swing forward and backward, *the fulcrum moves steadily in an ever-forward direction.* While we can pretty well say that in the last year or two our U.S. culture has been moving in a decidedly backward direction, it may bring hope to recognize that the fulcrum has been steadily moving forward over decades, centuries, and even millennia. Keeping this in mind, we will see that the pendulum will never swing back quite as far as it did the last time—we are not going back to slavery in this country! And, every time the pendulum swings forward, it goes just a little farther than it did the last time (who would have thought twenty years ago that we would now be discussing rights for transgender people?). While the pendulum may swing forward and backward, the fulcrum representing individual and cultural spiritual development inches slowly in an ever-forward direction. The chaotic crosscurrent—this frightening backward swing of the cultural pendulum in which we now find ourselves—may be painful, but it heralds a fairer, more equalized society for the future and a clearer view of spiritual maturity.

If indeed our society has a chance at moving in a forward, more inclusive, more spiritually mature direction, the question for each individual should be, "How can I cooperate with this process instead of holding it back?" One thing that holds back progress along the spiritual development trajectory is the way people tend to dig in their heels to defend their current beliefs. When new information is presented, instead of considering it fairly, they look for ways to disparage any concept that would shake up the status quo. We are faced with a choice between truth and comfort.

Chapter 10

One way to overcome this very human tendency, whether in ourselves or in others, is to allow the recognition that new information is always coming in. Our current beliefs were okay, given the information that was available until a certain point in time. But now, in the light of new information such as the many factors discussed in this book, our perspective needs to expand. A new, enlarged understanding is in order. It is not that we were wrong in our attachment to a given religion; rather, our seeing that religion as the *only* way simply suffered from an inability to see the larger picture. Accepting this reality, we can both excuse those who remain mired in more provincial understandings and allow ourselves to move on from them.

What Individual Spiritual Maturity Might Look Like

At this point we shall consider what traits an individual person would embody in spiritual maturity. One of the most crucial traits is that, because his or her values arise out of a personal sense of adequacy, the spiritual emmetrope responds to inevitable changes in a healthy way. No longer attached to the outer forms of things, such a person can see how to obey the spirit of the law, even while the letter of the law may be being breached.

As I have mentioned, the spiritual emmetrope understands that our existence is so much bigger than our own personal story. Someone I met not long ago serves as a sharp *counter* example: At a luncheon, this woman rushed up and introduced herself and in no time began bragging about being very happy living in Texas and owning an RV that got (yes, in 2015!) *eight* miles per gallon. She went on to say that people in Austin (*not* where she lives) were crazy about their green values and that their values were *wrong* because, whenever green issues are taken into consideration, the

Prognosis: A Transformed Society

economics don't work out. Even though this woman was trying to be very friendly to me, my reaction in this briefest of conversations was mostly negative, without my understanding why. It was only later in the day that the reason for my unease dawned on me. Her breezy comments spurred what I think is an important realization: Considering the long view of things, if we don't take ecology seriously now, no amount of money will afford a comfortable lifestyle for that woman's great-grandchildren or for mine. Without respect for ecological concerns, the economy becomes irrelevant. This is an example of what I mean by spiritual myopia. I am sure if she thought about it, that woman's concern for her future great-grandchildren is no less than anyone else's. But, blinded by her current immediate reality, she could not see how her actions today would contribute to an impoverished future for the generations to come.

Native Americans had an inherent wisdom regarding this concept. Their seventh-generation principle advises that we set aside our own self-interest in favor of considering the effect that each of our decisions will have on our descendants seven generations into the future. Like many indigenous cultures, Native Americans have cultivated intuitive wisdoms that people today would do well to study.

The ability to take more than our own little personal story into account—to perceive a reality bigger than just our own little part of it—is an important factor in overcoming spiritual myopia. What may be temporarily less comfortable for the spiritual emmetrope is no problem if it leads to a greater good for others, either in the moment or into the future. The question becomes whether it is worth suffering mild limits on one's own use of resources for the sake of those in other parts of the world and of those for several generations to come. To perceive it as worthwhile to limit our own consumption for such

Chapter 10

a larger value, it takes a longer, less myopic view of life and a more expansive view of the greater reality to which we are connected.

Writing in the early 1900s, Evelyn Underhill gave us several excellent quotes about what she calls mysticism. Mysticism was undoubtedly rare in her day, but it, in fact, suggests the very form of spiritual emmetropia to which large numbers of us are being called today.

Underhill tells us the goal is to emerge from concern with the self and "enlarge [our] boundaries and become the citizen of a greater, more joyous, more poignant world, the partaker of a more abundant life."[6] Moreover, "This unmistakable experience has been achieved by the mystics of every religion; and when we read their statements, we know that all are speaking of the same thing . . . we must remember . . . they are speaking from a plane of consciousness far above the ideas and images of popular religion."[7] In one of my favorite analogies of all time, Underhill points out that the Shepherd carries the lambs in his bosom, but "the sheep are expected to walk, and put up with the inequalities of the road, the bunts and blunders of the flock. It is to vigour rather than to comfort that you are called . . . [you are now raised] into a position of creative responsibility . . . you correspond too with a larger, deeper, broader world."[8] We can interpret the "lambs" as the people comforted by the certainties of popular religion who allow those certainties to fence them off from the rigors and vicissitudes of life. In contrast, the "sheep"— in the sense not of mindless, passive followers but of full adults distinguished from baby lambs needing protection—are the spiritual emmetropes of today. Like the mystics of Underhill's time, such a person will engage with the world with energy and vigor to become "an active and impassioned servant of the Eternal Wisdom."[9]

As I've mentioned, the spiritual emmetrope will also have done away with the need for exact answers. Instead of demanding closure

Prognosis: A Transformed Society

for complex existential matters, he will find the mystery exciting and be willing to live in the questions. He will have grown out of the need to be right. Unfortunately, far too many of our leaders are still shunning this perspective. Religious leaders still preach the unique correctness of their teachings. Political messages still promote binary reasoning, presenting matters in black-and-white terms and discouraging complex consideration of complicated matters. They do this mainly for their own purposes, to gain control over their listeners. It is important to recognize that the more we fall prey to such tactics, the deeper we fall into spiritual myopia. The spiritual emmetrope will resist group-think and consider important issues on his own. He will ignore propaganda disguised as news; and he will question the motives of religious leaders promoting exclusivity and of political leaders promoting selfish, divisive tactics designed to benefit only one limited portion of our demographic.

The spiritual emmetrope's perception of reality is free of the delusion of existential certainties; she will abstain from denying scientific findings in favor of biblical proclamations. The spiritual emmetrope will react appropriately to societal changes and will obey the dictate that adaptability to change is a value to be cultivated, a sign of good mental health. The spiritual emmetrope will have learned to diminish the self and the ego in favor of a larger entity, a larger "self" that includes everyone and everything in the universe.

This concept has been explained by many, but it is hard to relate to without the understanding that spiritual growth itself involves a process of expansion in which what is seen as "SELF" grows to include everyone, even as the individual, personal self diminishes in importance. So, to review a concept that has been presented earlier, the least evolved among us perceive themselves as just one individual person, apart from all others. This is the Lawless level in spiritual development theory. Such people are *egocentric*. Those at the Faithful level see themselves as part of a particular group. They are *ethnocentric*. Those at the Rational level see themselves as part of all of humanity. They are *worldcentric*. Finally, those at the Unitive level see themselves as part of everything in the universe. Their worldview is *universal*. Their "SELF" *is* the universe, so their small, personal self becomes far less important. Hence, when we say that the spiritual adept experiences ego diminution, what we mean is that his concern for the small, personal self takes a back seat to the larger SELF that includes the entire universe.

The above explains how it is that the spiritual emmetrope will experience a deep sense of interconnectedness. He will not be just connected; he will be part of it all. As a part of the same entity that includes everyone and everything, he will see clearly that what benefits one person benefits everyone. And what harms one person, or one animal, one tree, etc., harms everyone and everything, because we are all One.

Considering all the factors mentioned so far, we begin to glimpse the type of spiritual stance, *or faith*, to which our postmodern reality is calling us. Many authors have described this stance in different ways. In truth, there are probably about as many ways to describe a post-religious, post-conventional, postmodern, post-rational, post-denominational, post-critical, post-literal faith as there are real life examples of it. The bottom line is to understand that they all represent movement beyond both the Faithful, fixed belief systems of premodernity and the skeptical, Rational, secular mindset of modernity. They open the door to a different kind of faith that is now offering itself to us in the postmodern Western world.

A spiritually emmetropic faith will represent, not just an opportunity, but an imperative among those of us who are awakening to the fullness of our unity with a beneficent universe. It will impel us to open ourselves fully to both feeling and expressing the type of universal Love that such a faith will inspire.

Harvey Cox tells us that scholars of religion refer to the overall trend in religion today as a "move to horizontal transcendence" or a "turn to the immanent." But he says it would be more accurate to think of it as a "rediscovery of the sacred *in* the immanent, the spiritual *within* the secular."[10]

As mentioned in chapter 9, the distinction between *belief* and *faith* becomes crucial in curing our spiritual myopia. Both words are defined similarly: 1) complete trust or confidence in something or someone; and 2) intellectual assent to something that cannot be proven. But assigning the first definition to the word *faith* and the second to the word *belief* helps clarify an important concept. Beliefs, at least religious ones, arise from the happenstance of the culture into which we are born. People or institutions introduce us to concepts that are commonly held by others in the particular time, place, and culture in which we find ourselves. We choose either to accept or to reject the beliefs handed to us by our tribe. By contrast, faith is not so much culturally determined but rather develops from our individual wrangling with the circumstances of our personal reality. For some, this wrangling will result in a basic posture of existential trust—trust that life has some meaning and that despite all the trials and tribulations, there is something good about the overall picture of our reality. And trust in that goodness informs our feelings, our choices, and our overall posture toward reality—our *faith*. For others, wrangling with reality points them toward fear, suspicion, and divisiveness and an inability to trust in the overall goodness of the big picture—a *lack* of faith. Since all people from every age, all cultures, and all parts of the

Chapter 10

world will face some form of struggle, all people have the opportunity to choose between faith and fear, regardless of the happenstance of the culture into which they were born. So, where beliefs are culturally determined and imposed from without, faith must be inspired from within. *Faith*, in the sense the word is used in this book, comes from the heart and not from the head; it is about existential trust rather than intellectual assent to culturally imposed propositions.

The faith that finds a place in this book is about a basic posture of trust and confidence in the mysteries of our existence. In the light of all that has been discussed, it becomes evident that parroting a fixed set of beliefs laid out by others cannot be a very advanced form of spirituality or faith. The move beyond belief toward faith *is*, in fact, a transformation, a sign of progress, whether in an individual or in the overall society. Only a person willing to allow herself to be broken open with wonder at the miracle of our existence, with awe at the splendor of the universe, and with a heartrending love for and sense of connection with all that exists can experience the kind of faith we refer to here.

Harvey Cox tells us that in the arising Age of the Spirit specific creeds (beliefs) are fading in importance.[11] Hierarchies are wobbling. Faith as a way of life or a guiding compass has once again begun. The *experience of* the Divine is replacing theories *about* it.

Creative Faith

Westar Fellow Don Cupitt describes one example of a faith that approaches the spiritually emmetropic ideal in his book, *Creative Faith*.[12] It involves a stance more courageous than conventional religion, more dangerous (in a good sense!) than a closed-ended, self-protective belief system meant to assure salvation in the next world, and more

Prognosis: A Transformed Society

open to the joys and pains of meeting reality in a fully authentic way. Cupitt uses the metaphor "solar living" to describe an extroverted faith that expends itself in everyday living in this world, therefore having no need for an "afterlife." In solar living, or creative faith, the highest wisdom is "what *feels* right, what works *in life*, may be taken for true, *for the present*."[13] (Though Cupitt makes no such distinction, I assume that this stance is recommended only to a person who has already attained the self-governance of the Rational level.) In solar living, we acknowledge that "the external world is projected out from within our own hearts and tends to reflect our own feelings for good or ill."[14] He then continues:

> We must not call for divine intervention in support of our cause. . . . To make [this world] a better place we need to live without value-contrasts that divide . . . our own people from heathen Others, and short-term from long-term well-being. We need to live as completely without oppositional, ambivalent thinking and feeling as we can be [sic], even to the point of not hating our bitterest enemies and critics, and not even dreaming of seeing them get their comeuppance. . . . It is possible to have joy in life even while one is under the sentence of death. Solar living is "eternal life" in that it makes possible an indestructible happiness here and now. . . . The self is not preserved 'unto everlasting life': in solar living it simply, joyfully, and wholly expends itself.[15]

To a Faithful- or Rational-level reader, these ideas probably sound like nonsense. But, as someone caught between the Rational and the

Chapter 10

Mystic levels (and from my discussions, I believe there are lots of us—with one hand holding on to Rational certainties and the other extended toward, but not yet quite ready to grasp, Mystic or Unitive awareness), I can appreciate the great beauty in Cupitt's solar living.

Cupitt's is but one man's description of the more expansive faith that we may realize at the post-religious, post-rational, post-critical, postmodern levels. The crucial factor in overcoming spiritual myopia is to appreciate the spiritual development *process* and to trust that this process will bring each person to a personally authentic, but perhaps not objectively recognizable, endpoint.

How Can We Acquire Clear Spiritual Vision?

In chapter 3 I mentioned the Google Alert I have set up to send me notice whenever the term *spiritual maturity* appears anywhere on the Internet. Often posts that come in will be about a person becoming more deeply entrenched in the tenets and beliefs of one particular religion. While this development may represent the most mature level in that specific tradition, it cannot represent the most comprehensive form of spiritual maturity overall. If it fails to acknowledge that any religion is only one culture's way of connecting with the existential meaning in our lives, it leaves out all the truths of other religions and cannot be the most mature form of spirituality. If it fails to deal effectively with the changes to which our globalized world is bringing us, it must necessarily be provincial in its understandings. If it avoids dealing with the implications of spiritual development theory, it mires its adherents in a decidedly myopic blur. If it turns its back on the comparative wisdom of the perennial philosophy, it ignores a large part of truth. In short, becoming deeply entrenched in a particular religion today lacks the depth of the kind of spiritual maturity to which

Prognosis: A Transformed Society

our current circumstances call us. Religious maturity does not equal spiritual maturity. Spiritual maturity in a postmodern sense is much larger and more comprehensive than the highest level of maturity within any given religion.

While many terms exist to describe post-critical faith, or the Unitive level of spirituality, we must assume that some appeal to a larger number of people than others do. William Bloom, a leading British mind-body-spirit figure, proposes a term in *The Power of the New Spirituality* that I believe may hold particular appeal.[16] Before the U.S. edition of his book referred to *New Spirituality* in the title, the British version was entitled *The Power of Modern Spirituality*, which I personally feel is a bit of misnomer since much of what he describes is more typical of postmodern thought. Elsewhere, Bloom refers to "contemporary" spirituality. But the most poignant term he uses is *holistic spirituality*.[17]

Most people are familiar with the term *holistic* as it applies to medicine: treatment of the whole person, taking into account mental and social factors, rather than just the physical symptoms of a disease.[18] In spirituality, this term affirms that we can appreciate the whole only by taking all its parts into consideration. We can understand a part only by looking at its whole. I propose that each of our organized religions is a part of the totality of human spirituality, while the whole is something that approaches Bloom's definition of a holistic spirituality: "the natural human connection with the wonder and energy of nature, cosmos and all existence, and the instinct to explore and understand its meaning."[19]

We cannot understand the roots and significance of any given religion unless we consider it in relation to all other religions. Even to begin to understand spirituality as a whole, we must include perspectives from all different religions. We must study the motives that have caused every society since the time of the earliest humans to develop some way of relating to the transcendent level of Reality, and we must consider all the various ways that people from all cultures and belief systems connect to the spiritual today. We must include the myriad ways in which anyone living in the past, the present, or the future has found or will find to connect to the wonder and energy of nature, the cosmos, and all of existence—as well as the ways in which they obeyed, obey now, or will obey the instinct to explore and understand life's meaning.

A holistic spirituality would be an open-minded and openhearted one that respects the essence of all spiritual approaches. It would explore the crux of spirituality when it is stripped bare of its religious beliefs, symbols, mythologies, and metaphors.[20] Bloom invites readers toward this type of consideration. He opens his book by describing a study that showed that religious "believers performed better, had better health and greater happiness and lived longer than nonbelievers."[21] But recalling the angst that critical and post critical-level persons experience regarding what seem to them to be silly beliefs, our traditional religions may hold little appeal. How to experience, as Bloom puts it, the "benefits of religion and spirituality [without having to] buy into a set of beliefs, get into a faith box, or join an organized group"?[22]

What Bloom does not express is that a person would have to have moved beyond the earliest stages of spiritual development before this type of spirituality could hold any appeal. Holistic spirituality presupposes that a person has already moved beyond the need for the specific belief elements of Faithful-level religion. His or her behavior is largely self-regulating, in that rules such as the Ten Commandments have become second nature. Such people have grown beyond the need for

Prognosis: A Transformed Society

firm answers about where we come from or where we are going next. They identify with something larger than just one provincial group.

This approach also presupposes that a person has moved beyond the need for elements that predominate at the Rational level. They have acquired the humility not to gloat over having questioned the beliefs of traditional religion. They have acknowledged parts of our reality that do not submit to scientific explanation. They have come to appreciate the mystery in our reality, and they have recognized ways in which we all are connected.

To appreciate how Bloom's holistic spirituality offers a benefit over more conventional views, a person must have traveled through those earlier stages and be standing at the threshold of Unitive-level faith. Nevertheless, I do not believe that this most developed level is beyond our general reach. Having read numerous books on human spiritual evolution and its presumed "endpoint," which I am calling the Unitive level, I find Bloom's description best portrays an evolved spiritual stance as something attainable for the average person possessed of an open mind and an open heart.

In Bloom's conception, the new, contemporary, holistic, and *evolved* spirituality that is emerging involves no preaching, no sin, no guilt, no need for redemption, no insular beliefs, no miracles, no stories, no salvation, and no concern with the afterlife. His book supplies exercises to help readers attain this type of spirituality, which can be characterized in terms of just three elements: reflection, connection, and service.

Reflection

Bloom tells us that "one of the greatest struggles of contemporary life is that many of us are exposed relentlessly to never-ending information,

Chapter 10

stimulation, and choices."[23] Yet, he claims that the ability to step back and watch yourself is a crucial part of spiritual awakening and self-management, and a form of enlightenment. Undoubtedly, this is more difficult for the contemporary person than it was in the days before television and the Internet. In the old days, after all the chores were done, what else was there to do but sit on the porch for the few remaining minutes of light and think over what that day had brought and what challenges might arise in the next? At the same time, we must weigh the advantages of the perspective we can gain by having more information and stimulation—and more leisure time for contemplation—versus the quiet to process everything that may have been more prevalent in times past.

The ability to actively reflect, Bloom tells us, is a muscle that we must develop, exercise, and strengthen. To become more conscious, we want to carve time and space out of our busy schedules to observe and reflect on our lives as detached witnesses. We need to find a place or activity that leaves us free of distractions and interruptions from the outside world. Conditions that allow us to connect in this way will vary from one person to another. Bloom cites the example of a man he once knew who found those conditions most present while working on an antique car engine in his garage.

As a personal example, I can share that swimming is an activity that allows me access to realizations to which I may be blind even when actively trying to solve a problem. I almost never get in a pool unless I can spend an uninterrupted forty-five minutes or so completing my mile. (I am a strong swimmer, but speed is not my goal.) Swimming laps is a fairly solitary activity, despite the presence of any number of people in the pool at the same time and occasionally a careless or overzealous body impinging on my immediate space in the same lane.

Prognosis: A Transformed Society

You can't or generally needn't speak, there is little to look at, and, for the most part, earplugs restrict you from hearing anything quieter than a lifeguard's whistle.

Years ago, I had contracted with an architect and a builder to remodel my professional office. After many months of planning, we had decided on an exact layout that was going to be expensive to build but would greatly improve patient flow, efficiency, and the overall functionality of the office. However, one day just before signing the contract for the work to be done, I was swimming; and, in the solitude of that activity, my mind began casually reviewing the architectural drawings. Suddenly an alternate plan popped into my head that was much simpler and far less expensive but would allow the same functionality. When I presented the idea to the architect and builder, they agreed that it was a definite improvement, but they good-naturedly forbade me any further swimming until the project was completed.

While this is not a very spiritual story, I think it does show that removing ourselves from the noise of everyday input from the outside world and quieting our active, conscious mind can allow realizations to which we may otherwise not have access. Since that day, any time I jump in the water I confirm that I am open to receive any type of wisdom that might surface; and often I emerge with some new solution to a problem, some realization or connection my conscious mind could never have dreamed up, or even some new wording for the next thing I am trying to write.

Bloom's example and mine show that reflection need not be restricted to a meditator's deliberate, cross-legged stance in a solitary corner. For some of us, less structured environments may allow some access to realizations the universe might be trying to bring us. We may meditate and not even know we are doing it. As Bloom says, "Any time you are relaxed, [comfortable in your body,] and watching the world go by with good humor, you are in a natural state of contemplation and meditation."[24] It may happen any time we engage in quietly watching our thoughts and feelings as opposed to checking our text messages or turning on the TV. The only difference is that in deliberate meditation a person is conscious and self-aware about the fact that he is meditating.

Bloom discusses the advantages brought to us through reflection. While you would have to read his book to gain a full understanding, suffice it to say that reflection or meditation can offer at least these following benefits:

1. It can help us break free of our usual psychological and social conditioning. This relates to the Rational stage in spiritual development theory. Before we can become spiritually adult, we must consciously reflect on the truths about life that were imposed upon us, often tacitly, by our tribe. We must own the values by which we are living, and that often means breaking free, as Bloom asserts, of the conditioning with which we grew up. Reflection, consciously observing our lives as detached witnesses, helps us do that.

2. Conscious reflection can also help with healing and emptying ourselves from the ill effects of earlier personal traumas. This is a complex topic on which I do not feel qualified to expand. However, I take comfort in Bloom's assertion that such exploration is best conducted from within the context of a benevolent cosmos. If we are genuinely experiencing connection, we

Prognosis: A Transformed Society

will be genuinely supported by the contact with Spirit that comes to us through reflection. Bloom tells us that it is often during periods of stress and crisis that the heart opens and consciousness wakes us up, leading to personal and spiritual growth. If our reflection points to something we have done that we regret, rather than sink into guilt, shame, despair, or depression, we seek ways we can learn from it.[25] Reflection and ownership of the causes that lie behind our negative attitudes and behaviors, Bloom tells us, is often 90 percent of what it takes to transform beyond the hold such factors have on us.

3. Besides emptying us from the effects of crises and trauma, conscious reflection also leads us to a highly beneficial type of unknowing. The concept of unknowing is exceedingly absent from our conventional understandings. Contact with mainstream society leads us to believe that we need quick, definite answers to even the most difficult problems. Take, for example, the issue of politicians and war. I recall a time when a certain man running for political office was criticized by his opponents for his ambivalence about war. Even though I knew little about the man, this criticism stung me, because all I could think was that anyone who lacked ambivalence about war must be hiding from a huge part of reality. How bad does a political situation have to be before it justifies risking even one life to solve it? Anyone who thinks they have a clear answer to that question suffers from a spiritual myopia this book has no hope of clearing up.

In addition to the merits of war, other issues not solved by unilateral thinking include the ethics of surrogate parenting and genetic manipulation. In our postmodern world, all these dilemmas and countless others call us to move beyond limited and provincial thought patterns that may have worked in the past—except when they didn't. Certain elements in our society deliberately seek to restrict critical reflection and preclude our willingness to unknow something. So, while most of conventional society would assume that unknowing something refers to a particular form of ignorance, in spiritual terms unknowing means to have eschewed the need for certainty and the need to be right. It means remaining open to further insights from whatever source they might arise.

Bloom also masterfully uses his chapters on reflection to lead us to the realization of how some or most of the certainties our major religions assert are but ways we humans have developed to allay our anxieties. "Every time the word *God* is used as if the universal mystery were in some way similar to a giant human being," he says, "we know that confabulation and projection are at work.... How positive and hopeful it would be if every priest, priestess, and cleric taught self-reflection, emptying and unknowing alongside their own sacred scriptures."[26] Rather than provide definite answers to the unknowable, Bloom asserts that if only self-reflection were encouraged in our religious traditions, it would help people see their way clear to more universal recognitions. Extended self-reflection leads us to a willingness to "unknow" the very things about which the Faithful level demands certainty. It helps us develop a tolerance for ambiguity and for the mysterious and sometimes paradoxical spiritual appreciations called for in a postmodern worldview.

Connection

Bloom asks us to reflect on what it is in our personal experience that allows us to connect to the wonder and energy of life. Bloom claims

Prognosis: A Transformed Society

that this exercise can help develop anyone's sense of spiritual connection, regardless of—or even despite—any dogmatic religious beliefs. Bloom lists almost sixty activities that others have reported as having let them connect in this way. The activities include some decidedly spiritual acts such as prayer, meditation, and participating in ceremonies. They include some inspirational elements such as art, music, drumming, and chanting. But he also lists some everyday activities that most of the conventional world would not consider spiritual in any way—geometry (or math in general), walking, gardening, teaching, as well as "flow" activities at work.

What are "flow" activities? In his book, *Flow: The Psychology of Optimal Experience*, Hungarian psychologist Mihaly Csikszentmihalyi describes an enhanced mental (or spiritual) state triggered by certain activities that differ from one person to the next.[27] For some of us, work activities may trigger flow, but for others it may be family gatherings, community service activities, certain sports, or even hobbies. What is required to attain the flow state is that the person be completely absorbed, that the activity use all his skills to the utmost extent, and that the level of challenge it presents be in perfect balance with the skills required. The activity must be neither too hard nor too easy; it must require the doer's full concentration to the extent that awareness of temporal concerns such as time, tiredness, hunger—and even awareness of one's self as being separate from the activity—drop away. In the flow state, a person's concentration is fully engaged; his consciousness is completely ordered (as opposed to the psychic *disorder* that occurs with anxiety, boredom, and despair).

Bloom includes the flow state as one that can allow a person to connect to the wonder and energy of life. I will assert that this can happen whether the person consciously senses this connection or not.

Chapter 10

People who experience flow in their everyday lives are able to tap into something greater than themselves quite naturally and may have less need for conventional religious personifications.

What counts here—what makes any activity spiritual—is that it transports us outside ourselves, diminishes our sense of ourselves as separate from the whole, and allows us to connect to something greater. It allows us to experience being part of something that is greater, vaster, and more important than our own little self-serving self. For some people, the only way they can recognize this feeling is as part of an organized religion. In this sense they need their religion for salvation—not so much in the sense of salvation in the next world, but to save themselves from focusing solely on themselves in *this* world. Others of us recognize this feeling of selfless connection through our relations with family, through causes we support, through our professions and careers, and/or through certain types of leisure activities. This is as good an argument as any to choose a career focused on doing something useful and good in the world, as opposed to just making money. It is also a good argument for choosing a career based on our passions, since engaging in our passions regularly leaves us more likely to experience the flow state on a regular basis.

Somehow, these seemingly everyday activities that allow the flow state can carry us through all the inevitable difficulties, and sometimes far outside our comfort level, in the name of something that we see as more important than our own immediate gratification. While more intense experiences may take experienced meditators to much deeper levels of connection, we are not wrong to call our more everyday "self-naughting" experiences spiritual. To the conventional mind, the term *self-naughting* holds a negative connotation, something like

Prognosis: A Transformed Society

self-effacement. But in the spiritual world it is known that diminution of the personal ego—that is, recognition of the ego as a very small part of something much larger, and of feeling connected to that much larger entity—is the very essence of spiritual maturity.

Some of us can experience spiritual connection when we allow a piece of music or art or a starry night sky to inspire us. The feeling we get is of being caught up in something wonderful that we probably cannot explain: we are profoundly moved beyond and outside of ourselves. This, too, is spiritual connection.

Once we recognize the above factors, we can see that an engaged spirituality does not require us to follow outmoded rules or believe improbable religious certainties in a literal sense. A spiritual emmetrope knows that it is possible to cooperate with a timeless and universal human search for connection and meaning in life in many ways and that traditional churches are just one of them. In an engaged spirituality, a person is called to develop his or her own principles for what helps them move beyond the tyranny of the self and toward the "something more" that comes from greater connection with the world.

As far back as the nineteenth century, William James, considered the father of American psychology, recognized this truth. In his still revered *Varieties of Religious Experience*, he says of the process of unification: "However it come, it brings a characteristic sort of relief; and never such extreme relief as when it is cast into religious mould. Happiness! Happiness! . . . But to find religion is only one out of many ways to reaching unity; and the process . . . need not necessarily assume the religious form."[28]

The obvious conclusion is that the more often we engage in activities that take us outside ourselves, and the more varied those activities are, the more readily we can become more unitive in our understandings. As that process occurs, the less we will be satisfied with limited and provincial religious understandings.

Service

Bloom points out that there is no use in developing our connection with the magic of life if it does not spill over to serve others. An authentically expanded consciousness will result in an enhanced instinct for compassion and caring. He carefully lays out different aspects of service in which a person might engage—seeing the best in others, looking out for our neighbor's needs, and caring for the environment. He summarizes this type of service as being willing to go outside ourselves to "release what is trapped—emotions, animals, plants, people—into freedom."[29]

One of the most interesting aspects of service that Bloom describes is what he calls *vibrational service*. *Vibration* is a word that seems to raise the hackles in many people. In a scientific sense, the word refers to an oscillation of an electromagnetic wave. It can also refer to any kind of tremor or shaking, such as what happens during an earthquake. Bloom uses the term *vibration* metaphorically to denote the attitudes that we emanate out into the world, the general atmosphere that surrounds our being and that spreads to others and influences their reality.

Bloom says that every religion, every culture has recognized a natural vitality and energy that supposedly suffuses the entire cosmos. The words *prana* in Hindu, *qi* (chuuuh) in Taoism, or *chi* in popular spirituality all represent the same idea as *shekinah* in Judaism, *sakina* in Islam, and even the Holy Spirit in Christianity. However, where our Western religions have repressed the universal nature of this concept, a holistic spirituality will openly and explicitly *celebrate* this vast field of energy in which we all live and that connects us all.

Central to acknowledging this vast field of energy is appreciating that each of our own words and actions contribute directly to it. Everything we each say, do, and even think becomes part of this field and influences everyone else's experience of it. This important idea calls every one of us to a greater level of interpersonal responsibility than what has been recognized by any of the worldviews or mindsets preceding it. It means that we create part of the here-and-now world in which others must live. And it brings with it an ethical imperative to radiate a *positive presence* in the world wherever possible. This ethical imperative calls for us to take personal responsibility for the *vibrations* we put out into the universe. It defines a new kind of *vibrational ethics* that we all would do well to consider.

A major goal in holistic spirituality is to have a positive effect on others and, wherever possible, to clear up negativity. A person is expected to reign in any of her own thoughtless or selfish behavior and do nothing that would add to social injustice, the economic distress of others, or the ecological distress of the planet. A successful life is judged, not by one's worldly achievements, but by the quality of the effect a person has had on the universe in general. Has he been able to do more good than harm? Has she been able to radiate more good vibrations than bad ones?

Once we come to recognize a universal field of energy connecting us all, we cannot deny the importance of consciously choosing what type of attitudes we as individuals impose on that field. The outlooks we share influence the way those in our sphere of influence experience reality. The impressions, opinions, and feelings we put out into the world dramatically affect those around us.

Chapter 10

Awareness brought to us through holistic spirituality calls us to take personal responsibility for the words, attitudes, and moods we impose on others. Are we doing our best to contribute positive vibrations wherever possible? Do we seek opportunities to express love, appreciation, inclusiveness, and compassion? Or do we sink into the self-defeating trap of spreading negative vibrations such as fear, hate, judgment, and divisiveness? Do the vibrations we emit tend to uplift the reality of those around us? Or do we spread negativity that brings down the overall tone level of others? The best way to enhance our own experience is to act so that others may experience their world in the most positive way possible.

A helpful guideline for deciding what to share with others is found in what is said to be an ancient Arabian proverb, but similar variations of the same notion have been attributed to everyone from Socrates to Quakers. Before we say something, we want to ask ourselves, "Is it true, is it kind, is it necessary, and does it improve upon the silence?" Any readers of this book who are media folks or politicians will note that this guideline specifically excludes considerations such as, "Will it sell more news? Will it convince people that someone in the other political party is evil?"

Holistic values include inclusion and respect for every individual; care for the environment; recognition of spirituality as a normal and healthy part of daily life, as people experience the wonder and nature of all creation; and a commitment to celebrate the many paths that explore this wonder and its meaning. Other values include a commitment to respectful, loving, and positive relationships; a lifestyle and livelihood that confer benefit and do no harm; and a dedication actively to engage in building community, alleviating injustice, and relieving suffering—to deplore any situation that limits the rights,

Prognosis: A Transformed Society

development, and fulfillment of any being. (Imagine the world we would have if only our CEOs and our politicians would ascribe to this value!)

Don Cupitt's Creative Faith and solar living is one articulation of post-religious, post-critical, postmodern faith, and Bloom's is yet another. Countless others exist. For me, Bloom's New Spirituality is one that speaks most clearly, both describing a philosophy and prescribing a praxis for attaining it. His articulation of the type of faith we may want to aim for helps me see beyond the spiritual myopia of our times and most closely approaches the spiritual emmetropia toward which we might aim. I wish all readers of this book luck in finding a formula that works as well for them.

What a Spiritually Mature Society Might Look Like

Today in postmodernity it becomes evident that it is time for a bigger story. Our traditional—and necessarily provincial—understandings about religion and spirituality no longer hold water. Considering all the factors discussed in this book, it becomes evident that we need a bigger story about religion and a bigger story about spirituality. That bigger story is that each religious founder in history offered a system that worked for the time and the location in which it arose. Each "revelation" was valid for that time and that place. Each revelation was the attempt on the part of one local culture to fill that basic and timeless human need: to connect with something larger than the self. To repeat, the timeless and universal human need that drove the formation of all religions and all of spirituality is the need to connect to something larger than the self.

Seen this way, it becomes clear that spiritual truth is not about the specific existential proclamations of any given religion; it is not

Chapter 10

about following rules that lead to salvation in some dubious afterlife. Rather, spiritual truth is something that informs our everyday life in this world, the only world we know for sure exists. We know that the intense desire some people have for connection can be met in ways that take them outside the limits of consensus reality. Most of our belief systems are the result of the original founder's experiences outside the consensus reality. Many individuals have sought, and some have found, ways to experience connection with something outside the consensus reality. Some call it God.

Hence, it becomes evident that spiritual experience is what leads to spiritual growth, and spiritual growth comes from experiencing that which draws us outside of ourselves. We can be drawn outside ourselves in many ways, and religion, or membership in a church, is only one such way to meet that need. It should be evident that church is, indeed, one valid way of connecting to something larger than ourselves. But it should also be evident that many ways of meeting that need exist that have nothing to do with religion or spirituality per se. Ways such as art, music, gardening, community service, and even, or especially, professional satisfaction can easily be missed by those not prone to notice them.

We in postmodernity now have a greater chance than ever before to develop a spiritually emmetropic society, and issuing forth from that will be the chance to have peace among the religions. With all the factors considered in this book, we have a chance to become a society that has overcome the spiritual myopia that has prevailed up until this moment. The spiritually mature society we now have a chance to develop will take on more universal qualities than what currently exist. It will not only permit but will welcome and celebrate diversity of every sort. It will draw on the richness of all the colorful

Prognosis: A Transformed Society

and wondrous rituals and traditions that humans from all over the world have developed to address their spiritual yearnings. It will allow all people freedom of expression in beliefs, lifestyle, dress, and mores. People from all different cultures will live and work in close vicinity with no fear of their differences, no attempt to convert others to their way of thinking, no attempt to control or take advantage of one another. The only things that will be prohibited are those that might limit any individual's right to that expression or to live freely, provided he or she is not hurting anyone else.

In the spiritually mature society we now have a chance to develop, it will be generally recognized that people need to go through the spiritual development stages. Those exhibiting Faithful-level, ethnocentric values will be understood as just being in a certain stage of spiritual growth. We will allow them freedom to dwell at that level as long as necessary, but the wisdom of the larger group will recognize the folly in granting them powerful positions in religion or in government, where their less-evolved values could lead others astray. Rational-level people will be free to continue their reasoning and scientific exploration. But hints at a larger Reality than what can be determined through science and reason will abound, so that those people may be challenged to include less cut-and-dried elements in their explorations.

Most importantly, it will be generally accepted that all these various religions and spiritual traditions have one goal in common. It is the same thing that caused all cultures from every part of the world to form religions and spiritual practices in the first place: to allow people a sense of connection with something greater than themselves. In the spiritually mature society we are being called to develop, it will be clearly recognized that each individual religion has been just

Chapter 10

one culture's way of meeting that need. The common feature that all religions and all spiritual traditions share is the need to connect to something greater than the self. The extraneous elements of the given religions—such as the existence of an afterlife, the need for salvation, the various rules and the punishments—will be recognized as cultural idiosyncrasies. It will be considered acceptable for each group to hold these elements personally, but they will not be seen as universal concepts everyone should adopt. These realizations will allow peace among the religions.

Further, it will be acknowledged that people at the various spiritual levels can meet the universal human need to connect to something greater in ways other than religion. My personal understanding is that, currently, people at each level tacitly meet their need to connect in different ways. All that is necessary to religious tolerance is to recognize the different ways in which the need to connect may be met. Speaking very broadly, people at the Faithful level meet their need to connect through religion. They call that something greater to which they connect *God*, and God as an actual being separate from themselves is very real to them. People at the Rational level are more inclined to find connection through the FLOW activities of daily life. Hence, they don't need to reach outside the everyday consensus reality for their sense of connection. At the Unitive level, connection with the larger Reality is felt more viscerally, and in many cases this feeling becomes a desire to serve that larger reality.

Organizations and groups that support a spiritually emmetropic mentality are beginning to proliferate. The Charter for Compassion is one such entity. Founded by author Karen Armstrong with seed money from her 2008 TED prize, the charter has been signed by many and now enjoys an extensive list of worldwide partners. The charter calls

Prognosis: A Transformed Society

upon "all men and women to restore compassion to the centre [sic] of morality and religion.... Born of our deep interdependence, compassion is essential to human relationships and to a fulfilled humanity. It is the path to enlightenment, and indispensable to the creation of a just economy and a peaceful global community."[30]

The Shift Network is another organization promoting spiritual emmetropia. Their mission statement tells us "we know we are one sacred family and are united in our divinity, while celebrating our diversity. We hold a vision where, not only are everyone's basic needs met while living in peace, but the very best in all of us is expressed and humanity's full creative potential is set free." [31]

The Association for Global New Thought (AGNT) is another example: "New Thought is a spiritually motivated way of life that embraces the ancient wisdom traditions of east and west ... AGNT is committed to global healing achieved through personal transformation, community-building, interfaith, intercultural, and interdisciplinary understanding, and compassionate activism." The list of core beliefs posted on their website says it all:

> Love and the Sacred are One
> We are born blessed
> Prayer is actively creative
> The Beloved Community is our credo
> Compassion heals, compassion unites
> Violence in all forms is unacceptable as a way of solving problems
>
> No human being is illegal
> Black lives matter. Brown and white lives matter—
> enforcement of law must be color-blind

Chapter 10

All faiths, ethnicities and cultural identities are
worthy of respect and deserve security

All genders are whole, holy and good
Women have agency over their bodies
Equality, liberty and justice for all is a birthright

Science is Real
Climate change is an immanent challenge
to which we must respond
We are all interconnected and interdependent as
is all sentient life and the ecosystem, itself

Corporations are not people
Equal pay is due for equal work
Wealth should not wield power when its privileges are abused[32]

Brahma Kumaris, the largest spiritual organization in the world led by women, also characterizes spiritual emmetropia. Founded in 1937 and headquartered in India, the BKs have spread to over 110 countries on all continents as a worldwide spiritual movement dedicated to personal transformation and world renewal. They support the cultivation of a deep collective consciousness of peace and of the individual dignity of each soul. Raj Yoga meditation is the primary tool the BKs employ in this mission. This type of meditation is a "journey inwards,"... taking time out to enable a return to a centred [sic] place of being."[33]

Sister Jenna is the leader of the BKs in Washington, DC, near where I live. Sister Jenna runs two local mediation museums that

Prognosis: A Transformed Society

feature interactive displays of various faith traditions and offer numerous classes and workshops promoting peace, love, acceptance, compassion, and inclusion and eschewing fear, anger, separation, and competition. Her America Meditating Radio show promotes awareness of personal empowerment and peace as a way of increasing harmony despite the many great uncertainties in our culture. These activities, among too many other efforts to list, all contributing to enhanced spiritual vision and an improved humanity, recently earned Sister Jenna an honorary doctorate degree from St. Thomas Aquinas College. If Sister Jenna's efforts are any indication of the spiritual breadth typical of the BKs, then this group offers something truly amazing to the planet.

The Parliament of the World's Religions is an organization created to cultivate harmony among the world's religious and spiritual communities; its goals are spiritually emmetropic. The Parliament's website tells us that "here religious and cultural fears are replaced with understanding and respect. . . . The world's most powerful and influential institutions move beyond narrow self-interest to realize common good." More from their website:

> Interreligious harmony . . . is an attainable and highly desirable goal. Such an approach respects, and is enriched by, the particularities of each tradition. Moreover, within each tradition are the resources (philosophical, theological, and spiritual teachings and perspectives) that enable each to enter into respectful, appreciative and cooperative relationships with persons and communities of other traditions. . . . Too often, religion is misused as an instrument for division

Chapter 10

and injustice, betraying the very ideals and teachings that lie at the heart of each of the world's great traditions ... [but] when these diverse communities work in harmony for the common good, there is hope that the world can be transformed.[34]

If spiritual development theory can be trusted, we will always have people at various points along the spiritual path. But as more people begin to understand spiritual development, they will come to recognize the Lawless, Faithful, and even the Rational levels as necessary steps we should all strive to surpass on the way to a more integrated, more mature, and more inclusive form of spirituality. People will realize that the Faithful level does not represent a suitable basis on which to build a responsible adult life in an integrated, globalized society. Instead of encouraging literalist personifications and insular, triumphalist proclamations about access to exclusive truth, religious leaders will encourage their congregants toward broader, more inclusive understandings. In place of the black-and-white logic and existential certainties espoused at both the Faithful and the Rational levels, people will welcome *both/and* reasoning as a closer approximation of reality than *either/or*, and they will come to appreciate the beauty in the mystery, the excitement of the unknown, and the value in developing our connections to the universal.

What becomes important in a spiritually emmetropic society is not what a person's religious beliefs are, not what behaviors will afford them salvation in an afterlife, but rather what will draw them outside themselves and lead to greater meaning and fulfillment in this life. A society that has overcome its spiritual myopia will recognize that this answer will necessarily be very individual and

Prognosis: A Transformed Society

unique to each person. Parents, teachers, and religious or spiritual leaders will encourage people to find connection in whatever milieus work for them.

However comfortable our current religious understandings may be, we cannot undo or turn back the paradigm shift that we in the Western world are currently experiencing. Attempting to hold back these changes, trying to put the proverbial cat back into the bag, represents a refusal to accept the challenge or even to acknowledge its inevitability. It confines us to a spiritual blur that works only to our own detriment and that of our society. We now know how to begin to overcome the self-centered and divisive spiritual myopia in which certain elements in our culture would keep us mired. The only way forward is to rise boldly above the fray, teach ourselves and encourage others to deal effectively with our postmodern challenges, and find a way to work for good in the world by maximizing the effects of opportunities for growth that are presented to us.

One day an amalgam of inevitable forces—cultural intermixing, historical and scientific research, and globalized perspectives—will inspire the critical mass of society to enlarge its understandings beyond the valid *but partial* truths revealed to each single culture. The insular, triumphalist, and exclusive teachings of each single religion will give way to broader appreciation of our universal connectedness. At that time, we may begin to hope for peace among the religions.

The prescription for overcoming spiritual myopia in terms of religion is to find a tradition or spiritual community that speaks to you and participate in it fully. Respect its rich history and rituals, but engage with them as symbols of something larger. Participate in a way that allows you to experience spiritual connection without falling prey to righteousness, triumphalism, or the need to convert others.

Chapter 10

Or don't join anything, but participate in other life opportunities in that same way. What is important is not which tradition you follow, but the depth and breadth of your universal connections.

In spiritual emmetropia, the brilliant and beautiful lights emitted by our universe come to a point focus in exactly the perfect spot. Clear spiritual vision is not focused too far out, on a future afterlife that may or may not come true; nor is it focused on traditions and beliefs of the past. The perfect focus point for our spiritual appreciations is *this* life, *this* day, *this* minute. In spiritual maturity, our light is focused on exactly the right spot—the here and the now. Furthermore, we no longer seek light to shine on us, since the particulars of our own little lives have diminished in importance. Rather, in spiritual emmetropia we have been drawn outside of ourselves; we have emerged beyond the "tyranny of the self" that dominates our conventional society. We have progressed to a point where the light of the universe emanates *from within us* and *shines out* toward others. We find ourselves called to cooperate with the efforts of a benevolent Universe (or whatever personification of same resonates with our understanding) to illuminate the lives of others, causing us to feel connected to, and do the most good for, the most people we possibly can in this place and at this time.

Afterword

Thank you for reading *Overcoming Spiritual Myopia*. The topics you just read about are keys in moving beyond the outmoded notions of premodernity and modernity. Sadly these realizations go largely missing in our society. I doubt I have articulated them with the poignancy they deserve, but I have done my best. I hope this book has given you some ideas to see through those aspects of those insular religious models that cause divisiveness and exclusivity. I hope it has opened up a more expansive and more inclusive view of the role religion and spirituality can play in bringing about peace and unity.

I am sure at this point you have some opinions on this topic. Whether you loved this book or hated it, I would love for you to talk about it with others. Only by bringing the discussion out into the open can we ever hope to solve the increasing problem of how cultural intermixing and the democratization of knowledge are weakening the insular aspects of religious belief. We need to work together to broaden understanding about how the universal human search for meaning and connection can be upheld and respected, even as the traditional formats are losing power in a changing world.

Afterword

Why not register your views about this? Why not discuss it with others, both to open their minds and hearts and to further develop your own sentiments? Bring it up at the dinner table, host a discussion in your living room, talk about it online.

The term *Spiritual Myopia* holds a lot of power. Once the concept is introduced, I believe it becomes almost impossible to avoid seeing signs of spiritual myopia playing out at all levels of society. Please use this term to describe limited spiritual perspectives wherever you see them. Hashtag #spiritualmyopia is available to facilitate this online.

This is a great book for group discussions. Suggested discussion questions:

Chapter 2

1. Why do you think all different cultures since the beginning of recorded history sought some type of religious or spiritual connection?

2. Do you believe religions should be able to change over time, as new information comes in?

3. Why do you think some books were removed from the Bible under the Emperor Constantine?

4. How did Christianity become so focused on specific beliefs when the original faith in Jesus' time was more centered around a way of life?

5. Technology—the printing press in the fifteenth century and the internet today—tends to "democratize" information (make

it increasingly available to the average person) Is this a good thing or a bad thing?

6. Are you inclined to think we still live in the time of modernity, or can you see how we are moving into postmodernity?

7. Do the societal changes postmodernity is bringing us give you hope or cause fear?

Chapter 3

8. Had you ever heard of the general concept of Spiritual Development Theory—in any format or terminology or through the work of any theorist?

9. Does the spiritual development concept bring you hope, or cause fear?

Chapter 4

10. Consider each element of spiritual myopia—personification, literalism, fundamentalism, triumphalism, spiritual blindness, binary logic and the need for certainty. How does each of these hold people back from greater spiritual perspective?

Chapter 5

11. Have you had any experiences with people of other cultures that led you to question the religious or cultural ideas you grew up with?

12. Do you believe all cultures since the beginning of time formed religions for similar reasons? Is there a universal need within

humans to connect with something greater? What does that say about religions that claim their beliefs were divinely revealed?

13. Is the interfaith movement a positive development or is it causing confusion and weakening long-standing religious traditions?

Chapter 6

14. Does the Unitive level of spiritual development mean anything to you? Does it interest you to learn more about it? Can you see it playing out in certain individuals with whom you are acquainted and in various elements of society?

15. Why do you think you don't often hear explicit messages about the Unitive level of faith?

16. The idea of one's worldview expanding to include ever more of the universe is a simple, yet elegant concept. Why does most of our culture seem designed to keep us from recognizing universality as a spiritual goal? Why does most of society ignore spiritual development principles?

Chapter 7

17. Do you believe humanity is growing through stages similar to the individual spiritual development stages? What type of things could you do to get more information about it?

Chapters 8–10

18. If you had to come up with your own "bigger story" about religion and spirituality, what would it be?

Suggested Discussion Questions

19. Can you see evidence of Harvey Cox's "Age of the Spirit" coming into play in recent years? Can you see backlash elements trying to hold it back?

20. What causes backlash against human cultural (and religious and spiritual) progress?

21. Do you feel much of our society still suffers from spiritual myopia? Is overcoming spiritual myopia a good thing?

22. Do you suffer from spiritual myopia? What might you do to help overcome it?

23. What can you do to help our society overcome spiritual myopia?

24. How can overcoming spiritual myopia lead to peace among the religions?

Notes

Dedication

1. https://en.wikipedia.org/wiki/Standing_on_the_shoulders_of_giants. Accessed July 18, 2018.

Introduction

1. John R. Mabry, *Growing into God: A Beginner's Guide to Christian Mysticism* (Wheaton, IL: Quest Books, 2012), 13.

2. ibid., 137.

3. ibid., 13, 14.

Chapter 1

1. https://www.brienholdenvision.org/myopia-prevalence.html; accessed September 1, 2017.

2. B. A. Holden, T. R. Fricke, D. A. Wilson, et al., "Global prevalence of myopia and high myopia and temporal trends from 2000 through 2050," *Ophthalmology* 123, no. 5 (May 2016):1036–42.

3. https://www.merriam-webster.com/dictionary/myopia; accessed December 9, 2017.

4. Don Cupitt, *Creative Faith: Religion as a Way of Worldmaking* (Salem: Oregon: Polebridge Press, 2015), 73.

Chapter 2

1. http://www.wisegeek.org/which-are-the-oldest-religions-in-the-world.htm; accessed August 16, 2015.

2. ibid.

3. ibid.

4. Joanna Dewey, "Marcus J Borg: Jesus: Uncovering the Life, Teachings and Relevance of a Religious Revolutionary," *The Fourth R* 29, no. 1 (Jan–Feb 2016): 12.

5. Elaine Pagels, *Beyond Belief: The Secret Gospel of Thomas* (New York: Vintage Books, 2003), 40–41.

6. Harvey Cox, *The Future of Faith* (New York: Harper One, 2009), 58–59.

7. ibid., 61.

8. ibid., 62

9. ibid.

Chapter 3

1. https://www.ted.com/talks/megan_phelps_roper_i_grew_up_in_the_westboro_baptist_church_here_s_why_i_left; accessed April 3, 2017.

Chapter 4

1. https://en.wikipedia.org/wiki/The_Force_(Star_Wars); accessed November 13, 2107. (Quoting the 2000 documentary *The Mythology of Star Wars*.)

2. http://starwars.wikia.com/wiki/George_Lucas; accessed November 13, 2017.

3. https://en.wikipedia.org/wiki/The_Force_(Star_Wars); accessed November 13, 2107. (Quoting Steve *Silberman*, "Life After Darth," *Wired, May 1, 2005)*.

Notes

4. http://world.time.com/2013/06/20/extremist-buddhist-monks-fight-oppression-with-violence; accessed November 13, 2017.

5. Rev. Carol E. Richardson, *Truth and Illusion* (Rockville, MD: Highest Harmony Healing & Coaching, 2017), 209.

6. M. Scott Peck, *The Different Drum: Community Making and Peace* (New York: Touchstone, 1987), 187.

7. https://en.wikipedia.org/wiki/Les_Mis%C3%A9rables_(musical), https://en.wikipedia.org/wiki/Les_Mis%C3%A9rables; accessed November 15, 2017.

Chapter 5

1. http://sociology.emory.edu/faculty/globalization/issues04.html; accessed November 17, 2016.

2. Jim Kenney, *Thriving in the Crosscurrent: Clarity and Hope in a Time of Cultural Sea Change* (Wheaton, Il: Quest Books, 2010), 188.

3. Gregory C. Dahl, *One World, One People: How Globalization Is Shaping Our Future.* (Wilmette: IL: Baha'i Publishing, 2007), 257.

4. Susan Faludi, *Backlash: The Undeclared War against American Women* (New York: Doubleday, 1991).

5. http://sociology.emory.edu/faculty/globalization/issues01.html; accessed October 14, 2015.

6. Kenney, *Thriving*, 186.

7. ibid.

8. https://www.barna.com/research/competing-worldviews-influence-todays-christians/?utm_source=Barna+Update+List&utm_campaign=d2b24df6dc-EMAIL_CAMPAIGN_2017_05_9&utm_medium=email&utm_term=0_8560a0e52e-d2b24df6dc-172138909&mc_cid=d2b24df6dc&mc_eid=928a3aaec4; accessed November 15, 2017.

9. Aldous Huxley, *The Perennial Philosophy* (New York: Harper, 1945).

10. ibid., 83.

Notes

11. ibid.

12. ibid., 85. Huxley is quoting someone else here, but he does not say whom. He is talking about Shankara at the time.

13. ibid., 52–53.

14. Arthur Versluis, *Perennial Philosophy* (Minneapolis: New Cultures Press, 2015), 59.

15. ibid., 106.

16. ibid., 109.

17. https://www.westarinstitute.org/membership/westar-fellows; accessed March 31, 2016.

18. http://westarinstitute.org/wp-content/uploads/Ethos-Protocols.pdf; accessed March 31, 2016.

19. https://www.westarinstitute.org/projects/; accessed March 31, 2016.

20. https://www.westarinstitute.org/about/; accessed March 31, 2016.

21. Charles A. Bobertz and Stephen J. Patterson, "Christianity before Christianity: Orthodoxy and Heresy in Earliest Christianity," Jesus Seminar on the Road, Washington, DC, St. Mark's Episcopal Church, April 16, 2016.

22. http://www.jesuswalk.com/philippians/nicene-creed.htm; accessed April 15, 2018.

23. Other scholars consider 1 Corinthians to be the first creed.

24. From loose handout presented at the Jesus seminar, adapting the verses from Galatians 3:23–29.

25. Parenthetical comment added verbally by the presenter.

26. Loose untitled handout from seminar above; emphasis added by the author.

27. https://next.ft.com/content/a3eec9aa-36ba-11e3-8ae3-00144feab7de, http://www.huffingtonpost.com/deepak-chopra/god-is-the-new-physics_

Notes

b_6327472.html, https://www.quantamagazine.org/20140122-a-new-physics-theory-of-life, accessed April 25, 2016.

28. David Fideler, *Restoring the Soul of the World: Our Living Bond with Nature's Intelligence* (Rochester, Vermont: Inner Traditions, 2014).

29. ibid, 193.

30. Harow Shapley, "Man's Fourth Adjustment," *The American Scholar* 25, no. 4 (Autumn, 1956): 453–57.

31. ibid., 454 (emphasis added).

32. ibid., 455.

33. ibid., 457.

34. Pope John XXIII called the Second Vatican Council (or Vatican II) into existence in 1959, and four sessions were conducted between 1962 and 1965. Over two thousand bishops met and generated sixteen documents, the purpose of which was to address relations between the Roman Catholic Church and the modern world.

35. http://www.vatican.va/archive/hist_councils/ii_vatican_council/documents/vat-ii_decl_19651028_nostra-aetate_en.html; accessed October 9, 2015.

36. ibid.

37. ibid.

38. Gustav Niebuhr; https://books.google.com/books?id=UNogJNuZtYIC&pg=PT80&lpg=PT80&dq=Niebuhr,+Gustav+Rabbi+Jerome+Davidson&source=bl&ots=Ni-Cf6WF5R&sig=TJ9uVuchZ3ztaE1n4pAoDXpe7VQ&hl=en&sa=X&ved=0ahUKEwjj2r3np-nXAhWwQd8KHfFjBE0Q6AEIKTAA#v=onepage&q=Niebuhr%2C%20Gustav%20Rabbi%20Jerome%20Davidson&f=false; accessed December 1, 2017.

39. http://iipdigital.usembassy.gov/st/english/publication/2008/08/20080819131356cmretrop0.9265711.html#axzz3nhLsMw9t; accessed October 9, 2015.

Notes

40. https://www.ifyc.org/about; accessed October 9, 2015.

41. http://www.huffingtonpost.com/rev-donald-heckman/why-the-interfaith-movement-must-rebrand_b_2849432.html; accessed October 11, 2015.

Chapter 6

1. See K. Helmut Reich, *Developing Horizons of the Mind: Relational and Contextual Reasoning and the Resolution of Cognitive Conflict* (Cambridge: Cambridge University Press, 2002).

2. ibid., 25.

3. Harvey Cox, "The Market as God," advance book talk, Westar Institute Fall Meeting, Atlanta, GA, November 20, 2015.

4. Evelyn Underhill, *Practical Mysticism* (Columbus, OH: Ariel Press, 1942).

5. Abraham Maslow, *Religions, Values, and Peak Experiences* (New York: Viking, 1970), 22.

6. Underhill, *Practical Mysticism*, 23.

7. ibid., 90.

8. ibid., 93.

9. ibid., 94.

10. ibid., 114–15.

11. "Second naïveté" is a term used by French philosopher, Paul Ricoeur. What he called the "first naïveté" and the "critical distance" corresponds roughly to our Faithful and Rational stages, respectively. His second naïveté corresponds roughly to our Universal stage. It denotes a returned openness to spirituality, a deeper form of faith than that which occurs in the Faithful (first naïveté) stage. This was explained in much greater detail in *Faith Beyond Belief*. See Paul Ricoeur, "Religion, Atheism, and Faith," in *The Conflict of Interpretations: Essays in Hermeneutics* (Evanston, IL: Northwestern University Press, 1974), 467.

12. http://www.joanchittister.org/node/56; accessed March 25, 2017.

Notes

13. http://www.azquotes.com/quote/505138; accessed March 25, 2017.

14. http://www.azquotes.com/quote/818316; accessed March 25, 2017.

15. http://www.azquotes.com/quote/1369987; accessed March 25, 2017.

16. http://www.azquotes.com/quote/1053225; accessed March 25, 2017.

17. James Fowler, *Stages of Faith: The Psychology of Human Development and the Quest for Meaning* (San Francisco: Harper & Row, 1981), 183.

18. ibid., 198.

19. ibid., 211.

Chapter 7

1. http://www.bibliotecapleyades.net/ciencia/esp_ciencia_life23.htm; accessed March 26, 2017.

2. http://www.infoplease.com/spot/christmas1.html; accessed March 26, 2017.

3. Cupitt, *Creative Faith*, 125 (see ch. 1, n. 4).

4. ibid., 124.

5. http://www.businessinsider.com/where-iphone-parts-come-from-2016-4; accessed November 5, 2017.

6. https://carm.org/what-relativism; accessed April 24, 2016.

Chapter 8

1. Wayne Teasdale, *The Mystic Heart: Discovering a Universal Spirituality in the World's Religions* (Novato: New World Library, 1999).

2. ibid., 10.

3. Kurt Johnson and David Robert Ord, *The Coming Interspiritual Age* (Vancouver: Namaste Publishing, 2012).

4. ibid., 292.

5. ibid., 293.

6. The author saw Ken Wilbur speaking on this subject in a video several years ago and has not been able to find it in any of his writings. If anyone has information about the source, please contact the author at mpjauthor.com.

7. Raymond Moody, *Life After Life: The Investigation of a Phenomenon—Survival of Bodily Death* (Atlanta: Mockingbird Books, 1975).

8. http://www.iands.org/about-ndes/key-nde-facts.html?start=1; accessed October 17, 2015.

9. Eben Alexander, *Proof of Heaven: A Neurosurgeon's Journey into the Afterlife* (Colorado Springs: WaterBrook, 2012).

10. Mary C. Neal, *To Heaven and Back: A Doctor's Extraordinary Account of Her Death, Heaven, Angels, and Life Again; A True Story* (Colorado Springs: WaterBrook, 2012).

11. http://www.deathreference.com/Me-Nu/Near-Death-Experiences.html; accessed October 18, 2015.

12. http://www.beliefnet.com/faiths/galleries/12-absolutely-amazing-miracles.aspx; accessed April 13, 2016.

13. http://www.adishakti.org/_/hindus_have_received_their_religion_through_revelation.htm; accessed April 13, 2017.

14. http://bahaiteachings.org/stage-development-model-human-spiritual-maturation; accessed April 13, 2017.

Chapter 9

1. Cox, *The Future of Faith*, 22 (see ch. 2, n. 6).

2. http://www.philosophyforlife.org/exploring-the-multiverse-of-spiritual-pluralism; accessed April 4, 2016.

3. Larry Culliford, *Seeking Wisdom: A Spiritual Manifesto* (Buckingham: University of Buckingham Press, 2018), 101.

4. ibid.

5. ibid.

6. Jack Good, *The Dishonest Church* (Haworth, NJ: St. Johann Press, 2008), 221–25.

7. http://www.yesmagazine.org/happiness/the-ancient-greeks-6-words-for-love-and-why-knowing-them-can-change-your-life; accessed April 22, 2016. Article originally appeared in *Sojourners*, https://sojo.net/articles/have-you-tried-six-varieties-love, December 5, 2013; accessed February 1, 2018.

Chapter 10

1. Steven Pinker, *The Better Angels of Our Nature: How Violence Has Declined* (New York: Penguin, 2011).

2. Kenney, *Thriving*, 11, (see ch. 5, n. 2).

3. ibid., 3.

4. ibid., 41.

5. https://quoteinvestigator.com/2012/11/15/arc-of-universe/; accessed April 30, 2018.

6. Underhill, *Practical Mysticism*, 115 (see ch. 6, n. 4).

7. ibid., 162–63.

8. ibid., 177–78.

9. ibid., 181.

10. Cox, *Future of Faith*, 2 (see ch. 2, n. 6).

11. ibid., 19.

12. Cupitt, *Creative Faith*, 53 (see ch. 1, n. 4).

13. ibid., 53.

14. ibid., 103.

15. ibid., 104.

16. William Bloom, *The Power of the New Spirituality* (Wheaton, IL: Quest Books, 2011).

17. ibid., 11.

18. https://www.google.com/webhp?sourceid=chrome-instant&ion=1&espv=2&ie=UTF-8#q=holisitic; accessed April 10, 2016.

19. http://www.f4hs.org/education/contemporary-spirituality-paper.htm; accessed April 10, 2016.

20. Bloom, *Power of the New Spirituality*, 11.

21. ibid., 1.

22. ibid., 2.

23. ibid., 115.

24. ibid., 106.

25. ibid., 104–10.

26. ibid., 145–46.

27. Mihaly Csikszentmihalyi, *Flow: The Psychology of Optimal Experience* (New York: Harper, 1990).

28. William James, *The Varieties of Religious Experience: A Study in Human Nature; The Gifford Lectures on Natural Religion Delivered at Edinburgh in 1901–1902* (New York: Longmans, Green, and Co., 1902), Lecture 8.

29. Bloom, The Power of the New Spirituality, 180.

30. https://charterforcompassion.org/charter/charter-overvew; accessed December 18, 2017.

31. https://shift.theshiftnetwork.com/about; accessed April 30, 2018.

32. https://www.agnt.today/core-beliefs; accessed April 28, 2018.

33. http://www.brahmakumaris.org/meditation/raja-yoga-meditation; accessed April 28, 2018.

34. https://parliamentofreligions.org/about/mission; accessed April 28, 2018.

Bibliography

NOTE: All biblical quotations are from the English Standard Version. http://biblehub.com/esv.

Alexander, Eben. *Proof of Heaven: A Neurosurgeon's Journey into the Afterlife.* New York: Simon & Schuster, 2012.

Bloom, William. *The Power of the New Spirituality: How to Live a Life of Compassion and Personal Fulfillment.* Wheaton, IL: Quest books, 2012.

Chittister, Joan. *Welcome to the Wisdom of the World and its Meaning for You.* Grand Rapids: Eerdmans, 2007.

Cox, Harvey. *The Future of Faith.* New York: Harper One, 2009.

Csíkszentmihályi, Mihály. *Flow: The Psychology of Optimal Experience.* New York: Harper Perennial, 1991.

Culliford, Larry. *Seeking Wisdom.* Buckingham: University of Buckingham Press, 2018.

Cupitt, Don. *Creative Faith: Religion as a Way of Worldmaking.* Salem, OR: Polebridge Press, 2015.

Dahl, Gregory C. *One World, One People: How Globalization Is Shaping Our Future.* Wilmette, IL: Bahá'í Publishing, 1998.

Bibliography

Dewey, Joanna. "Marcus J. Borg: Jesus: Uncovering the Life, Teachings, and Relevance of a Religious Revolutionary." *The Fourth R* 29, no. 1 (Jan–Feb, 2016).

Faludi, Susan. *Backlash: The Undeclared War against American Women.* New York: Anchor Books (Doubleday), 1991.

Ferrer, Jorge N. *Revisioning Transpersonal Theory: A Participatory Vision of Human Spirituality.* Albany: State University of New York Press, 2001.

Fideler, David. *Restoring the Soul of the World: Our Living Bond with Nature's Intelligence.* Rochester: Inner Traditions, 2014.

Fowler, James W. *Stages of Faith: The Psychology of Human Development and the Quest for Meaning.* San Francisco: Harper & Row, 1981.

Fox, Matthew. *One River, Many Wells: Wisdom Springing from Global Faiths.* New York: Tarcher Perigee, 2004.

Good, Jack. *The Dishonest Church.* Haworth, NJ: St. Johann Press, 2008.

Huxley, Aldous. *The Perennial Philosophy.* New York: Harper Perennial, 1945.

James, William. *The Varieties of Religious Experience: A Study in Human Nature; The Gifford Lectures on Natural Religion Delivered at Edinburgh in 1901–1902.* New York: Longmans, Green, and Co., 1902.

Johnson, Kurt and David Robert Ord. *The Coming Interspiritual Age.* Vancouver: Namaste, 2012.

Johnston, Margaret Placentra. *Faith Beyond Belief: Stories of Good People Who Left Their Church Behind.* Wheaton, IL: Quest Books, 2012.

Kenney, Jim. *Thriving in the Crosscurrent: Clarity and Hope in a Time of Cultural Sea Change.* Wheaton: Quest Books. 2010.

Mabry, John R. *Growing into God: A Beginner's Guide to Christian Mysticism.* Wheaton, IL: Quest Books, 2012.

Maslow, Abraham H. *Religions, Values, and Peak-Experiences.* New York: Viking, 1970.

Bibliography

McIntosh, Steve. *The Presence of the Infinite: The Spiritual Experience of Beauty, Truth, and Goodness.* Wheaton, IL: Quest Books, 2015.

Moody, Raymond. *Life After Life: The Investigation of a Phenomenon—Survival of Bodily Death.* Atlanta: Mockingbird Books, 1975.

Neal, Mary C. *To Heaven and Back: A Doctor's Extraordinary Account of Her Death, Heaven, Angels, and Life Again; A True Story.* Colorado Springs: WaterBrook, 2012.

Niebhur, Gustav. *Beyond Tolerance: Searching for Interfaith Understanding in America.* New York: Viking/Penguin. 2008.

Pagels, Elaine. *Beyond Belief: The Secret Gospel of Thomas.* New York: Vintage Books, 2003.

Peck, M. Scott. *The Different Drum: Community Making and Peace.* New York: Simon and Schuster, 1987.

———. *Further Along the Road Less Traveled: The Unending Journey Toward Spiritual Growth—The Edited Lectures.* New York: Simon & Schuster, 1998.

———. "Introduction." *People of the Lie: The Hope for Healing Human Evil.* New York: Simon and Schuster, 1983.

———. *The Road Less Traveled: A New Psychology of Love, Traditional Values, and Spiritual Growth.* New York: Simon and Schuster, 1978.

Pinker, Steven. *The Better Angels of Our Nature: Why Violence Has Declined.* New York: Penguin Books, 2011.

Reich, K. Helmut. *Developing the Horizons of the Mind: Relational and Contextual Reasoning and Resolution of Cognitive Conflict.* Cambridge: Cambridge University Press, 2002.

Richardson, Rev. Carol E. *Truth and Illusion: The Politics of Spirituality and How One Person's Lie Is Another One's Truth.* Rockville, MD: Highest Harmony Healing & Coaching, 2017.

Bibliography

Ricoeur, Paul. "Religion, Atheism, and Faith." Translated by Charles Freilich. In *The Conflict of Interpretations: Essays in Hermeneutics*. Edited by Don Ihde. Evanston, IL: Northwestern University Press, 1974.

Roper, Megan Phelps. "I Grew Up in the Westboro Baptist Church. Here's Why I Left." TED talk. TEDNYC. Filmed February 2017. https://www.ted.com/talks/megan_phelps_roper_i_grew_up_in_the_westboro_baptist_church_here_s_why_i_left.

Spong, John Shelby. *A New Christianity for a New World: Why Traditional Faith Is Dying and How a New Faith Is Being Born*. San Francisco: HarperSanFrancisco, 2001.

———. *Resurrection: Myth or Reality? A Bishop's Search for the Origins of Christianity*. San Francisco: HarperSanFrancisco, 1995.

Teasdale, Wayne. *The Mystic Heart: Discovering a Universal Spirituality in the World's Religions*. Novato, CA: New World Library, 1999.

Teresa of Avila. *The Interior Castle*. Translated by E. Allison Peers. Radford, VA: Wilder Publications, 2008.

Underhill, Evelyn. *Practical Mysticism*. Columbus, OH: Ariel, 1942.

Versluis, Arthur. *Perennial Philosophy*. Minneapolis: New Cultures Press, 1959.

Walsch, Neale Donald. *Conversations with God: An Uncommon Dialogue*. Book 1 (New York: Putnam, 1995). Book 2 (Charlottesville, VA: Hampton Roads, 1997). Book 3 (Charlottesville, VA: Hampton Roads, 1998).

Index

Note: *f* **indicates figure**

A
Absolute Truth, 153
acceptance, 91, 133–34
active engagement, 134–35
agape (selfless love), 192
Age of Belief, 34, 154
Age of Faith, 34, 154
Age of Reason, 39
Age of the Spirit, 34, 153–56, 206
Alexander, Eben, 166
ambiguity, 81
America Meditating Radio, 229
Amish, 54
animism, 26
anthropocentrism, 107
antiquity, 29–30
antisocial, 76
apostolic authority, 32
aristocracy, 30
Armageddon, 32
Armstrong, Karen, 98, 226–27
arrested development, 60

Association for Global New Thought (AGNT), 227–28
astigmatism, 16
    spiritual, 17
atheists, 60
authority
    in Christianity, 32, 37
    obedience to, 195
    outer, 51
    personal, 51
    religious, 35–36, 48, 74, 89, 153
    of science, 39–40
    spirit as, 121, 133
awakening, 7

B
Backlash: The Undeclared War Against American Women (Faludi), 87
Bahá'i, 29, 172
Bahá'u'lláh, 172
Barna Group, 89–92
belief
    Christian, 29–34, 100–101

compared to faith, 188–89, 205–6
literalism and, 53, 72, 92
religious, 84, 92, 110–11
Benedict XVI (pope), 154
Better Angels of Our Nature: How Violence Has Declined, The (Pinker), 194
Beyond Belief: The Secret Gospel of Thomas (Pagels), 31
Beyond Tolerance: Searching for Interfaith Understainding in America (Niebuhr), 109
Bible, 69, 161–64
Big Bang, 105
Big History, 105–8
binary logic, 1, 49–50, 79–82, 114–15, 133, 203
black-and-white reasoning, 117, 133, 151, 203, 230
blame, 134
blind men and elephant (tale), 179–80
Bloom, William, 209–11, 213–16, 223
Book of Mormon, 172
books, 35
Borg, Marcus, 98
born-again experience, 62, 77
bottom-up globalization, 88
Brahma Kumaris, 228
Buddhism, 27, 28*f*, 96

C

Catholic Church, 154
censure, 54
certainty, 49, 79–82
changes. *See also* cultural changes
fear of, 71
as inevitable, 23, 189, 200
as progress, 22, 35
to religions, 29–34, 36–38
to social order, 22, 87, 196
in technology, 35–36
chaos, 139, 149, 151, 196–97
Chaotic Antisocial Stage, 76. *See also* Lawless stage/level
Charter for Compassion, 226–27
chi (energy), 220
children
development of, 59–60, 156–57
religious training of, 185
Chittister, Joan, 131
Christian, David, 105–6
"Christianity before Christianity" (seminar), 99
Christians and Christianity
belief in, 29–34, 142
creation myths and, 142
development of, 28*f*, 177
early, 31–32, 143
metanarrative of, 43
modern, 143–44
as monotheistic, 27–28
New Spirituality and, 91
nonconformists and, 54
in premodernity, 33–34
revelation and, 172
Roman tyranny and, 32
as time-dependent, 95
values in early, 33
Christmas, 142–43
Chung Hyun Kyung, 131
clarity, 18
clergy, 20–21, 128, 258
cognitive dissonane, 55
cognitive relativism, 152–53

Index

Coming Interspiritual Age, The (Johnson and Ord), 160–61
common humanity, 92
community, 134–35
competition, 135–36
complexity
 binary thinking and, 79–82, 115
 Faithful stage and, 51
 Rational stage and, 56–57, 115–16
 in reasoning, 115
conditioning, 214
conformity, 195
Confucianism, 27
Conjunctive Faith, 133
connection. *See also* oneness; unity
 in born-again experience, 77
 developing sense of, 216–20
 Faithful stage and, 77
 invisible, 79, 123
 Rational stage and, 78–79
 spiritual, 41, 216, 219, 231
 spiritual blindness and, 75–76
 in spiritual maturity, 73
 Unitive stage and, 125
consciousness
 expansion of, 88, 181, 187, 215, 220
 four levels of, 125–26
 reality arising from, 105
 unity, 161, 165
 unseen, 124–25
consensus reality, 119, 124, 224
Constantine, 32–34, 50–51, 141–42
contemplation, 66–67, 212
contemplative science, 97
Conversations with God (Walsch), 163–64

Copernican revolution, 107
cosmology, 105
Council of Nicea, 33, 141–42
Cox, Harvey
 on Age of the Spirit, 34, 154, 156, 205–6
 on early Christianity, 31–32
 on media, 117
 on religions in every society, 176–77
creation myths, 106, 141
Creative Faith (Cupitt), 18–19, 143, 206–8, 223
creator deities, 26
critical analysis, 99, 102–3, 143–44
Critical Distance, 127
Csikszentmihalyi, Mihalyi, 217
Culliford, Larry, 183–84
cultural changes. *See also* changes
 fear of, 71
 increasing spiritual maturity, 157, 181–82
 as pendulum swings, 199
 in postmodernity, 145–47
cultural evolution, 44, 88, 139–58, 177, 187, 197
cultural intermixing, 54, 67–68, 84–95, 197, 231, 247
Cupitt, Don, 18–19, 143, 206–8, 223

D

Dahl, Gregory, 86–87
Dark Ages, 33
Davidson, Jerome, 109–10
Davies, Paul, 103
December 25, 142–43
deities, creator, 26
despair, 133–34

developmental stages, in fetus, 139–40
Different Drum, The (Peck), 127–28
direct spiritual experience, 164–65
Dishonest Church, The (Good), 191
divisiveness, 130
domination, 30, 73
dominion, 72–73

E
ecumenism, 180
ego, 120–21, 135, 218–19. *See also* self
egocentrism, 59–60, 62, 122, 204
egotism, seven forms of, 120
emmetropia (perfect focus), 16–17, 169. *See also* spiritual emmetropia
Empire Strikes Back (film), 66
emptying, 215
end-times, 32
energy field, 220–21
enlightenment, 7
Enlightenment (era), 39, 104
entanglement, 105
eros (romantic love), 191–92
eternity-based philosophies, 95–96
ethics, 156, 221
ethnocentrism, 49, 57, 122, 204
Evans, Jules, 180–81
evolution
    cultural, 44, 88, 139–58, 177, 187, 197
    human, 88, 160
    technological, 34–38
extroversion, 47

F
faith
    compared to belief, 188–89, 205–6
    creative, 206–8, 223
    spiritually emmetropic, 204–5
    trust and, 89
Faith Beyond Belief: Stories of Good People Who Left Their Church Behind (Johnston), 5, 45, 52, 113–14
Faithful stage/level
    binary thinking in, 50, 53, 133
    ethnocentrism in, 49, 53, 122, 204
    fundamentalism and, 71–72
    group attachment in, 49
    literalism in, 48–49, 53, 69–71
    pre-critical thinking in, 50
    relativism and, 150–53
    religious authority in, 48, 74, 153
    role in mature society of, 225–26
    traits of, 48–50, 50*f*, 58*f*, 61*f*, 126*f*–27*f*
    triumphalism and, 63, 74
    values of, 197–98
    view of Lawless stage, 60
Faludi, Susan, 87
farsightedness, 16–17
fear, of change, 22, 63–64, 71
Ferrer, Jorge N., 180–81
fetus, development of, 139–40
Fideler, David, 104
First Adjustment, 107
First Näiveté, 127
flow activities, 217, 226
flow state, 217–18
Flow: the Psychology of Optimal Experience (Csikszentmihalyi), 217
focus, perfect, 16, 169, 232
focus on world, 135, 232
Force, in *Star Wars,* 66

Index

forces of nature, 64–65, 103–4, 140
foresight, 15
forgiveness, 134
forward direction, 140, 153, 193, 198–99
Fourth Adjustment, 107
Fowler, James, 133–35
Fox, Matthew, 180
Francis (pope), 154
fulcrum (analogy), 198–99, 198f
fundamentalism, 32, 71–73, 153
Future of Faith, The (Cox), 31–32, 34

G
Gabriel (angel), 172
Galatians, Epistle to the, 101–2
Gandhi, Mahatma, 135
gender revolution, 152
generosity, 136
global communications, 84–85
globalization, 85–86, 147–48, 160
Globalization website, 87–88
God
    Big History and, 107
    concepts of, 190–91
    as culturally determined, 68
    direct experience of, 125
    evolution of thought and, 140–41
    gender and, 67–68
    in Hinduism, 27
    as light, 191
    as love, 191–92
    love of, 32
    as metaphysical force, 66–67
    in monotheistic religions, 27–29
    as music, 191
    personifications and, 169
    praying to, 91
    Rational stage and, 78–79
    as specific being, 48
God and the New Physics (Davies), 103
godless, 60
gods
    creator, 26
    forces of nature as, 64–65, 103–4, 140
God Seminar, 99
good, 91
Good, Jack, 191
gratitude, 134
groupthink, 55–56, 203
Growing into God (Mabry), 7
Gutenberg, 36

H
handicapped parking, 194–95
healing, 214–15
Heckman, Donald, 111
hierarchy of needs, 186
Hinduism, 25, 27, 28f, 96, 172
holistic spirituality, 209–11
holistic values, 222–23
Holy Spirit, 220
homosexuality, 152
Hugo, Victor, 76–77
human cultural evolution. *See* cultural evolution
humanism, 56
humility, 121, 124, 135
Huxley, Aldous, 93, 95, 186, 192
hyperopia (farsightedness), 16

I
inclusiveness, 92, 153, 203–4
individuality, 90, 195

individuals
    in antiquity, 30
    factors in spirituality of, 175–76
    knowledge available to, 42–43
    Renaissance elevation of, 38
    working with social change, 199–200
information, siloed, 179, 186
inner reality, 19, 146
intercessory prayer, 169
interfaith, term, 110–11
Interfaith Conference of Metropolitan Washington, 109
Interfaith Movement, 108–11
Interfaith Youth Core (IFYC), 110
International Association for Near-Death Studies (IANDS), 166
Internet, 42
interspirituality, 111, 153, 159–60
introversion, 47
intuition, 124
Islam, 28f, 29, 42, 95, 172

J

Jainism, 27
James, William, 219
Jehovah's Witnesses, 54
Jenna, Sister, 162, 228–29
Jesus, 30–32, 70
Jesus Seminar, 98–99
Jesus Seminar on the Road (seminars), 99
John 14:6, 70
Johnson, Kurt, 160
Johnston, Margaret Placentra, 5–6, 8–9, 34–35, 130–31, 145–46
Judaism, 27, 28f, 54, 95, 161, 172
judgment, 47–48

K

Kenney, Jay, 86, 88, 196–98
King, Jr., Martin Luther, 135, 199
knowledge
    availability of, 3–4, 35–36
    democratization of, 42–43, 247
    experiential, 124, 179
    literacy and, 35
    in postmodernity, 42–43
    as progress, 39
    spread of, 38–39
Kroiter, Roman, 66

L

labyrinth, 162–63
lambs (analogy), 202
language, 94
Lawless stage/level. *See also* Chaotic Antisocial Stage
    egocentrism in, 59–60, 62, 122, 204
    as pre-religious and godless, 60
    spiritual blindness in, 61, 75–76
    traits of, 59–61, 61f, 126f–27f
    triumphalism and, 75
    as unconnected to others, 60
legal blindness, 75
lenses, new, 83–111, 178–79
Les Misérables (Hugo), 76–77
Life After Life (Moody), 166
life force energy, 169–71
life review, 166
light, God as, 191
Lipsett, Arthur, 66
literacy, 35–36
literalism, 48–49, 53, 69–71, 88–89, 161

INDEX

love
    disinterested, 94–95
    God as, 191–92
    Greek terms for, 191–92
Lucas, George, 66
ludus (playful love), 192
Luther, Martin, 37

M

Mabry, John, 7
"Make America Great Again," 87, 158
"Man's Fourth Adjustment" (Shapley), 107
mantras, 125–26
Market as God, The (Cox), 117
Marxism, 90
Maslow, Abraham, 118, 186
materialism, 145
meaning
    humanistic view of, 56
    near-death experiences and, 167
    new ways of finding, 41–42, 182
    oneness and, 91
    in postmodernity, 149
    through spiritual connection, 140, 160, 168, 219
media, 1, 4–5
metanarratives, 43
metaphorical interpretation, 132–33
metaphysical force, 66–67
Middle Ages, 33
miracles, 171–72
modernity
    characteristics of, 39–44
    science in, 40, 141
    values of, 196
    as wave, 196–98
monotheism, 27

Moody, Raymond, 166
morality, 51, 72
mores, changing, 195–96
Mormonism, 172
Moses, 172
mountain (analogy), 180
moveable type, 36
multiculturalism, 146–47
music, God as, 191
myopia (shortsightedness or nearsightedness), 2–3, 13–17, 14*f*
mystical worldview. *See* unitive worldview
Mystic/Communal stage, 127–28. *See also* Unitive stage/level
Mystic Heart, The (Teasdale), 159
mysticism, 97, 118, 120, 202

N

narcissism, 60
nationalism, 87–88, 148
Native Americans, 201
natural forces, 64–65, 103–4, 140
NDEs. *See* near-death experiences
Neal, Mary C., 166
near-death experiences (NDEs), 165–68
nearsightedness. *See* myopia
negativity, 4–5, 220–22
New Age, 6–7, 90, 155–56
New Physics, 103–5
"new" spirituality, 6–7
New Spirituality, 89–92, 155–58, 223
news sources, 1, 4–5
Nicene Creed, 100–101
Niebuhr, Gustav, 109
non-peakers, 118
nontheistic religions, 27–28

259

INDEX

nonvisible world, 123
Nostra Aetate, 108–9

O
obedience, 195
ocean (analogy), 180
oneness, 124–25. *See also* connection; unity
One River, Many Wells (Fox), 180
One World, One People: How Globalization is Shaping Our Future (Dahl), 86–87
"ontogeny recapitulates phylogeny," 139–40
open heart, 43, 183, 211
open-mindedness, 54, 117, 183
optimism, 47
Ord, David Robert, 160
other, 73, 196

P
Pagels, Elaine, 31
paradigm shift, 231
paradox, tolerance of, 133
Parliament of the World's Religions, 229–30
partial blindness, 75, 78
Patel, Eboo, 110
Patterson, Stephen J., 101
Paul, St., 101–2
Peace Village, 162
peaker, 118
peasants, 30, 32
Peck, M. Scott, 76, 127–28
pendulum (analogy), 198–99, 198*f*
perennial philosophy, 93–97, 160
Perennial Philosophy (Versluis), 96
Perennial Philosophy, The (Huxley), 93

personal authority, 51
personal responsibility, 50
personification, 63–69, 78–79, 169
pessimism, 47
Phelps, Fred, 52
Phelps-Roper, Megan, 52–55
philautia (love of self), 192
philia (brotherly love), 192
Piaget, Jean, 59
Pinker, Steven, 194
pluralism, 110
polytheism, 26–27
popular religion, 48, 179, 186, 202
positive presence, 221
postmodernity
    communications and knowledge in, 42–43
    cultural changes in, 145–47
    meaning in, 149
    spiritually emmetropic society in, 223–24
    worldviews of, 89–90
Power of Modern Spirituality, The (Bloom), 209
Power of the New Spirituality, The (Bloom), 209–11
Practical Mysticism (Underhill), 117
practice, spiritual, 183–84
pragma (love in compromises), 192
prana (energy), 220
prayer
    Reiki and, 169–71
    types of, 168–69
pre-critical thinking, 50
premodernity
    Christianity in, 33–34
    gods in, 140–41

Index

pre-religious, 60
presbyopia, 16
printing press, 35–36
progress
    knowledge and, 39
    in lives of common people, 38–39
    in science and technology, 35, 40
    societal, 22
progressive revelation, 172
Proof of Heaven: A Neurosurgeon's Journey into the Afterlife (Alexander), 166

Q
qi (energy), 220
Quakerism, 96
quantum physics, 104–5, 145

R
Rational stage/level
    binary thinking in, 133
    cognitive dissonance and, 55
    complexity and, 56–57
    critical thinking in, 55, 114
    humanism and, 56
    mystical experiences and, 118
    role in mature society of, 225–26
    scientific method and, 56
    spiritual blindness at, 78–79
    traits of, 55–57, 58f, 126f–27f
    triumphalism and, 74–75, 114
    as truth seeker, 114
    view of Faithful stage, 56–59
    Westar and, 99
    worldcentrism in, 56–57, 62, 122, 204
Reality, 120
reality, inner, 19, 146
reason, 56, 175–76
reasoning levels, 80–81, 114–16
reflection, 211–16
Reformation, 36–37
refractive myopia, 13–17, 21
Reich, K. Helmut, 80–81, 114–15
Reiki, 169–71
relationships, 92
relativism, 150–53
religions
    academic study of, 97–100
    categories of human inquiry and, 180
    comparing, 92
    creation myths of, 106
    current trend in, 205
    development of, 28f
    in every society, 176–77
    evolution of, 25–29
    insular traditional, 2
    Interfaith Movement and, 108–11
    literalism and, 88–89, 161
    myopia in leaders of, 20–21
    popular, 48, 179, 186, 202
    resurgence of interest in, 148–49
    spiritual feeling in, 218
    as traditions, 188–89
    Unitive stage and, 125
    universal truth in, 93
    as weapons, 72
Religions for Peace, 109, 111
religious maturity, 209
religious pluralism, 110
Renaissance, 36–38
responsibility, personal, 50, 90, 181, 221–22

Restoring the Soul of the World (Fideler), 104
revelation, 96, 172–73, 223
Revelation, Book of, 32
Richardson, Carol E., 73
Ricoeur, Paul, 127
righteousness, 71
Rishis, 172
river (analogy), 180
rules of behavior, 195

S

sakina (energy), 220
salvation, 135, 141
science
    authority of, 39–40
    quantum, 104, 145
    Rational level and, 56, 59, 144
scientific method, 19–20, 40, 56
SDP. *See* Spiritual Development Programme
Second Adjustment, 107
Second Näiveté, 127
Second Vatican Council, 108–9
secularism, 90
secular modernity, 40–41, 144–45
Seeking Wisdom: A Spiritual Manifesto (Culliford), 183–84
self, 177–78, 203–4. *See also* ego
self-effacement, 218–19
self-importance, 60
self-naughting, 218–19
self-reflection. *See* reflection
separation, 73
September 11, 2001, 110
service, 220–23
seventh-generation principle, 201

Shapley, Harow, 107
shekinah (energy), 220
Shepherd (analogy), 202
Shift Network, 227
shortsightedness. *See* myopia
shunning, 54
Sikhism, 28f, 29
siloed information, 179, 186
Smith, Joseph, 172
social order, changes to, 22
societal norms, 21, 60, 151
society, religions in every, 176–77
solar living, 207, 223
solitude, 134–35
spiraling curriculum, 8–9
spirit authority, 121, 133
spiritual amaurosis (blindness), 61
spiritual astigmatism, 17
spiritual blindness, 61, 75–79
Spiritual Development Programme (SDP), 183–84
spiritual development theory. *See also* Faithful stage/level; Lawless stage/level; Rational stage/level; reasoning levels; Unitive stage/level
    compared to human cultural evolution, 177
    definition of, 45–46
    finding way beyond myopia, 138
    near-death experiences and, 168
    as nonjudgmental, 47–48
    stages in, 46–47
    trajectory of, 46–47, 56, 121, 140, 187, 196–99
spiritual emmetropia
    faith and, 204–5
    perception of reality in, 203–4

Index

personifications and, 169
response to change and, 200–203
term, 18
traits of, 18–19, 184, 200
spiritual farsightedness, 17
spiritual immaturity, 73, 148
spirituality. *See also* New Spirituality
concept of, 9
factors in, 175–76
holistic, 209–11
as mountain, 180
"new," 6–7
new interest in, 149–50
as ocean, 180–81
as river, 180
as symphony, 181
spiritual maturity
connection and oneness in, 73
individual, 200–223
at Rational stage, 56
in society, 223–32
universal worldview in, 130
use of term, 46, 208–11
spiritual myopia
binary thinking and, 79–82
at cultural level, 184–85
factors in, 63–82
forms of, 17–23
fundamentalism and, 71–73
increase of, 21
literalism and, 69–71
need for certainty and, 79–82
personification and, 63–69
prevention of, 185–87
societal messages and, 137
spiritual blindness and, 75–79
term, 9

treatments for, 176–85
triumphalism and, 74–75
spiritual path, 177, 183–84
Spiritual Stage 1, 76
spiritual truths, 116
Spong, John Shelby, 98
Stages of Faith (Fowler), 133
Star Wars (films), 66
storge (family love), 192
subatomic particles, 104–5
"Suppressive Persons," 54
Suzerainty Treaty, 72–73
symphony (analogy), 181

T

Taoism, 27
Teasdale, Wayne, 159
technological evolution, 34–38
Ten Commandments, 51, 172
Teresa, Mother, 135
Third Adjustment, 107
Thomas, Gospel of St., 31
Thriving in the Crosscurrent: Clarity and Hope in a Time of Cultural Sea Change (Kenney), 86, 196–98
time-dependent philosophies, 95
To Heaven and Back: A Doctor's Extraordinary Account of Her Death, Heaven, Angels, and Life Again: A True Story (Neal), 166
tolerance of paradox, 133
top-down globalization, 86, 88
tradition, compared to religion, 188–89
traits
of Faithful stage, 48–50, 50*f*, 58*f*, 61*f*, 126*f*–27*f*

INDEX

of Lawless stage, 59–61, 61*f,*
126*f*–27*f*
of Rational stage, 55–57, 58*f,*
126*f*–27*f*
of spiritual emmetropia, 18–19
of Unitive stage, 121–27,
126*f*–27*f,* 132–38
transcendence, 96, 118, 205
traumas, healing, 214–15
travel, 84–85
triumphalism, 20, 74–75, 102, 131, 144
trust, 189–90
truth
absolute, 153, 186
divine and revealed, 39–40, 93,
141, 144, 153, 161, 172–73
relativism and, 152–53
2012 (year), 160–61
21-87 (film), 66

U

Underhill, Evelyn
on acceptance, 133–34
on active engagement, 134–35,
202
on mysticism, 117, 120
unification, process of, 219
union, 7
Unitive stage/level. *See also* Mystic/
Communal stage
acceptance in, 133–34
community and, 134–35
competition and, 135–36
focus on world in, 135
forgiveness and, 134
generosity in, 136
gratitude and, 134
humility in, 121, 124, 135
intuition at, 124
love at, 192
metaphorical interpretation in,
132–33
mystical experience and, 118
spirit authority and, 121, 133
term, 113–14
tolerance of paradox in, 133
traits of, 121–27, 126*f*–27*f,*
132–38
unseen connections in, 123–24
unitive worldview, 7–8, 125, 130, 162,
178, 204
unity, 96–97, 126, 161, 165, 177. *See
also* connection; oneness
Universalizing Faith, 134–35
universe, 106–8
unknowing, 215–16

V

values
holistic, 222–23
modern, 177–78, 196–98
rules and, 152
Varieties of Religious Experience
(James), 219
Vedas, 172
Versluis, Arthur, 96–97
vibration, 220
vibrational ethics, 221
vibrational service, 220
violence, 194
vision, lack of, 21
vitality, 220–21

INDEX

W

Walsch, Neale Donale, 163–64
wave (analogy), 196–98
Westar Institute, 97–100, 206
Westboro Baptist Church, 52–55
Western World, 29–30
"What's Wrong with the Perennial Philosophy?" (Evans), 180–81
"Why the Interfaith Movement Must Rebrand" (Heckman), 111
Wilbur, Ken, 164–65
women
    backlash against, 87
worldcentrism, 56–57, 62, 122–23, 204
worldviews
    challenges to, 85
    competing, 89
    conservative, 178
    ethnocentric, 49, 53, 122, 204
    expanding, 117, 121–23
    generational, 89
    inclusive, 177
    of postmodernity, xx
    rigid fundamentalist, 71–72
    of secular modernity, 144–45
    unitive/universal, 7–8, 125, 130, 162, 178, 204
    worldcentric, 56–57, 62, 122–23, 204

Z

Zoroastrianism, 27

Things you can do to help promote (or refute) awareness about Spiritual Myopia

- Comment online about related issues using the hashtag #spiritualmyopia
- Post comments about the book *Overcoming Spiritual Myopia* online
    - Facebook
    - Twitter
    - LinkedIn
    - Amazon
    - GoodReads
- Take a selfie with the book for Instagram or Facebook.
- Write a blogpost about #spiritual myopia
- Give *Overcoming Spiritual Myopia* as a gift
- Invite a few people over (or to a coffee shop) to talk about it
- Invite Margaret to visit or Skype in to this discussion
- Invite Margaret to speak (in person or over Skype) at your church, community or Meetup group
- Ask your library to carry *Overcoming Spiritual Myopia*

Also by Margaret Placentra Johnston

*Faith Beyond Belief: Stories of Good People Who Left
Their Church Behind (Quest Books, 2012)*

*GOLD WINNER of the 2013 Nautilus Book Awards
in Religion/spirituality (Western)*

About the Author

As a practicing Optometrist for over three decades, Dr. Margaret Placentra Johnston has dedicated her life to helping people see better in the physical world. In the last decade, her mission has also included offering a clearer vision of a different kind—a broader view of religion and spirituality than that recognized in the conventional world.

Her first book *Faith Beyond Belief: Stories of Good People Who Left Their Church Behind* (Quest Books, 2012) brings together the works of twelve spiritual development theorists from different centuries, different disciplines and different parts of the world to illuminate some rarely described steps necessary on the road to spiritual maturity. It was named GOLD WINNER of the 2013 Nautilus Book Award in (Western) Religion/spirituality.

About the Author

In *Overcoming Spiritual Myopia: A View Toward Peace Among the Religions* Margaret provides further perspective. Many factors in Western culture are calling us to enlarge our understanding of religion and spirituality beyond the "truths" dispensed in our typical organized religions. New perspectives emerging now challenge us to recognize and appreciate the universal nature of our spiritual connections. Through this lens, Margaret can see the way forward to toward a kinder, more gentle world, and an outlook that can finally allow peace among the religions. She writes to help these new perspectives become part of the common knowledge in our culture.

Dr. Johnston holds a Bachelor of Arts (BA) and Master of Arts (MA) in Education from the Catholic University of America; a Bachelor of Science (BS) and a Doctor of Optometry (OD) degree from the Pennsylvania College of Optometry (now called Salus University.) She offers courses and speaks to groups on the topic of spiritual development, and has been interviewed on numerous radio shows. Margaret has two grown sons and lives with her husband in Northern Virginia.

MPJauthor.com

www.ingramcontent.com/pod-product-compliance
Lightning Source LLC
Chambersburg PA
CBHW020359080526
44584CB00014B/1087